Normativity in African Regional Relations

VALUES AND IDENTITIES: CROSSING PHILOSOPHICAL BORDERS

Series editors

Paul Crowther is professor of philosophy at the National University of Ireland, Galway

Tsarina Doyle is lecturer in philosophy at the National University of Ireland, Galway

How do values define human identity and the different activities through which this identity finds expression? Values and Identities: Crossing Philosophical Borders publishes research-led monographs and edited collections that face this problem head on. Titles in this series investigate specific forms of value and, in particular, how they interact across societal contexts to form more complex identities.

Recent Titles

Charles Taylor's Doctrine of Strong Evaluation: Ethics and Ontology in a Scientific Age, Michiel Meijer
On Music, Value and Utopia: Nostalgia for an Age yet to Come?, Stan Erraught
Partial Values: A Comparative Study in the Limits of Objectivity, Kevin DeLapp
The Reality of Money: The Metaphysics of Financial Value, Eyja M. Brynjarsdóttir
Sovereignty as Value, Edited by André Santos Campos and Susana Cadilha
Stoic Philosophy and the Control Problem of AI Technology: Caught in the Web, Edward Spence
Normativity in African Regional Relations, Frank Aragbonfoh Abumere
Ideals and Meaningfulness, André Grahle (forthcoming)
Psychosis, Refusal and Autonomy: A Phenomenological Study of Mental Health Detention, Owen Earnshaw (forthcoming)
Inhabiting Difference: Harnessing Lived Experience for Creative Social Change, James Abordo Ong (forthcoming)

Normativity in African Regional Relations

Frank Aragbonfoh Abumere

ROWMAN & LITTLEFIELD
Lanham • Boulder • New York • London

Published by Rowman & Littlefield
An imprint of The Rowman & Littlefield Publishing Group, Inc.
4501 Forbes Boulevard, Suite 200, Lanham, Maryland 20706
www.rowman.com

British Library Cataloguing in Publication Information Available

Library of Congress Cataloging-in-Publication Data

Names: Abumere, Frank Aragbonfoh, author.
Title: Normativity in African regional relations / Frank Aragbonfoh Abumere. Other
    titles: Values and identities.
Description: Lanham : Rowman & Littlefield, 2022. | Series: Values and identities:
    crossing philosophical borders | Includes bibliographical references and index. |
    Summary: "Combining moral philosophy, political philosophy, political theory,
    and international relations, this book explores the possibility of using normative
    international relations as a realistic resolution to the problem of domination of,
    and discrimination against, minorities, specifically or especially migrants on the
    African continent"-- Provided by publisher.
Identifiers: LCCN 2022018307 (print) | LCCN 2022018308 (ebook) |
    ISBN 9781786615893 (cloth) | ISBN 9781786615909 (ebook)
Subjects: LCSH: Minorities--Legal status, laws, etc.--Africa. | Emigration and
    immigration law--Africa. | Africa--Emigration and immigration. | Africa--Ethnic
    relations. | Africa--Foreign relations.
Classification: LCC JV8790 .A32 2022 (print) | LCC JV8790 (ebook) |
    DDC 304.8096--dc23/eng/20220421
LC record available at https://lccn.loc.gov/2022018307
LC ebook record available at https://lccn.loc.gov/2022018308

Contents

Introduction

The African Continental Free Trade Area (AfCFTA) is expected to boost the free movement of goods, services, and capital on the African continent. While the Free Movement of Persons Protocol (FMP Protocol), as the name suggests, is expected to boost the free movement of persons on the continent. Therefore, ceteris paribus, a combination of AfCFTA and the FMP Protocol will ultimately boost the free movement of persons on the continent because predictably the free movement of goods, services, and capital will tend to ease restrictions on the free movement of persons on the continent, thereby resulting in a more integrated region or continent. Again, ceteris paribus, when this regional or continental phenomenon is added to the already existing free movement of persons, it may result in progress geometrically, or at least arithmetically.

Prima facie, boosting the free movement of persons on the continent is a positive thing. However, it comes with a pitfall due to the historical and current domination of, and discrimination against, migrants on the continent, and even minorities in general. Minority domination and discrimination can be a complex and multifaceted subject. Nevertheless, since the fundamental problems with minority discrimination are those of identity and difference, inclusion and exclusion, the scope of and the grounds for discrimination, and, above all, rights and justice, I set out to deal with minority discrimination in light of the ground situation of migrants on the African continent. There is a complexity to the discrimination against migrants in Africa, which not only makes the problem unique from many cases of discrimination but also makes it an important case to discuss. In the discrimination against migrants in Africa, there are multiple majority groups (host or receiving countries and their institutions and citizens) dominating a multitude of minority groups (migrants), and some nationalities are simultaneously victims and perpetrators or prey and predators. This makes the problem different from many other cases of discrimination, where it is usually one majority against one or few minorities.

The complex nature of the problem of discrimination against migrants reflects certain conditions that make for very specific kinds of discrimination against migrants in Africa. In view of the conditions, in the short run, one may be forced to adopt stopgap solutions to the problem, while at the same time accepting that ultimately a human rights framework and a minority rights framework would lead to a long-run possible resolution to the problem. However, walking step by step, from the short-run solution to the long-run solution is an arduous journey because the discrimination problem is intractable. The intractability of the discrimination problem does not mean that resolving the problem is impossible. Conscious that the host or receiving countries and their institutions and citizens have the capacity to interfere arbitrarily in certain choices migrants are in a position to make, I propose a realistic resolution to the problem.

My aim is to combine moral philosophy, political philosophy, political theory, and international relations in order to explore the possibility of using normative international relations as a realistic resolution to the problem of domination of, and discrimination against, minorities, specifically, or especially migrants, on the African continent. To this effect, I explain the grounds of domination of, and discrimination against, minorities and migrants; the nature of the domination of, and discrimination against, minorities and migrants; and why the domination of, and discrimination against, minorities and migrants seems to be an intractable problem. Then, I explain that in cases of domination of, and discrimination against, minorities, minority rights are the go-to solution. However, I show why minority rights is not a realistic resolution to the domination of, and discrimination against, minorities and migrants in Africa.

Consequently, without negating minority rights but also not relying on minority rights, I argue for normative international relations (which includes the adoption of minority rights but does not depend on minority rights) among African states as a realistic resolution to the domination of, and discrimination against, minorities and migrants on the African continent. Furthermore, I argue that the starting point of any realistic resolution to the problem must entail the adoption of normative international relations; then, I explain that to have normative international relations that transcends realist-rationalist fundamentalism, African states must be amenable to a fusion of horizons. This is not a policy book with a set of policies or recommendations that are actionable. Nevertheless, the book tells us where to start from if we are to have a set of policies that are actionable.

I divide the discussion into eight chapters. In chapter 1 ("Identities and Differences"), I focus on the conceptual and theoretical framework of the book, which revolves around the concepts of identity, minorities, and minority rights. Unless these three concepts (and the concept of domination that I explain in chapter 2) are explained in detail in order to lay a solid foundation for the discussions in the remainder of the book (chapters 2–8), the entire goal of the book—which is to show the ineffectiveness of minority rights in the face of discrimination against minorities, especially migrants in Africa— will be a project in futility. Based on the analysis of the three concepts of identity, minorities, and minority rights in chapter 1, in subsequent chapters I address issues such as the grounds of domination of, and discrimination against, minorities, especially migrants; the nature of the domination of, and discrimination against, minorities, especially migrants; why in cases of domination of, and discrimination against, minorities, minority rights are the go-to solution; why minority rights are not a realistic resolution to the domination of, and discrimination against, minorities, especially migrants, in Africa; and, consequently, instead of minority rights, why normative international relations among African states is a realistic resolution to the domination of, and discrimination against, minorities, especially migrants, on the African continent.

I have a twofold aim in chapter 2 ("The Problem of Domination and Discrimination, and the Right to Immigration"). My first aim is to explain what the concept of domination entails, while my second aim is to discuss whether migrants even have the right—in the first place—to migrate to their host countries where they are considered as minorities. The relationship between my first aim and my second aim is that those who discriminate against migrants do so mainly because they think that migrants do not have such rights in the first place. On the one hand, establishing that migrants have such rights necessarily makes the discrimination against them unjust. However, even if it is established that they do not have such right, this does not justify the kind of discrimination they face.

While I look at the concept of domination and migrants' right to immigration (in theory) in chapter 2, I look at the trajectory of immigration and the trend of discrimination against migrants (in practice) in chapter 3 ("Expected Migrant Minorities and Problematic Identities and Differences"). In chapter 4 ("Problems with Minority Rights Approach"), I discuss the legal and political approach to addressing the question of minority—that is, the problem of the domination of, and discrimination against, minorities. The basic point of the discussion is to weigh the strengths and weaknesses of the legal and political approach on a scale and see which one outweighs the other. Based on the result that the scale shows, the remainder of the book (i.e., chapters 5, 7, and 8, except chapter 6) extrapolate or deduce whether such a legal and political approach (notably minority rights) will lead to a realistic resolution to the discrimination against migrants. While my concern is with Africa as a whole, I focus on Nigeria for the purpose of contextualizing the discussion in chapter 4. This contextualization is important because being the most populous country in Africa, Nigeria represents a microcosm of Africa. Therefore, understanding the Nigerian case will probably give us insights into the other cases, or at least some of the other cases, on the continent.

Following the aforementioned trend of contextualization, my aim in chapter 5 ("A Preliminary Discourse on a Realistic Resolution to Domination and Discrimination") is to proffer ways to resolve the problem of discrimination discussed in chapter 4. Like I expected in chapter 4, proffering ways to resolve the Nigeria case may probably give us insights into other cases, or at least some of the other cases, on the continent because Nigeria, as the most populous country on the continent, is a microcosm of Africa.

I have a twofold aim in chapter 6 ("The Status of Minority Rights in Africa"). First, I contend that—at the theoretical and methodological level— unless we look at two kinds of explanations, we will not have a robust explanation for why African states widely reject minority rights. Second, I contend that—at the practical and policy level—when dealing with minority rights, unless African states disregard the internal and external dynamics, they may not "value" minority rights. To defend this second contention, I argue that by virtue of the features and functionality of minority rights, African states can see the protection of minority rights either as a categorical imperative or as a hypothetical imperative, and see minority rights as a universal human and helpful phenomenon rather than as a particular and harmful Western phenomenon—that is, as a harmful source of disunity.

In chapter 7 ("The African Union and Normative International Relations") and chapter 8 ("Future of Normative International Relations in Africa")—in view of the failure of the minority rights approach as discussed in chapters 4 and 5 and the compound nature of the problem as discussed in chapter 6—I argue for normative international relations among African states as a realistic resolution to the domination of, and discrimination against, migrant minorities. The normative international relations may include the adoption of minority rights, but it will not be limited to the adoption of minority rights. Essentially, it represents a constructivist reliance on norms in international politics in spite of the anarchical nature of international politics. Nevertheless, I am conscious, and I admit, that normative international relations is not a new theory—it is not even a theory at all in the sense in which realism and neorealism, liberalism and neoliberalism, social constructivism and constructivism, the English School and critical theories such as Marxist theory, postcolonial theory, feminist theory, and so on are theories. In view of the above consciousness and admission, in order to untangle normative international relations in ways that will make it adaptable to Africa, I untangle the relationship between normative international relations and realism, statism, internationalism, cosmopolitanism, idealism within the context of human rights (individual human rights), group rights (minority rights) protection in international politics, and global politics in a globalized world. In addition, stemming from a consciousness and admission that normative regional relations are often not actionable, I essentially delineate the scope and explain the content of normative international relations among African states.

Chapter One

Identities and Differences

In the preliminary discourse in this chapter, I focus on the conceptual and theoretical framework of the book, which revolves around the concepts of identity, minorities, and minority rights. Except these three concepts (and the concept of domination that I shall explain in the next chapter) are explained in detail in order to lay a solid foundation for the discussions in the remainder of the book (chapters 2–8), the entire goal of the book—which is to show the ineffectiveness of minority rights in the face of discrimination against minorities, especially migrants in Africa—will be a project in futility. Based on the analysis of the three concepts of identity, minorities, and minority rights in this chapter, in subsequent chapters I will address issues such as the grounds of domination of, and discrimination against, minorities, especially migrants; the nature of the domination of, and discrimination against, minorities, especially migrants; why in cases of domination of, and discrimination against, minorities, minority rights are the go-to solution; why minority rights are not a realistic resolution to the domination of, and discrimination against, minorities, especially migrants, in Africa; and, consequently, instead of minority rights, why normative international relations among African states is a realistic resolution to the domination of, and discrimination against, minorities, especially migrants on the African continent.

In this chapter, while I focus on the conceptual and theoretical framework of the book—that is, the concepts of identity, minorities, and minority rights through which all the analysis and narratives in the book are woven together—in the next chapter I simultaneously explain the concept of domination and deal with the contextual foundation of the subject matter of the book, and then in the third chapter I establish the factual and historical foundation of the issues discussed in the book. By so doing, chapters 2, in aid of chapter 1, contributes to laying a solid foundation for the remainder of the discussion in the book, while chapters 2 and 3 help me situate the problematic of the book within a historical and contextual background. In what follows in this chapter, appreciating that the problem definition and formulation will

benefit from comparative analyses, I conduct my narrative through a system-
atic review of the state of the art of the concepts of identity (in the first section
of the chapter), minorities (in the second section of the chapter), and minority
rights (in the third section of the chapter). I particularly rely on postcolonial
African thinkers to tease out the concept of identity. So the thoughts of thinkers such as Frantz Fanon (although he is not from continental Africa, as a
diasporic African, he is an African in a pan-Africanist sense), Chinua Achebe,
Kwame Gyekye, Kwasi Wiredu, Achille Mbembe, Kwame Anthony Appiah,
and Achie Mafeje pervade my narrative on the concept of identity.

THE QUESTION OR PROBLEM OF IDENTITY

The basic mission of philosophy, Kwame Gyekye (1995) says, includes, but
is not limited to, the following. First is the provision of a basic system of
beliefs that guides people's lives. Second is the determination of "the nature
of human values and how these values can be realized concretely in human
societies" (23). Third is the provision of "conceptual interpretations and
analysis of [human] experience, necessarily doing so not only by responding
to the basic issues and problems generated by that experience but also by sug-
gesting new or alternative ways of thought and action" (24). All this is made
possible through speculation about "the whole range of human experience"
(23). And fourthly is the provision of "conceptual responses to the problems
posed in any given epoch for a given society or culture" (27).

The aforementioned description of (some of) the basic tasks or (part of) the
basic mission of philosophy represents a general view of what the mission of
philosophy is. However, when spatiotemporal circumstances are considered,
the specificity of what the mission of philosophy is as far as people X are
concerned is almost always different from what it means as far as people Y
are considered. For instance, it is this kind of specificity that accounts for
Frantz Fanon's (1967) observation that Black people (both Africans on the
continent and diasporic Africans) have two dimensions, the one dimension is
with fellow Black people, while the other dimension is with White people.
Black people behave differently in one way (characterized by a sense of inferiority) in their interaction and relationship with White people and in another
way in their interaction and relationship with fellow Black people. For Fanon,
"That this self-division is a direct result of colonialist subjugation is beyond
question" (8).

Given the spatiotemporal circumstances of the African people, in terms
of both internal dynamics (internal interactions and relations in Africa) and
external dynamics (external interactions and relations between Africa and the
rest of the world) both historically and presently, Africans would appreciate

an approach to philosophizing that leads to "a call for a new Pan-Africanism that brooks neither external dependence nor internal authoritarianism and social deprivation" (Mafeje 2008 [2000], 113). Consequently, upon the spatiotemporal circumstances mentioned earlier, Kwasi Wiredu and Kwame Gyekye (1992) advise that "[p]hilosophers belonging to a given culture or era or tradition select those concepts or clusters of concepts that, for one reason or another, matter most and that therefore are brought to the fore in their analysis" (7). In view of the implications of spatiotemporal circumstances, Wiredu and Gyekye argue that "this is the time when there is the maximum need to study African traditional philosophy" (98) and, I think I am apt to say, African political thought in particular. When studying African political thought, "the starting points, the organizing concepts and categories" of contemporary African political thought should "be extracted from the cultural, linguistic, and historical background of African peoples if that philosophy is to have relevance and meaning for the people, if it is to enrich their lives" (Gyekye 1995, 33, 42).

I think any philosophizing that is to have relevance and meaning for the African people must deal with *an* African Zeitgeist. I used the indefinite article "an" rather than the definite article "the" to prefix African Zeitgeist because I think it is possible to have more than one Zeitgeist at the same time. Achille Mbembe (2001) says:

> [T]here is a close relationship between subjectivity and temporality—that, in some way, one can envisage subjectivity itself as temporality. The intuition behind this idea was that, for each time and each age, there exists something distinctive and particular—or, to use the term, a "spirit" [*Zeitgeist*]. These distinctive and specific things are constituted by a set of material practices, signs, figures, superstitions, images, and fictions that, because they are available to individuals' imagination and intelligence and actually experienced, form what might be called "languages of life." (15; emphasis in original)

I think in Africa today, considering the close relationship between subjectivity and temporality, identity is a Zeitgeist. A careful observation of the complex historical and ongoing experiences in Africa shows that the question or the problem of identity is the most intellectually absorbing, specifically something that African political philosophizing attempts to, and should, resolve. This is pertinent in our globalized world today partly because (among other things) "identity is increasingly used both as a weapon to further brutalise the weakest in our midst and as a leverage to claim a status of pure or authentic victim. To have been brutalised or to have been victimised, in turn, is increasingly seen as the most potent way to claim one's rights or one's access to care, justice, redress or reparation" (Mbembe 2019, s.p.).

At this juncture, I shall briefly explain my approach to the question or problem of identity. One can deal with the question or problem of identity by approaching identity as a category of practice or as a category of analysis. My focus is on approaching identity as a category of practice as opposed to approaching identity as a category of analysis. Nevertheless, I will use the approach to identity as a category of analysis to complement my approach to identity as a category of practice. All the while, I will be conscious of Rogers Brubaker and Frederick Cooper's (2000, 5) warning against the confusion of these two categories, and I will be conscious that the "preconceived treatment of identity is very common amongst researchers who continue to take it for granted as comprising a specific array of characteristics, rather than considering the mechanisms by which the concept is crystallized as reality" (Bray 2008, 303).

Alongside the earlier focus or approach, I shall avoid a reductionist approach to the question or problem of identity that takes the form of what Amartya Sen (2007) calls "identity disregard" and "singular affiliation" (20). As Sen says:

> [T]wo different types of reductionism seem to abound in the formal literature of social and economic analysis. One may be called "identity disregard," and it takes the form of ignoring, or neglecting altogether, the influence of any sense of identity with others, on what we value and how we behave. . . . In contrast with "identity disregard," there is a different kind of reductionism, which we may call "singular affiliation," which takes the form of assuming that any person preeminently belongs, for all practical purposes, to one collectivity only. (20)

It is not contentious to aver that identity is valuable to both individuals and collectives. In other words, for both individuals and collectives, identity is a value. Value can be understood in both a narrow sense and a broad sense. In a narrow sense, value "is that which is good, desirable, or worthwhile" (Mintz 2018, s.p.). In a broad sense:

> Values are basic and fundamental beliefs that guide or motivate attitudes or actions. They help us to determine what is important to us. Values describe the personal qualities we choose to embody to guide our actions; the sort of person we want to be; the manner in which we treat ourselves and others, and our interaction with the world around us. They provide the general guidelines for conduct.. . . . Values are the motive behind purposeful action. They are the ends to which we act. (s.p.)

On the one hand, identity as value in a narrow sense can be seen as a good, desirable, or worthwhile thing. On the other hand, identity as value in a broad sense is a basic and fundamental belief that guides or motivates attitudes or actions. It helps individuals or collectives to determine what is important to them. Identity as value describes the personal or group qualities individuals or collectives choose to embody to guide their actions, the sort of person or group they want to be, the manner in which they treat themselves and others, and their interaction with the world around them. Identity as value provides the general guidelines for individuals' or collectives' conduct, it is the motive behind individuals' or collectives' purposeful action, and it is the end to which they act. After all, "Identity is a matter of the significance of a thing, a question of purpose and perspective. The achievement of a sense of identity is most significant when it involves acquiring a sense of oneness from many separate distinct events or objects, when it is a question of parts and wholes" (Willard 1970, 6).

Kwame Anthony Appiah (1992) defines identity as "a coalescence of mutually responsive (if sometimes conflicting) modes of conduct, habits of thought, and patterns of evaluation; in short, a coherent kind of human social psychology" (174). He argues that "the African identity is, for its bearers, only one among many. Like all identities, institutionalized before anyone has permanently fixed a single meaning for them" (177). In other words, for him, "[B]eing African is, for its bearers, one among other salient modes of being, all of which have to be constantly fought for and rethought" (Ibid.). In the same vein, Mbembe (2002) argues that everyone, that is every African, "can imagine and choose what makes him or her an African" (258). However, on the one hand, he opines that "the state of war in contemporary Africa should, in fact, be conceived of as a general cultural experience that shapes identities, just as the family, the school, and other social institutions do" (267). Then, on the other hand, Appiah (1992) goes on to argue that, in Africa, it is the tribal identity "that provides one of the most useful models for such rethinking; it is a model that draws on other identities central to contemporary life in the subcontinent, namely, the constantly shifting redefinition of 'tribal' identities to meet the economic and political exigencies of the modern world" (177).

Appiah's (1992) claim that tribal identity provides one of the most useful models for rethinking identity in Africa seems to be corroborated by Chinua Achebe's (1982) self-description when he says that "*I'm an Ibo writer, because this is my basic culture*" (s.p.; emphasis mine). Nevertheless, Achebe goes beyond describing himself as an Ibo writer and describing his Ibo identity as his basic culture to also assert that he is a

Nigerian, African and a writer . . . no, black first, then a writer. Each of these identities does call for a certain kind of commitment on my part. I must see what it is to be black—and this means being sufficiently intelligent to know how the world is moving and how the black people fare in the world. This is what it means to be black. Or an African—the same: what does Africa mean to the world? When you see an African what does it mean to a white man? (s.p.)

Note that in the above self-description, Achebe (1982) described himself in five ways—that is, he self-identifies in five ways—namely, Ibo, Nigerian, African, Black, and writer. In a lexical order, Ibo comes first, Nigerian comes second, African comes third, Black comes fourth, and writer comes fifth. His identity as an African only comes before his identities as Black and writer, but it comes after his identities as Ibo and Nigerian. That Achebe gives precedence to his identities as Ibo and Nigerian over his identity as an African (this does not in any way suggest that he thinks the various identities are mutually exclusive) may be a function of the trajectory of the formation of the African identity understood in its singularity—that is as a singular identity—as opposed to African identities understood in their plurality—that is, as plural identities. Appiah (1992) argues that "[t]o speak of an African identity in the nineteenth century . . . would have been 'to give to aery nothing a local habitation and a name.' Yet there is no doubt that now, a century later, an African identity is coming into being. . . . This identity is a new thing; . . . it is the product of a history" (174).

Following the above argument by Appiah (1992), some may think that the African identity is evolving from its liquid form to a solid form. This does not tell us when the solidification of the African identity will happen; however, it suggests that in its liquid state there are only pluralities of African identities, and in its solid state there will be a singularity of African identity. I do not think a solid and singular African identity will necessarily replace liquid and plural African identities. However, I think the former can be superimposed on the latter or both can exist side by side. In other words, the existing plurality of identities will not evolve into a singular identity—that is, it will not necessarily be replaced by a singular identity. Rather, both will coexist in a condition whereby in a metaphysical sense the singular identity is the universal while the plural identities are the particulars, or in a taxonomic ranking, the singular identity is the genus while the plural identities are the species, or in an ordinary language sense, the singular identity represents the general identity while the plural identity represents specific identities. As Appiah says in his translation and interpretation of an Akan proverb, "Each of us . . . belongs to a group with its own customs" (180). The implication of these pluralistic identities for the singular African identity is that "[t]o accept that Africa can be in these ways a usable identity is not to forget that all of us belong to multifarious communities with their local customs; it is not to dream of a single African state and to forget the complexly different trajectories of the continent's so many languages and cultures" (Ibid.).

Preceding Appiah's (1992) argument, Achebe (1982) made an observation that is similar to Appiah's argument. In his observation, Achebe says:

> It is, of course true that the African identity is still in the making. There isn't a final identity that is African. But, at the same time, there *is* an identity coming into existence. And it has a certain context and a certain meaning. Because if somebody meets me, say, in a shop in Cambridge [England], he says, "Are you from Africa?" Which means that Africa means something to some people. Each of these tags has a meaning, and a penalty and a responsibility. All these tags, unfortunately for the black man, are tags of disability. (s.p.; emphasis in original)

Like other human identities, the African identity is not ahistorical, it is historical, and it is not unconstructed, it is constructed. Every human identity is simultaneously historical and constructed, and every human identity has its share of false presuppositions—that is, errors and inaccuracies that due to courtesy we refer to as myth, while religion refers to them as heresy and science refers to them as magic (Appiah 1992, 174). To understand the point about the construction of African identity in particular and human identity in general, we merely need to understand that "[i]nvented histories, invented biologies, invented cultural affinities come with every identity; each is a kind of role that has to be scripted, structured by conventions of narrative to which the world never quite manages to conform" (1992, 174).

That human identity is history and construction dependent affects whether it is shallow, deep, or middle-of-the-road between the former and the latter. The kind of histories invented and the ways they are invented, the kind of biologies invented and the ways they are invented, and the kind of cultural affinities invented and the ways they are invented determine the shallowness and deepness of human identity. Ordinarily, one may assume that in terms of time period, the longer one is aware or conscious of his or her identity, the deeper such identity is. Conversely, the shorter one is aware or conscious of his or her identity, the shallower his or her identity is. However, "[t]he duration of awareness, of consciousness of an identity, has really very little to do with how deep it is. You can suddenly become aware of an identity which you have been suffering from for a long time without knowing" (Achebe 1982, s.p.).

To illustrate the point about the deepness or shallowness of a human identity does not depend on the duration of one's awareness or consciousness of the identity. Achebe (1982) uses the Igbo identity as an example. He says that historically in his area—that is, the Igbo area of present-day Nigeria—the Igbo people did not self-identify as Igbo. They self-identify as people from one particular village or the other.

In fact, in some place "Igbo" was a word of abuse; they were the "other" people, down in the bush. And yet, after the experience of the Biafran War, during a period of two years, it became a very powerful consciousness. But it was real all the time. They all spoke the same language, called "Igbo," even though they were not using that identity in any way. But the moment came when this identity became very very powerful . . . and over a very short period. (s.p.)

The illustration by Achebe (1982) indicates three important things about human identities. First, it indicates that human identities "are complex and multiple and grow out of a history of changing responses to economic, political, and cultural forces, almost always in opposition to other identities" (Appiah 1992, 178). Second, it indicates that human identities flourish in spite of our misrecognition of their origins (Ibid.). In other words, human identities flourish in spite of "their roots in myths and in lies" (Ibid.). Third, it indicates that, consequently, there is "no large place for reason in the construction—as opposed to the study and the management—of identities" (Ibid.). For Appiah, "One temptation, then, for those who see the centrality of these fictions in our lives, is to leave reason behind: to celebrate and endorse those identities that seem at the moment to offer the best hope of advancing our other goals, and to keep silent about the lies and the myths" (Ibid.).

In the construction of human identities, we are tempted to celebrate and endorse identities that advantage us and keep silent identities that disadvantage us because "[a] sense of identity can be a source not merely of pride and joy, but also of strength and confidence" (Sen 2007, 1). A sense of identity can be a positive thing in that having a sense of identity is capable of making vital "contribution to the strength and the warmth of our relations with others, such as neighbors, or members of the same community, or fellow citizens, or followers of the same religion. Our focus on particular identities can enrich our bonds and make us do many things for each other and can help to take us beyond our self-centered lives" (2007, 2).

However, just as a sense of identity can be a positive thing in the way described earlier, it can also be a negative thing because "[t]he adversity of exclusion can be made to go hand in hand with the gifts of inclusion" (Sen 2007, 2–3), and when this happens, "a sense of identity can firmly exclude many people even as it warmly embraces others" (2007, 3). Of course, identity can also be neutral—that is, neither positive nor negative. But looking around the world, both historically and presently, we see time and places when and where identity has been a source or even *the* source of negativities such as wars, discrimination, domination, and other atrocities and violations and the consequent suffering and dehumanization of the victims at the hands of the perpetrators. As Sen (2007) reminds us, "[I]dentity can also kill—and kill with abandon. A strong—and exclusive—sense of belonging to one group can in many cases carry with it the perception of distance and divergence from other groups. Within-group solidarity can help to feed between-group discord" (2).

Considering identity in its negative sense as described earlier, Sen (2007) asks a very important question, "If identity-based thinking can be amenable to such brutal manipulation, where can the remedy be found?" (3). Responding to the question, he argues that the remedy to such brutal manipulation of identity-based thinking

> can hardly be sought in trying to suppress or stifle the invoking of identity in general. For one thing, identity can be a source of richness and warmth as well as of violence and terror, and it would make little sense to treat identity as a general evil. Rather, we have to draw on the understanding that the force of a bellicose identity can be challenged by the power of competing identities. These can, of course, include the broad commonality of our shared humanity, but also many other identities that everyone simultaneously has. This leads to other ways of classifying people, which can restrain the exploitation of a specifically aggressive use of one particular categorization. (3–4)

Looking at Africa, both historically and presently, evidently the brutal manipulation of identity-based thinking exists on the continent. Alarmingly, the trajectory of the manipulation of identity-based thinking on the continent shows that the future (at least the near future) is certain (or at least highly probable) to converge with the past and the present. Whether in Central Africa (e.g., Democratic Republic of Congo—DRC—and Cameroun), West Africa (e.g., Nigeria and Mali), East Africa (e.g., Kenya and Uganda), Southern Africa (e.g., South Africa and Zimbabwe), or North Africa (e.g., Libya and Egypt), the brutal manipulation of identity-based thinking pervades the continent.

In Africa, it is imperative that we find a remedy for the brutal manipulation of identity-based thinking since there will always be strangers in our midst, and at least some of us if not many of us, and at least sometimes if not often, we too are strangers in the midst of others. As Toyin Falola (2006) says, "Africans have always been on the move, ever since the time they created civilization and scattered it around the continent and elsewhere" (1). Moreover, there is no doubt that "[t]he interpenetration of so many different foreign cultures with so many varying indigenous ones makes culture clash a problem for every new African state" (Willard 1970, vii). For this reason, when commenting on the predicament of African identities, without rejecting the realities of such identities, V. Y. Mudimbe (2003) warns against "the potential dangers of perspectives that in the name of difference would value as essences what was in actuality engineered by the colonial library" (212).

Contemporary identity is manifested in the self being true to itself—that is, being authentic. In other words, contemporary identity stresses its authenticity and listening to its inner voice (Taylor 1994). David Campbell (1992) says, "[I]dentity is an inescapable dimension of being. Nobody could be without it" (9). Ted Hopf (1998) avers that absent identity a "world of chaos, a world of pervasive and irremediable uncertainty, a world much more dangerous than anarchy" (175) will be the order of the day. If Campbell and Hopf are right, then identity is very important. Among thinkers who theorize about the concept of identity, there is a consensus that "identity has become indispensable to contemporary political discourse" (Heyes 2020, sec. 1). At the same time, they are agreed that identity "has troubling implications for models of the self, political inclusiveness, and our possibilities for solidarity and resistance" (sec. 1).

As already mentioned in the preceding section, identity can be employed positively, neutrally, or negatively. This is not only true of domestic politics, it is also true of international politics. Felix Berenskoetter (2017) says, "'[I]dentities' manifest our ontology of the international and play a central role in politics" (1). Bruce Cronin (1999) observes that "identities provide a frame of reference from which political leaders can initiate, maintain, and structure their relationships with other states" (18). While Anthony Burke (2006) even goes as far as asserting that "there is . . . no world politics without identity, no people, no states, no international system" (394).

Whether in domestic politics or international politics, identity represents a major distinction line between the self and the other. But as Mbembe (2015) says, "The self is made at the point of encounter with an Other. There is no self that is limited to itself. The Other is our origin by definition" (s.p.). In the encounter between the self and the other, the self may oppress the other or the other may oppress the self. While this is not always the case, unfortunately it is sometimes the case in both domestic and international politics, and it is often the case in African domestic politics and in Africa's and Africans' encounter with the rest of the world. This situation gives rise to, or at least engenders, identity politics on the African continent.

Identity politics represents a significant departure from pre-identitarian politics of recognition, and what makes the former a significant departure from the latter is that the former demands "recognition on the basis of the very grounds on which recognition has previously been denied" (Kruks 2001, 85). For instance, based on identity politics, Blacks *qua* Blacks would demand recognition from Whites, Africans *qua* Africans would demand recognition from Europeans, and so on. The point here is that a group or groups demand(s) equality with another group or other groups not based on common humanity but rather simply based on the identity of the group or groups that is/are demanding for equality. Note that although the group(s) is/are oppressed in the first place based on their identity, they insist that they should be treated with equality based on that same identity. "The demand is not for inclusion within the fold of 'universal humankind' on the basis of shared human attributes; nor is it for respect 'in spite of' one's differences. Rather, what is demanded is respect for oneself as different" (2001, 85).

The starting position of identity politics is analyses of oppression, discrimination, domination, and that kind of social injustice. Then, it goes on "to recommend, variously, the reclaiming, re-description, or transformation of previously stigmatized accounts of group membership. Rather than accepting the negative scripts offered by a dominant culture about one's own inferiority, one transforms one's own sense of self and community" (Heyes 2020, sec. 1). However, as positively useful as it is and in spite of its worthy aim of equalizing identities, identity politics poses its own danger. The danger is that identity politics "casts as authentic to the self or group a self-understanding that in fact is defined by its opposition to a dominant identity, which typically represents itself as neutral. Reclaiming such an identity as one's own merely reinforces its dependence on this Other, and further internalizes and reinforces an oppressive hierarchy" (2020, sec. 2).

The aforementioned danger posed by identity politics pales in comparison with the danger of othering that identity itself poses. If the danger posed by identity politics is worth worrying about, then othering deserves to be worried about even more. Othering is "a process . . . through which identities are set up in an unequal relationship" (Crang 1988, 61). It simultaneously constructs

> the self or in-group and the other or out-group in mutual and unequal opposition through identification of some desirable characteristic that the self/in-group has and the other/out-group lacks and/or some undesirable characteristic that the other/out-group has and the self/in-group lacks. Othering thus sets up a superior self/in-group in contrast to an inferior other/out-group. (Brons 2015, 70)

Othering is a situation involving moral agents on opposite sides of a relationship or interaction in which on the one side we have the subject who is/are active in the relationship or interaction—that is, doing the othering—and on the other side we have the object who is/are passive in the relationship or interaction—that is, suffering the othering. The active subject is the self while the passive object is the other. The other is a construction that opposes and thereby constructs the self (Simone de Beauvoir 1949). Put differently, othering involves self-other distantiating in which the self dehumanizes the other (1949, 70). In essence, generally, othering echoes Hegelian dialectic of self-other relationship and specifically Hegelian master-slave relationship. Nevertheless, othering does not necessarily have to take the form of an affirmation of self-superiority and other-inferiority. Although othering often sets up a superior self/in-group in contrast to an inferior other/out-group, it can also create distance between self/ in-group and other/out-group by means of a dehumanizing over-inflation of otherness. The other then, is not so much (implicitly) inferior, but radically alien. In either case, the effect is a near impenetrable border between the self/in-group and the inferior and/or radically alien other/out-group, "justifying" social exclusion, discrimination, and/or subjection. (1949, 72)

Othering occurs when identity differences are turned into otherness and the otherness takes the form of a negative, rather than a positive or neutral, categorization. In other words, othering occurs when identity differences result in the self negatively, rather than positively or neutrally, stereotyping the other. This is the case because

[a]n identity is established in relation to a series of differences that have become socially recognized. These differences are essential to its being. If they did not coexist as differences, it would not exist in its distinctness and solidity. Entrenched in this indispensable relation is a second set of tendencies, themselves in need of exploration, to conceal established identities into fixed forms, thought and lived as if their structure expressed the true order of things. When these pressures prevail, the maintenance of one identity (or field of identities) involves the conversion of some differences into otherness, into evil, or one of its numerous surrogates. Identity requires differences in order to be, and it converts difference into otherness in order to secure its own self-certainty. (Connolly 2002, 64)

A look at both history and the present shows that it is not far-fetched to claim that othering is dangerous. Just to mention of the well-known havocs othering has wreaked in our world, I shall borrow the following words from Slavenka Drakuli´c (1992): "I understand now that nothing but 'otherness' killed Jews, and it began with naming them, by reducing them to the other. Then everything became possible. Even the worst atrocities like concentration camps or the slaughtering of civilians in Croatia or Bosnia" (145). To the aforementioned atrocities that occurred because of othering, we can add the following: DRC in which King Leopold II and his fellow Belgians exterminated over ten million Congolese and the Rwanda genocide, the infamous "100 days of slaughter" (BBC 2019), in 1994, in which within one hundred days extremists from the ethnic majority Hutu massacred around 800,000 people mostly from the ethnic minority Tutsi. The list of the atrocities that have occurred because of othering can go on and on, but the aforementioned atrocities both in Africa and outside Africa suffice to illustrate the danger of othering.

WHO ARE MINORITIES?

As shown in the previous paragraph, minorities are usually at the receiving end of the atrocities of othering. One may ask, Why are minorities usually at the receiving end of the atrocities of othering or what is it about minorities that make them the targets of othering? To answer the question satisfactorily, it is helpful to first of all know, or at least clarify, who minorities are. To clarify this, one must in turn attempt to specify exactly, or at least clarify, what the concept of minority is. The concept of minority seems to be an essentially contested concept—that is, a concept whose users inevitably engage in endless disputes about the proper uses of the concept (Gallie 1956, 169). Essentially contested concepts have no generally agreed upon meaning. Although they have their own original meanings, the original meanings are "jettisoned or only retained by some users, while other users invent their own meanings of the concepts. In short, an essentially contested concept means different things to different people, and none of these different meanings are taken to be the standard meaning of the concept" (Abumere 2019, 1).

Steven Wheatley (2005) says, "[I]n any consideration of the meaning of the term 'minority,' reference is invariably made to the . . . definitions, proposed respectively by Francesco Capotorti and Jules Deschênes" (18). On the one hand, Capotorti (1977) defines minority as a

> group numerically smaller to the rest of the population of the State, in a non-dominant position, whose members—being national of the State—possess ethnic, religious or linguistic characteristics differing from those of the rest of the population and show, if only implicitly, a sense of solidarity, directed towards preserving their culture, traditions, religion or language. (E/CN.4/ Sub.2/384/Rev. 1, para. 568, quoted in United Nations 2010, 2)

On the other hand, Deschênes (1985) defines "minority" as

> a group of citizens of a State, constituting a numerical minority and in a non-dominant position in that State, endowed with ethnic, religious or linguistic characteristics which differ from those of the majority of the population, having a sense of solidarity with one another, motivated, if only implicitly, by a collective will to survive and whose aim [is] to achieve equality with the majority in fact and in law. (para. 181)

Arguably, the most popular definition of minorities is that propounded by Capotorti, the former Special Rapporteur of the United Nations Sub-Commission on Prevention of Discrimination and Protection of Minorities. There are familiar problems with the definitions, especially Capotorti's definition. For instance, the definition assumes that minorities cannot be in a dominant position within their state. This problem is not only familiar, it is also instantly evident when we look at Capotorti's definition, prima facie. But there are other problems that are not instantly evident when we look at the definition, prima facie. These other problems only become evident after a careful look at, and a deep scrutiny of, the definition. In the following paragraphs, these problems are examined to know to what extent Capotorti's definition is close to or far away from what we may refer to as the abstract ideal concept of minorities although such an abstract ideal concept is not concretely defined anywhere.

Capotorti's conception of a minority as "a group numerically inferior to the rest of the population of a state" (E/CN.4/Sub.2/384/Rev. 1, para. 568, quoted in United Nations 2010, 2) is subtly contentious. Prima facie, one does not see any problem with the conception because the term *minority* implies something smaller in number than the majority, which is bigger in number. The above description of minority is merely quantitative. Admittedly, Capotorti combined quantitative and qualitative aspects in his definition of minorities: He did not stop at saying that minorities must be numerically inferior to the rest of the population (quantitative aspect); he went on to ascribe certain qualitative characteristics to such a numerical inferior group; and these qualitative characteristics include nationality or ethnicity, religion and language. However, the problem with Capotorti's insistence that minorities must be numerically inferior to the rest of the population surfaces when we remember times and places such as apartheid South Africa. In apartheid South Africa, the Blacks and Coloreds (Indians and racially mixed persons) who faced discrimination were not numerically inferior to the rest of the White population.

In apartheid South Africa, the Blacks alone—without adding the Coloreds— were numerically superior to the rest of the population, yet they were racially discriminated against by the Whites, who were numerically inferior to the rest of the population. Based on Capotorti's definition—that is, his notion of numerical inferiority—apartheid would not be a problem for minority rights. In other words, it would not be a case of minority discrimination. Nevertheless, while the "letter" of Capotorti's definition would not see apartheid as a problem for minority rights or as a case of minority discrimination, the "spirit" of his definition—in view of the qualitative characteristics he ascribed to minorities—would certainly condemn apartheid as minority discrimination and violation of minority rights. Therefore, more important than being numerically inferior is that the victims of discrimination are not the dominant group of the population.

If the notion of dominancy takes precedence over the notion of numerical inferiority, then perhaps the word *minority* in the concepts of minority discrimination and minority rights should be revisited. Nevertheless, such revisitation is not within the remit of this paper or project—for I am not merely, and only, working with the letters of the concepts but more importantly working with and interested in the spirit of the concepts. Ultimately, the requirement to be in a nondominant position remains important. In most instances, a minority group will be a numerical minority, but in others a numerical majority may also find itself in a minority-like or nondominant position, such as Blacks under the apartheid regime in South Africa. In some situations, a group that constitutes a majority in a state as a whole may be in a nondominant position within a particular region of the state in question (United Nations 2010, 2–3).

Capotorti's definition implies that persons or people can only be a minority in their own state—in a state in which they hold citizenship. The definition does not permit that residents, even longtime residents, who have no citizenship, can be classified as minorities in their state of residence. On whether noncitizens and residents can be considered as part of a minority group in a state, the stance of the United Nations (UN) as explained by the Working Group on Minorities—in the Commentary on the United Nations Minorities Declaration—is that

> while citizenship as such should not be a distinguishing criterion that excludes some persons or groups from enjoying minority rights under the Declaration, other factors can be relevant in distinguishing between the rights that can be demanded by different minorities . . . those who have been established for a long time on the territory may have stronger rights than those who have recently arrived . . . the best approach appears to be to avoid making an absolute distinction between "new" and "old" minorities by excluding the former and including the latter, but to recognize that in the application of the Declaration the "old" minorities have stronger entitlements than the "new." (E/CN.4/Sub.2/AC.5/2005/2, paras. 10–11; United Nations 2010, 4–5)

What this quotation shows is that in addition to the criteria enumerated by Capotorti, the UN has added an extraneous condition to what qualifies a group to be a minority. However, the UN does not tell us why, apart from longer stay, historical or old minorities should have stronger right claims than new minorities. What, in this case, is special about longer stay? We can deduce that those who have stayed longer have—in comparison with new minorities—participated more in the affairs of the state, interacted more with other groups in the state, contributed more to the well-being and welfare of the state, become so accustomed to life in the state that they may not be able to fit in in other states, or having lived so long in the state they have no entitlements in any other state—that is, they have nowhere else to go.

However, it is not always true that historical or old minorities fulfill the above-listed conditions more than new minorities. In many states, a historical or an old minority may fulfill all, many, some, or one of those conditions more than a new minority, but this may not necessarily be the case in all states. Even if we were to grant that historical or old minorities everywhere fulfill the conditions more than new minorities, we will still have a problem left, and I refer to this problem as the problem of indeterminacy. This problem says that although we can determine—in terms of period of stay—that one minority has stayed longer than the other minority, we cannot actually determine which rights to grant minorities and which rights to deny minorities when we have a series of minorities with periods of stay ranging from 0 to 1 on a spectrum.

On the spectrum, let us say between 0 and 0.1 is less than ten years, 0.1 is ten years, 0.2 is twenty years, 0.3 is thirty years, 0.4 is forty years, 0.5 is fifty years, 0.6 is sixty years, 0.7 is seventy years, 0.8 is eighty years, 0.9 is ninety years, and 1 is one hundred years. It is clear that any minority on 0.1 is new while any minority on 0.9 is old comparatively. Therefore, we may say that the latter has stronger right claims than the former. But what if we have minorities on 0.4, 0.5, and 0.6, is the minority on 0.4 new and the minority on 0.6 old? If so, what about the minority on 0.5, is it new or old? How much stronger should the 0.5 minority's right claims be than the right claims of 0.4 minority, and how much weaker should it be than the right claims of 0.6 minority?

Intuitively, perhaps, it is understandable to think that historical or old minorities should have stronger right claims than new minorities. Nevertheless, rather than the distinction between "old" and "new," the emphasis should be on discrimination. If a group of minorities are discriminated against, whether they are old or new should not be the determinant of whether their right claims are justified or not. The fact of discrimination alone is enough to justify their right claims. However, adopting the distinction between negative freedom, positive freedom, and republican freedom, let us adapt the distinction to distinguish between three facets of rights—namely, negative rights, positive rights, and republican rights—and see how old and new minorities will fare in the various facets. In terms of positive rights—that is, what should be done for minorities—old minorities are likely going to get more because it is easier to argue for their entitlements by virtue of their long stay. This is purely a practical matter—it does not mean that morally, and in theory or in principle, new minorities do not deserve as much. But when it comes to negative rights—that is, what should not be done to minorities— neither in theory nor in practice is there any justification to cause any group of minorities moral harm simply because they are new, when this moral harm is unjustifiable to be caused to old minorities.

Furthermore, in view of republican rights—that is, minorities should not be dominated—allowing minority groups to be dominated because they are "new" is not different from permitting discrimination on the ground of the period of stay. If the length of stay is a justified reason for discrimination against new minorities, why not, say, the color of their skin, the language they speak, the ethnicity they belong to, the faith they profess, or their sexual orientation, health status, gender, age, and so on? If Catholics and Protestants, Christians and Muslims, Hindus and Buddhists, Kikuyu and Luo, Arabs and Indians, Blacks and Whites, heterosexuals and lesbian, gay, bisexual, transgender or intersexual persons (LGBTs), and so on are all deemed to be equal by the United Nations Minorities Declaration, why should a minority group that is considered to be "new" be less equal than a minority group that is considered to be "old"? This is the case in practice, but it should not be the case in theory and principle. It may be plausible in law, but it tends to be implausible in morality.

A definition should not overstretch itself to cover "everything," otherwise it becomes meaningless. To retain its meaningfulness, a definition must delimit itself to capture the essentials of the phenomenon it attempts to define. But overdelimitation too is a danger; it may lead a definition to overlook certain essential aspects of the phenomenon that is being defined. Does Capotorti's definition overdelimit itself when it restricts the concept of minority to national or ethnic, religious, and linguistic groups? While there is no shortcut answer to the above question, it is worth pondering that "[t]he question often arises as to whether, for example, persons with disabilities, persons belonging to certain political groups or persons with a particular sexual orientation or identity (lesbian, gay, bisexual, transgender or intersexual persons) constitute minorities" (United Nations 2010, 3). My answers to these questions are in the affirmative!

Whether we answer these questions in the affirmative or negative, we should note:

> While the United Nations Minorities Declaration is devoted to national, ethnic, religious and linguistic minorities, it is also important to combat multiple dis-crimination and to address situations where a group belonging to a national or ethnic, religious and linguistic minority is also discriminated against on other grounds such as gender, disability or sexual orientation. Similarly, it is impor-tant to keep in mind that, in many countries, minorities are often found among the most marginalized groups in society and severely affected by, for example, pandemic diseases, such as HIV/AIDS, and in general have limited access to health services. (Ibid.)

We can go on enumerating the limitations of Capotorti's definition, but the fact is that there is no definition that has been able to aptly define the concept of minority. Nevertheless, although the nature and essence of minority are very difficult to succinctly capture in a definition, at least we know and we agreed that minorities exist, and that what it means to be a minority involves "so and so" characteristics in "so and so" context. Hence, while "[t]here is no internationally agreed definition as to which groups constitute minorities" (Ibid., 2) at the same time "[i]t is often stressed that the existence of a minority is a question of fact and that any definition must include both objective factors (such as, the existence of a shared ethnicity, language, or religion) and subjective factors (including that individuals must identify themselves as members of a minority)" (Ibid.).

On the question of subjective identification, one can identify herself as a member of a certain minority group, yet she may be objectively identified by the minority group itself, the dominant majority group, or both of the groups as not being a member of the minority group. In this case, while other members of the minority group are discriminated against, she may not be discriminated against. Hence, as far as discrimination is concerned, her subjective identification is trumped by the objective identification of others. So also a person may refuse to subjectively identify himself as a member of a certain minority group, yet others may identify him objectively as a member of the minority group. Consequently, when members of the minority group are being discriminated against, he too may be discriminated against. Hence, as far as discrimination is concerned, his subjective identification is trumped by the objective identification of others. My argument here is not to negate the very important value of subjective identification. But the aim is to show that objective identification too is very important.

The subjective identification as minorities and the objective identification of minorities have serious consequences that I shall discuss in subsequent chapters. It is due to such consequences that at the Paris Peace Conference in 1919, shortly after the First World War, Woodrow Wilson—the then president of the United States of America—argued for the founding of the League of Nations. In defense of the formation of the League of nations, he argued that "nothing, I venture to say, is more likely to disturb the peace of the world than the treatment which might in certain circumstances be meted out to minorities" (as quoted in Krasner 1999, 93). Certainly, Wilson was basing his argument on the circumstances of the First World War. Moreover, the argument was even more true in view of the circumstances of the Second World War. In our current world, contrary to Wilson's fear or assertion, the domination of, and discrimination against, minorities may not be the most likely factor to disturb domestic, international, regional, and global peace. Nevertheless, such treatments are still some of the potent factors that are causing and/or enabling domestic, international, regional, and global crises and conflicts.

Although Wilson was referring to European minorities in general, it is notable that the specific minorities that were at the receiving end of the domination and discrimination that led to the First World War may be referred to as migrants even though they became settlers and subsequently citizens. In other words, in the events that led to the First World War, these migrants or settlers who later became citizens were the most affected group of minorities as far as domination and discrimination are concerned. November 11, 2018, was the centenary of the end of the First World War. In this centenary and since the end of the Second World War, there is no doubt that, generally, European states have made some progress in the protection of minorities. However, the current treatment of migrants (especially migrants of African descent, Middle Eastern descent, and South East Asian descent—arguably in that order) in Europe shows that, after all, the French writer, Jean-Baptiste Alphose Karr, might be right when he wrote in 1849, *plus ça change, plus c'est la même chose* (the more things change, the more they stay the same). On these grounds, one may be right to argue that the apparent change to the discrimination against minorities in Europe after the Second World War is merely superficial as far as migrants from Africa, the Middle East, and South East Asia are concerned. In other words, the discrimination against minorities in Europe *essentially* remains the same. It is not only in Europe that migrants are currently being discriminated against. From North America to South America to Asia to Africa, migrant minorities are discriminated against. Therefore, in the third chapter, I will tease out some ways in which global, regional, and subregional affairs affect how migrants are treated in Africa. For now, in the next section, I will discuss the go-to solution for the domination of, and discrimination against, minorities—that is, the usual or normal approach, namely, minority rights, to the problem of domination of, and discrimination against, minorities.

MINORITY RIGHTS

Reviewing the literature on minority rights, Kymlicka (n.d.) concludes:

> In much of the political science and law literatures, the term "minority rights" is used to refer to legal provisions that have two key features: first, they are intended to recognize or accommodate the distinctive needs of non-dominant ethnic or racial groups; and second, they do so by adopting minority-specific measures, above and beyond the non-discriminatory enforcement of universal individual rights that apply regardless of group membership. (s.p.)

In Kymlicka's (n.d.) description of minority rights, as presented earlier, he only mentioned nondominant ethnic or racial groups as minorities. But, as we know, there are other categories of minorities such as nondominant religious groups, nondominant linguistic groups, and so on. Therefore, seeing that the description in question is insufficient and may even be reductionistic, let us add to it these other categories of minorities in order to make it a better and robust description of minority rights. Assuming that the description contains these other categories of minority rights, let us proceed with our discussion. Predicated on the above description of minority rights, according to Kymlicka, "minority rights are often distinguished from anti-discrimination policies, as two distinct (but complementary) tools for protecting minorities from injustice at the hands of dominant groups. . . . Minority rights . . . involve positive group-specific measures, not just the non-discriminatory enforcement of universal human rights." (s.p.)

As we have seen in the foregoing description, minority rights do not only treat individuals as members of a minority group, but crucially, they also especially treat individual members of a minority group as a collective. So, for minority rights, minority groups have two sides: The one side is the individual members who make up a minority group; and the other side is the collective minority group. On the former side we see the individuals not just as ordinary individuals but also as individuals who are members of a certain minority group. On the latter side, we do not look at individuals, but we look at the collective; hence, we do not see individual members, but we see a certain collective minority group. These two sides are not two different entities; rather, they are two complementary sides of the same entity. This individual and collective distinction will be revisited and dealt with in detail in chapter 4.

Critics and criticisms of minority rights abound. One key criticism has always been that individual human rights are enough and minority rights are unnecessary. As Kymlicka (n.d.) says, "Not everyone agrees that minority rights are appropriate or needed; some commentators believe that anti-discrimination is sufficient" (s.p.). Those who argue that antidiscrimination policies are sufficient—therefore minority rights are not needed—base their argument on two cojoined grounds: The protection of human rights—that is, individual human rights—is sufficient, hence there is no need of minority rights; and minority groups are made up of individuals; once the rights of these individuals are not violated, their membership of a minority group is inconsequential. In both instances, what these critics of minority rights commit is the fallacy of composition. The fallacy of composition is the assumption that if something is true of, good for, bad for, or—in the case of the above argument—sufficient for a part, some parts, or every single part, then it necessarily means that it is also true of, good for, bad for, or—in the case of the above argument—sufficient for the whole as a unit.

In opposition to the above fallacy, the fulfilment of the individual human rights of the individual members of a minority group does not necessarily mean that the group as a collective does not suffer any rights infringement.

And the nonviolation of the individual human rights of the individual members of a minority group does not necessarily mean that the group as a whole does not suffer any rights violation. As a unit, although the group is the sum total of all its individual members, the group is more than a mere aggregate of the individual members. As a collective, the individual members now have an additional, but not less important, identity—that of the group. That "the category 'minority rights' is now widely accepted as a legitimate component of international human rights" (Ibid.) is based on the realization of the above fact that the collective unit of a minority group is more than a mere aggregate of the individual members of the minority group.

Some critics have even taken their criticism as far as to say that minority rights negate individual human rights. It is in this vein that critics have said that "the Council of Europe's norms of minority rights . . . impose ethnic identities on individuals, and . . . privilege[s] cultural differences over our common humanity" (Ibid.). It is in the same vein that Alain Finkielkraut (1988) said:

The United Nations, founded to propagate the universalist ideals of Enlightened Europe, now speaks on behalf of every ethnic prejudice, believing that peoples, nations and cultures have rights which outweigh the rights of man. The "multicultural" lobby dismisses the liberal values of Europe as "racist", while championing the narrow chauvinism of every minority culture. (quoted in Kymlicka 2007, 6)

In contrast to the assumption of critics that minority rights negate individual human rights, the fact and reality is that both in theory and in practice, and both historically and currently, "the rights of minorities and indigenous peoples are an inseparable part of a larger human rights framework, and operates within its limits" (Kymlicka n.d., s.p.). All the international declarations and conventions on minority rights assert the above position (Ibid.). Moreover,

both the UN and Council of Europe are unambiguous that minority rights cannot be used to "outweigh the right of man." The UN's Declaration on Minority Rights states that any rights recognized in the Declaration "shall not prejudice the enjoyment of all persons of universally recognized human rights and fundamental freedoms." Similarly, the Council of Europe's Framework Convention says that the Convention must be interpreted in a way that complies with the European Convention on Human Rights. (Ibid.)

It is a misconception to see minority rights as posers of dangerous threats to states. Positively, minority rights are concerned with many facets of the collective life of minorities. While there are multitudes of concerns for minority rights, there are key concerns that other various concerns, arguably, revolve around. These key concerns can be summed up as "survival and existence, promotion and protection of the identity of minorities, equality and non-discrimination, and effective and meaningful participation" (United Nations 2010, 7).

For the past three and half decades, the recognition and acceptance of minority rights has been in ascendancy. On the global level, The UN adopted a "Declaration on the Rights of Persons belonging to National or Ethnic, Religious and Linguistic Minorities" in 1992, and a "Declaration on the Rights of Indigenous Peoples" in 2007. At the regional level, the Council of Europe adopted the "European Charter for Regional or Minority Languages" in 1991, and the "Framework Convention for the Protection of National Minorities" in 1995 (Ibid.). While the recognition and acceptance of minority rights is currently in ascendance, the nonrecognition and rejection of minority rights was the order of the day for most part of the post–world war period in the international community (Kymlicka, n.d., s.p.) Moreover, even today, Africa still lags behind Europe, North America, and South America. As Kymlicka (n.d.) says:

> At the regional level, while both the council of Europe and the Organization of American States have seriously debated minority and indigenous rights, the topic has been largely neglected by other regional organizations, such as the African Union, the Arab League or ASEAN. Indeed, it remains a taboo topic in many post-colonial countries in Asia, Africa and Middle East, where state minority issues remain heavily "securitized", treated as issues of state security rather than as issues of human rights or even of free and open democratic debate. (s.p.)

While the problem of minority discrimination is found in all parts of the world and while the protection of minority rights is a major concern in all parts of the world, some parts of the world have done better than others in the commitment to protect minority rights. The depth of commitment to minority rights varies markedly around the world (Ibid.). Alarmingly, currently the global situation is that

> [s]upport for minority rights varies not only by region, but also by different types of group. While there has been an impressive level of international support for the claims of indigenous peoples, there has been much less support for the claims of national minorities, and even less for the rights of immigrants and refugees, who have arguably faced a situation of declining international protection in the same period that indigenous peoples have gained greater rights and recognition. While indigenous peoples are widely seen as weak and innocent victims who pose no threat to the larger state, other types of minorities are often seen as

either posing a dangerous threat to break up the country (national minorities) or as undesirable and undeserving outsiders who do not belong (migrants). (Ibid.)

While a plethora of minority rights problems are sprinkled all over the subcontinent, the subcontinent has not done enough to protect minority rights. This is no surprise because not even (individual) universal human rights have been adequately protected on the subcontinent. There is more work, in fact a lot of work, to be done in getting more multilateral organizations, states, multinational corporations (MNCs), international nongovernmental organizations (INGOs), nongovernmental organizations (NGOs), and persons committed to minority rights, widening the scope of commitment, and raising the level of commitment. A cursory look at the continent, from West Africa to East Africa, to Central Africa, to Southern Africa to North Africa, will glaringly reveal the enormous work that is beckoning on the proponents of minority rights in these parts of the world (I shall say more about this in chapter 4).

Minorities lacking differentiated group rights implies that multiculturalism—which ensures that minorities have differentiated group rights—is largely absent in Africa. In the absence of multiculturalism, guaranteeing minority rights becomes a herculean task or even a project in futility. Consequently, one may aver that, in Africa, the problem of domination and discrimination will remain intractable unless multiculturalism is accepted and minority rights are seen as the *conditio sine qua non* and the *conditio per quam* through which multiculturalism is practiced on the continent. In subsequent chapters, I shall explain why I am not sanguine about this kind of argument. For now, it suffices to look at how Africa stands in comparison with other regions as far as minority rights are concerned.

However, multiculturalism and minority rights are rejected in Africa due to a combination of internal and international dynamics. In chapter 4, I shall explore these dynamics and then explain how we may be transcended to arrive at the possibility of acceptance of multiculturalism and minority rights. In chapter 3, I will explore why practically the ill-treatment of migrants in Africa is likely to remain the norm for a long time even if there are constitutional guarantees for the protection of minorities through multiculturalism and minority rights. In the next chapter, I explain what the concept of domination entails and discuss whether migrants even have the right—in the first place—to migrate to their host or receiving countries where they are considered as minorities. After all, those who discriminate against migrants do so mainly because they think migrants do not have such right in the first place.

REFERENCES

Abumere, Frank Aragbonfoh. 2019. "Rule of Law." In *The Palgrave Encyclopedia of Global Security Studies*, edited by Scott Romaniuk, Manish Thapa and Peter Marton. Cham: Palgrave Macmillan.

Achebe, Chinua. 1982. "Interview with Anthony Appiah, D. A. N. Jones and John Ryle." *Times Literary Supplement*, February 26, 1982.

Appiah, Kwame Anthony. 1992. *In My Father's House*: *Africa in the Philosophy of Culture*. Oxford: Oxford University Press.

BBC. 2019. "Rwanda Genocide: 100 Days of Slaughter." April 4, 2019.

Berenskoetter, Felix. 2017. "Identity in International Relations." *Oxford Research Encyclopedias, International Studies*, December 22, 2017.

Bray, Zoe. 2008. "Ethnographic Approaches." In *Approaches and Methodologies in the Social Sciences*: *A Pluralist Perspective*, edited by Donattela della Porta and Micheal Keating, 296–315. Cambridge: Cambridge University Press.

Brons, Lajos. 2015. "Othering, An Analysis." *Transcience* 6, no. 1: 69–90.

Brubaker, Rogers, and Frederick Cooper. 2000. "Beyond 'Identity.'" *Theory and Society* 29: 1–47.

Burke, A. 2006. "Identity/Difference." In *Encyclopedia of International Relations and Global Politics*, edited by M. Griffiths, 394–96. London: Routledge.

Campbell, D. 1992. *Writing Security*: *United States Foreign Policy and the Politics of Identity*. Manchester: Manchester University Press.

Capotorti, Francesco. 1977. "Study on the Rights of Persons Belonging to Ethnic, Religious and Linguistic Minorities." UN Doc. E/CN.4/Sub.3/384/Add. 1–7.

Connolly, W. E. 2002. *Identity/Difference*: *Democratic Negotiations of Political Paradox*. Ithaca: Cornell University Press.

Crang, M. 1991. *Cultural Geography*. London: Routledge.

Cronin, B. 1999. *Community under Anarchy*: *Transnational Identity and the Evolution of Cooperation*. New York: Columbia University Press.

De Beauvoir, Simone. *Le Deuxi`eme Sexe*. Paris: Gallimard, 1949 (1976).

Deschênes, Jules. 1985. "Proposal Concerning a Definition of the Term 'Minority.'" UN Doc. E/CN.4/Sub.2/1985/31.

Drakuli´c, C. 1992. *The Balkan Express*: *Fragments from the Other Side of the War*. New York: Norton.

Falola, Toyin. 2006. "Welcome." Conference Program, Movements, Migrations, and Displacements in Africa, Africa Conference 2006, The University of Texas at Austin, March 25–27, 2006.

Fanon, Frantz. 1967. *Black Skin, White Mask*. London: Grove Press.

Finkielkraut, Alain. 1988. *The Undoing of Thought*. Translated by Dennis O'Keefe. London: Claridge Press.

Gallie, W. B. (1956). Essentially contested concepts. Proceedings of the Aristotelian Society, 56, 167–198.

Gyekye, Kwame. 1995. *An Essay on African Philosophical Thought*: *The Akan Conceptual Scheme*. Philadelphia: Temple University Press.

Heyes, Cressida J. 2020. "Identity Politics." *The Stanford Encyclopedia of Philosophy*, Fall edition. http://plato.stanford.edu/archives/fall2020/entries/identitypolitics/

Hopf, T. 1998. "The Promise of Constructivism in International Relations Theory." *International Security* 23: 171–200.

Krasner, Stephen. 1999. *Sovereignty: Organized Hypocrisy*. Princeton, NJ: Princeton University Press.

Kruks, Sonia. 2001. *Retrieving Experience: Subjectivity and Recognition in Feminist Politics*. Ithaca, NY: Cornell University Press.

Kymlicka, Will. 2007. *Multicultural Odysseys: Navigating the New International Politics of Diversity*. Oxford: Oxford University Press.

Kymlicka, Will. n.d. "Minority Rights." *Encyclopedia Princetoniensis: The Princeton Encyclopedia of Self-Determination*. http://pesd.princeton.edu/?q=node/256. Accessed: June 19, 2017.

Mafeje, Achie. 2008[2000]. "Africanity: A Combative Ontology." *CODESRIA Bulletin* third and fourth: 106–13.

Mbembe, Achille. 2001. *On the Postcolony*. London: University of California Press.

Mbembe, Achille. 2002. "African Modes of Self Writing." *Public Culture* 14, no. 1: 239–73.

Mbembe, Achille. 2015. "The State of South African Political Life." *African is a Country*, September 19, 2015. https://africasacountry.com/2015/09/achille -mbembe-on-the-state-of-south-african-politics

Mbembe, Achille. 2019. "Thoughts on the Planetary: An Interview with Achille Mbembe." In *New Frame*, edited by Sindre Bangstad and Torbjorn Tumyr Nilsen. September 5, 2019. https://www.newframe.com/thoughts-on-the-planetary-an -interview-with-achille-mbembe/

Mintz, Steven. 2018. "What are Values?." *Ethics Sage*, August 1, 2018. https://www .ethicssage.com/2018/08/what-are-values.html. Accessed: June 10, 2020.

Mudimbe, V. Y. 2003. "Globalization and African Identity." *CR: The New Centennial Review* 3, no. 2: 205–18.

Sen, Amartya. 2007. *Identity and Violence: The Illusion of Violence*. New York: W.W. Norton.

Taylor, Charles. 1994. "The Politics of Recognition." In *Multiculturalism: Examining the Politics of Recognition*, edited by Amy Gutmann, 25–74. Princeton, NJ: Princeton University Press.

United Nations. 2010. "Minority Rights: International Standards and Guidance for Implementation." N(E/CN.4/Sub.2/384/Rev. 1, Office of the High Commissioner for Human Rights, United Nations.

Wheatley, Steven. 2005. *Democracy, Minorities and International Law*. Cambridge: Cambridge University Press.

Willard, J. 1970. *Cameroon Federation: Political Integration in a Fragmentary Society*. Princeton, NJ: Princeton University Press.

Wiredu, Kwasi, and Kwame Gyekye. 1992. *Person and Community: Ghanaian Philosophical Studies*. Washington: The Council of Research in Values and Philosophy.

Chapter Two

The Problem of Domination and Discrimination, and the Right to Immigration

I have a twofold aim in this chapter. My first aim is to explain what the concept of domination entails, while my second aim is to discuss whether migrants even have the right—in the first place—to migrate to their host countries where they are considered as minorities. The relationship between my first aim and my second aim is that those who discriminate against migrants do so mainly because they think migrants do not have such a right in the first place. On the one hand, establishing that migrants have such a right necessarily makes the discrimination against them unjust. However, on the other hand, even if it is established that they do not have such a right, this does not justify the kind of discrimination they face. I shall discuss the kind of discrimination they face in chapter 3. To prepare the grounds for such a discussion, I shall proceed to explain the concept of domination and then discuss migrants' right, or lack of right, to migrate to their host or receiving countries.

THE CONCEPT OF DOMINATION

Max Weber (1978) famously conceives of domination as a situation in which the probability that a person will obey the command issued by another person is high (212–13). Specifically, somebody "dominates another if and only if they have a certain power over that other, in particular a power of interference on an arbitrary basis" (Pettit 1997, 52; see Weber 1978, 212–13)—Aki dominates Onyinye if Aki is arbitrarily capable of interfering in certain choices that Onyinye is in a position to make (Pettit 1997, 52). Therefore, the domination of migrants refers to a situation in which a host state, certain groups in the state, or nationals of the state are capable of arbitrarily interfering in

33

certain choices that migrants are in a position to make. In other words, the domination of migrants means the asymmetric relationship between migrants and the host state, certain groups in the state, or its nationals in which the latter negatively control, influence, or illegitimately exercise power over the former for the gains of the latter and to the detriment of the former. Constitutive of this asymmetric relationship is differential treatment in which members of the latter are given preferential treatment which advantages them while members of the former are ill-treated in ways that disadvantage them. This can be formal (ingrained in laws and procedures), informal (e.g., systemic biases), or both formal and informal (Abumere 2020).

While I am using the terms *domination* and *discrimination*, the former is the operative term because my conception of the former entails the latter. Discrimination can be moral, immoral, or amoral, and it can be positive, negative, or neutral. Throughout this book, I use the term *discrimination* in its negative sense. For instance, reverse discrimination such as affirmative action may be a positive thing. But discrimination that is quintessentially based on the grounds of identities and differences qua identities and differences will be a negative thing. This latter form of negative discrimination is what this book is concerned with.

In many societies in the global south, minority domination and discrimination is either implicitly or explicitly perpetrated by individuals, collective agents, organizations, institutions, and even the state itself. Racial, national or ethnic, linguistic, and religious supremacy are some of the oldest, most prevalent, most dangerous, and most immoral reasons for minority discrimination. But there are other reasons such as economic insecurity of a majority group, a majority group's fear of domination by a minority group, historical oppression of a majority group by a minority group, and so on. So minority domination and discrimination can be a complex and multifaceted subject. Nevertheless, the fundamental problems with minority domination and discrimination are those of identity and difference, inclusion and exclusion, the scope of and the grounds for domination and discrimination, and, above all, rights and justice.

Discrimination against minorities and minorities is not a new phenomenon in international politics. So too the consequences of such discrimination are not new in international politics. As mentioned in chapter 1, when arguing for the founding of the League of Nations at the Paris Peace Conference in 1919—shortly after the First World War—the then president of the United States, Woodrow Wilson, gave the following warning: "Nothing, I venture to say, is more likely to disturb the peace of the world than the treatment which might in certain circumstances be meted out to minorities" (quoted in Krasner 1999, 93). Certainly, Wilson was basing his warning on the circumstances of the First World War. Moreover, the argument was even truer in view of the circumstances of the Second World War. November 11, 2018, was the centenary of the end of the First World War. A century after the end of the war, there is no doubt that, generally, European states have made some progress in the protection of minorities. In our current world, the ill-treatment of minorities may not be the most likely factor to disturb domestic, transnational, international, subregional, regional, and global peace. Nevertheless, such treatment is still one of the potent factors that are causing and/or enabling domestic, transnational, international, and regional crises and conflicts in Africa.

It is a fait accompli that states discriminate against minorities. It is not only states that discriminate against minorities; organizations, collectives, and individuals also discriminate against minorities. The discrimination against minorities takes two forms: Minorities are discriminated against as a group—that is, as one people; and individuals are discriminated against individually, but because they belong to a minority group. But why is it the case that "persons belonging to national or ethnic, religious and linguistic minorities [etc.] are also often victims of multiple discrimination"? (United Nations 2010, 1). The answer to this question is context dependent. The reason minority *A* is discriminated against in state *X* may not be the same reason why minority *B* is discriminated against in state *Y*. While the particular and specific reasons for discrimination against minorities *A* and *B* may be different, the universal and general reasons for the discrimination by states *X* and *Y* are the same.

On a broader general level, the discrimination occurs because minorities *A* and *B* are minorities in states *X* and *Y*. And on a narrower general level, the discrimination occurs because *A* and *B* are racial minorities, national minorities, ethnic minorities, linguistic minorities, religious minorities, and so on in states *X* and *Y*. On the particular or specific level of reason for discrimination, while state *X* may discriminate against racial minority *A* for fear that *A* might dominate the rest of the country economically, state *Y* may discriminate against racial minority *B* for the irrational belief that members of *B* are less human than members of the majority group in the country. So too, while *X* may discriminate against religious minority *A* for the irrational belief that members of *A* are infidels, *Y* might discriminate against religious minority *B* for fear that *B* may dominate the rest of the country politically.

Generally, the grounds for domination and discrimination against minorities can be approached from two perspectives which are one and the same thing. The one approach is the "positive" perspective, while the other approach is the "negative" perspective. Here, the terms *positive* and *negative* do not have any moral connotations and denotations; I am using them in their arithmetic sense. In this arithmetic sense, positive should be taken to mean "part of"—sometimes, although not necessarily, an addition—while negative should be taken to mean "not part of"—sometimes, although not necessarily, a subtraction. In the positive sense, minorities are discriminated against because of the group they belong to—that is, because of the group they are "part of." In the negative sense, minorities are discriminated against because of the group they do not belong to—that is, because of the group they are "not part of."

The above explication of the general grounds for minority discrimination is important because, from a political philosophy and political theory point of view, it helps us see that it is incongruent to accept the validity of (individual) universal human rights[1] and at the same time discriminate against minorities. If we accept the validity of universal human rights, and we agree that most importantly, among other reasons, individuals have these rights by virtue of being human, then we should recognize that members of minorities are humans too and are entitled to universal human rights regardless of whether they are "part of" a minority group and "not part of" a majority group.

A brief discussion of certain philosophical arguments—although they were originally used in the context of global distributive justice—will suffice to explain the aforementioned incongruence. Relevant deductions should be made from the following discussion in this paragraph and the next one. Simon Caney (2005) argues that global distributive justice can be justified on the same fundamental grounds on which domestic distributive justice is justified (107). For Caney, domestic distributive justice rejects discrimination against fellow citizens not merely because they are fellow citizens but fundamentally because they are fellow humans and it is wrong to discriminate against fellow humans (ibid.). Since both citizens and noncitizens are all humans, and fellow humans, the standard justifications for domestic distributive justice principles can equally serve as the standard justifications for global distributive justice principles (Abumere 2015, 20; Caney 2005, 107). For Samuel Black (1991), to deny the aforementioned claim is to commit "the fallacy of restricted universalism" because an argument for distributive justice "that ascribes rights and claims on the basis of certain universal attributes of persons, cannot at the same time restrict the grounds for those claims to a person's membership or status within a given society" (357).

Making relevant deductions from the above discussion in the preceding paragraph, we can also argue that the rights of members of minority groups can be justified on the same fundamental grounds on which the rights of members of majority groups are justified. Individuals, collectives, organizations, and states reject discrimination against members of majority groups not merely because they are fellow members of a majority group but fundamentally because they are fellow humans and it is wrong to discriminate against fellow humans. Since members of both majority and minority groups are all humans, and fellow humans, the standard justifications for nondiscrimination against—and respect for the rights of—members of majority groups can equally serve as the standard justifications for nondiscrimination against—and respect for the rights of—members of minority groups. To deny this claim is to commit "the fallacy of restricted universalism" because an argument for nondiscrimination against—and respect for the rights of—members of majority groups "that ascribes rights and claims on the basis of certain universal attributes of persons, cannot at the same time restrict the grounds for those claims to a person's membership or status within a given society" (357).

As earlier mentioned, the fundamental problems with minority domination and discrimination are those of identity and difference, inclusion and exclusion, the scope of and the grounds for domination and discrimination, and, above all, rights and justice. There is a plethora of the domination of—and discrimination against—minorities in Africa because the minorities lack what Kymlicka (1995) refers to as differentiated group rights—namely, minority rights. If minorities in general are supposed to possess differentiated group rights, then migrants as a subset of minorities—that is, a special category of minorities, specifically, are supposed to possess differentiated group rights. However, those who discriminate against migrants think that migrants do not have the right, in the first place, to move to the host or receiving countries. So the question is do migrants have such right? This is not a simple question that requires a disjunctive answer "yes" or "no." It is a complex question that may not necessarily be answered in the affirmative or in the negative but must be thoroughly interrogated nonetheless. Such a task is the aim of the next section.

ETHICS OF MIGRATION AND CASES OF EXCEPTION

I divide the discussion into three parts. In the first section ("The Problem with the Relational Approach and the Nonrelational Approach"), I present an overview of the arguments relationists use in support of closed borders and nonrelationists use in support of open borders. Then, on the one hand, I offer preliminary arguments for why relationists ought to create exceptions for cases such as the X and Y case (cases of exception). On the other hand, I offer preliminary arguments for why, contra nonrelationists, open borders should be particular, for instance, in the X and Y case (cases of exception), rather than universal—that is, in all cases. In the second part ("Right to Immigration as Rectification for Historical Injustice"), I engage in a detailed and extensive analysis of the preliminary arguments in the first part. Using rectificatory justice as grounds of my cases of exception, I show, on the one hand, why relationists are wrong to extend closed borders to cases of exception such as the X and Y case. On the other hand, I show why nonrelationists are wrong to extend their open borders beyond cases of exception such as the X and Y

case. In view of the aforementioned problem with both the relational and the nonrelational approaches in respect of cases of exception, in the third part ("The Significance of the Problem") I argue for a complementary use of the approaches, explain what the complementary use is, give reasons for why it is necessary, and show how it resolves the problem with the relational and nonrelational approaches and how it is a perfect fit for cases of exception.

The Problem with the Relational Approach and the Nonrelational Approach

In the vast majority of political philosophy and political theory literature on migration, migration is mostly conceived of as an issue of global justice in which the relational approach and the nonrelational approach are pitted against each other. On the one hand, the relational approach is associative—that is, it is member based. It emphasizes that the common relationships that bind moral agents of justice (insiders, e.g., citizens, compatriots, etc.) together have moral significance. Moral agents (outsiders, e.g.. instance non-citizens, noncompatriots, etc.) who are not part of such relationships do not have right claims against insiders and have no duties of justice to the insiders. On the other hand, the nonrelational approach denies that justice is based on any special relationship such as citizenship, compatriotism, and so on. It asserts that justice is based on our common humanity and common human factors such as natural prerogatives, basic needs, and so on (Armstrong 2012, 25; Maffettone 2013, 127; Risse 2012, 8–9; Sangiovanni 2007). To illustrate relational and nonrelational duties, during the COVID-19 pandemic-induced lockdown across the world, Nigeria airlifting Nigerians, but not Ghanaians, who were stranded in South Africa, is a relational duty. Whereas, Nigeria receiving refugees and asylum seekers from Cameroon and respecting the international law principle of *nonrefoulment* is a nonrelational duty.

Generally, the relational approach supports the restriction on the right to immigration, whereas the nonrelational approach opposes such restriction. There are several arguments both for and against restricting the right to immigration. Arguments against restricting the right to immigration include cosmopolitan egalitarianism, libertarianism, democracy, and utilitarianism. Whereas arguments for the restriction on the right to immigration include culture, economy/efficiency, welfare states, political functioning/liberal nationalism, security, self-determination, democracy, jurisdiction, political realism, and indirect cosmopolitanism (Wellman 2020).

The relationists who argue for the status quo—that is, no right to immigration—include David Miller, Christopher Heath Wellman, Anna Stilz, and so on. While the nonrelationsists who criticize the restriction on the right to immigration include Joseph Carens, Kieran Oberman, Arash Abizadeh,

Ayelet Shachar, Sarah Fine, Phillip Cole, and so on. In view of Miller's and Carens' arguments being widely debated, using Miller on one side (those who argue for the status quo—that is, no right to immigration) and Carens on the other side (those who criticize the restriction on the right to immigration) will suffice to illustrate the views of both the relationists' and the nonrelationists' sides—that is, both the relational and the nonrelational approaches.

For Miller (2016), states' authority to control their borders can be seen as a necessary derivative of their sovereignty. However, this sovereignty argument is weak (too quick) because: (1) "[i]t assumes that the 'sovereign state' . . . is the best form of government" and (2) extends the state's authority to prospective immigrants (58). Due to the weaknesses of the "sovereign state argument," Miller turns to the "territorial jurisdiction argument." According to this argument, "[H]aving rights of jurisdiction over a given territory implies having the right to control the movement of people in and out of that territory, so that where a state can legitimately exercise jurisdiction it is also entitled to exclude immigrants if it so wishes" (58–59).

The right to territorial jurisdiction entails further rights: (1) "the right to control and use the resources that the territory contains" and (2) "the right to control the movement of goods and people across its borders" (Miller 2016, 60–61). Does the right to claim territorial jurisdiction necessarily entail the right to control immigration? Miller says, "Not in the strictest sense because a state might choose to pre-commit the resources to cover the rights of all the people who might wish to enter" (62). Therefore, "the argument about jurisdiction needs to be completed by an argument about self-determination in order fully to justify the right to close borders" (ibid.)—self-determination is "the right of a democratic public to make a wide range of policy choices within the limits set by human rights" (ibid.).

The above argument is criticized on the grounds that due to the human costs of closing borders, self-determination is not of sufficient value to do so. Nevertheless, self-determination matters because it gives citizens some degree of control over what happens to their political community in the future (Miller 2016, 62–63). Alongside self-determination, the function of democracy is an argument for border control (70). The overall size of their populations is another reason why states may have to control immigration. So, instead of grounding state's rights on sovereignty, territorial jurisdiction, and self-determination, the rights are based on the grounds of efficiency, culture, and so on.

However, it is not always the case that a smaller population is more governable both economically and politically than a larger population. Therefore, the efficiency argument is weak. Nevertheless, the culture argument is stronger than the efficiency argument. In spite of its strength, the culture argument still leaves ample room for challenges to states' right to control immigration for the following reasons. First, "the argument about the cultural composition of the demos mistakenly assumes that without immigration we would have a culturally homogenous body of citizens" (Miller 2016, 66). As Michael Blake (2003) argues, "To identify the purpose of the state with the preservation of a cultural group is inevitably to draw an invidious distinction against those citizens who do not happen to belong to that community" (232–33).

Second, even if immigration limits the scope of self-determination, "political self-determination is simply not an important enough value to outweigh the pressing claims to enter that immigrants may make" (Miller 2016, 66). Third, "excluding immigrants is a form of coercion, and no state can be justified in coercing outsiders without their agreement" (66–67). In spite of the above challenges, Miller thinks that immigration controls are not necessarily coercive: "The immigrant is being prevented from doing something . . . but he is not being coerced to do anything else in particular" (74).

Unlike Miller, Carens (2013) argues that "in principle, borders should generally be open and people should normally be free to leave their country of origin and settle in another" (225). He challenges the views that, first, "[t]he power to admit or exclude noncitizens is inherent in sovereignty and essential for any political community that seeks to exercise self-determination" (ibid.); second, "[e]very state has the legal and moral right to exercise control over admissions in pursuit of its own national interest and of the common good of the members of its community" (ibid.); and third, in most cases, states are under no obligation to accept immigrants (ibid.).

Analogically, Carens (2013) says, "[C]itizenship in Western democracies is modern equivalent of feudal class privilege—an inherited status that greatly enhances one's life chances" (226). He outlines a positive case for open borders: First, "[t]he institutions and practices that govern human beings are ones that human beings have created and can change" (ibid.); second, "in evaluating the moral status of alternative forms of political and social organization, we must start from the premise that all human beings are of equal moral worth" (ibid.); and third, "restrictions on the freedom of human beings require a moral justification" (ibid.).

In view of the above assumptions, Carens (2013) thinks there should be open borders, at least, prima facie, for the following reasons. First, "[f]reedom of movement contributes to individual autonomy" (227–28); second, "freedom of movement is essential for equality of opportunity" (227–28); and third, "[f]reedom of movement would contribute to a reduction of existing . . . inequalities" (227–28). Moreover, in the Cantilever Argument, he says, "[T]he freedom to move across state borders as a human right is a logical extension of the well-established democratic practice of treating freedom of movement within state borders as a human right" (237). The assumptions "undergird the claim to moral legitimacy of every contemporary democratic regime" (227). Therefore, supposedly, they are very strong assumptions or arguments!

Kieran Oberman (2016) thinks that the right to immigration protects certain fundamental interests that are valuable. Admitting that there are circumstances in which persons can be restricted from immigrating, Oberman argues for the right to immigrate. For Oberman, apart from such circumstances, no restriction on the right to immigrate can be morally justified. Arash Abizadeh (2016) concedes that citizens may owe to each other special obligations. However, he argues that such special obligations do not justify the restriction on the right to immigrate. Based on the grounds of equality, he argues that persons should have the right to immigrate. Denying such a right is tantamount to denying the equality of persons.

Sarah Fine (2016) thinks that the restriction on the right to immigrate is a form of racism and ethnicism. Michael Walzer's (1983) treatment of "white Australia" policy (47) corroborates this racism charge. Arguing that historically the emergence of borders were based on racism, Fine (2016) thinks, in effect that, if racism is not morally justifiable then restriction on the right to immigration is also not morally justifiable. Still, on the grounds of equality, Ayelet Shachar (2016) thinks that the merit-based immigration system is unfair because it discriminates against those deemed nonmeritorious and then treats them as less equal persons. In spite of all the above arguments for open borders, the status quo—both in theory and in practice—does not support the above claims. No wonder, while theorizing about refugees, Phillip Cole (2000) famously criticized liberal political theory of structural discrimination (61–63). In a nutshell, nonrelationists argue that we may base the rights of migrants on three desiderata—namely, equality, freedom, and vulnerability. On the grounds of equality, all humans are equal; prevention to enter is discrimination. On the grounds of freedom, if freedom of movement is valuable, it should not be limited to intrastate movement. On the grounds of vulnerability, as humans, we owe one another the duty to protect or help vulnerable people.

The relational approach (supporting restriction on right to immigration) and the nonrelation approach (opposing restriction on right to immigration) meet at a juncture at which the relational approach agrees that there are certain conditions that create grounds for the right to immigration. The refugee case is a prominent one. Although refugees are not citizens and have no special relationship with citizens, citizens have moral duties to them because of their humanitarian condition. The refugee case is a variant of what I refer to as cases of exception because they fit neither the norm of the relational approach nor the norm of the nonrelational approach. These cases are middle-of-the-road between the extremes of the relational and nonrelational approaches. Contra the relational approach, cases of exception show that certain conditions demand that insiders (citizens, compatriots, etc.) have duties of justice to outsiders (noncitizens, noncompatriots), and the latter have right claims against the former. Whereas contra the nonrelational approach, such conditions entail that the former owe the duties of justice only to the latter and not to all human beings, and only the latter and not all human beings have those right claims against the former. Therefore, an intermediary position between the relational and nonrelational approaches is the best fit for such cases.

For instance, to problematize the two approaches, I shall use the case of colonial historical relationships. Neither the relational approach nor the nonrelational approach can resolve the recent and current problem of migration—from former colonies to former colonizers, that is partly conditioned by colonial historical relationships. For instance, due to their colonial historical relationships, Nigerians tend to migrate to the United Kingdom, Ivorians to France, Congolese to Belgium, Angolans to Portugal, and so on. On the one hand, by using the term *partly*, I acknowledge that such migration is not only colonialism induced, it is also induced by other factors such as economics, conflicts, climate change, and so on. On the other hand, by focusing on recent and current migration that is partly conditioned by colonial historical relationship, I revolve the problem of infinite regression in relation to the question of time limit. By infinite regression, I mean going back to migration that is partly conditioned by colonialism during medieval times, ancient times, and so on. Recent and current migration, in the context of this article, include the following: migration from Africa to Europe as partially conditioned by the European colonization of Africa before and especially from the scramble for Africa and the partition of Africa at the 1884–1885 Berlin Conference; migration from the Middle East to Europe as partially conditioned by the 1916 Sykes-Picot Agreement; and similar colonialism-induced migration such as from India and Pakistan to the United Kingdom, and from Brazil to Portugal. To avoid the problem of infinite regression, my time line, admittedly arbitrarily, is from around 1800s to the present.

The relational approach thinks that as noncitizens of former colonizer X, citizens of former X's colony Y have no right claims against X, and X has no duty of justice to them. The relational approach is "shortsighted" in that it only sees one kind of special relationship that exists inside X (between citizens and government) but does not see another kind of special relationship that exists outside X (between X and its formal colonies, in this case Y). Whereas the nonrelational approach thinks that citizens of Y, as human beings, have right claims against X, and X has a duty of justice to them. However, the problem for both the relational and the nonrelational approaches is that the colonial historical relationship between X and Y suggests that (1) contra the relational approach, although citizens of Y are noncitizens of X, they may have certain right claims against X, and X may owe them certain duties of justice and (2) contra the nonrelational approach, other noncitizens of X who do not have such colonial historical relationship with X do not have such right claim against X, and X does not owe them such duty of justice.

I refer to cases, such as the above, as cases of exception because they fit neither the framework of the relational approach nor the framework of the nonrelational approach. Using cases of exception that are based on historical injustice, for instance, the colonial historical relationship between X and Y, I shall show a very important problem that both the relational approach and the nonrelational approach have in common. The problem is that neither the relational approach nor the nonrelational approach is sufficient as an approach to the global justice of migration. Then, I shall argue that the problem signifies that insights from the relational approach can be helpful for the nonrelational approach and vice versa.

I aver that the case of colonial historical relationships between former colonies and their former colonizers is another variant of cases of exception for the following reason. Using the X and Y example, it seems plausible to argue for Y citizens' right to immigration to the X based on two variants of the relational approach's grounds for justice within the state—namely, coercion and cooperation. On the coercion argument, the state owes its citizens duties of justice partly because the state coerces its citizens to do things that they may not do absent coercion, or to restrain from doing things that they may do absent coercion. On the cooperation argument, citizens owe one another duties of justice partly because the citizens of the state cooperate with one another as a collective to ensure the well-being of the entire citizens. In view of the coercion and cooperation arguments, as a former colony of X, Y citizens can demand justice from X because in certain ways X coerced them and they cooperated with X during colonialism.

In view of the coercion and cooperation that existed between former colonizers and the formerly colonized, it can be argued that former colonizers do not only owe the formerly colonized an obligation of reparation, but the former also owe the latter an obligation to distribute equitably the advantages that resulted from the coercion and cooperation that happened during colonialism (Amighetti and Nuti 2015; Ypi et al. 2009). Likewise, in view of the coercion and cooperation that existed between X and Y citizens, it can be argued that X simultaneously owes Y citizens an obligation of reparation for the harms that resulted from the coercion and an obligation to distribute the advantages that resulted from the cooperation.

However, one may rebut my argument in the penultimate and preceding paragraphs by arguing that while there was cooperation and coercion between X and Y citizens, such cooperation and coercion are not as intensive and extensive as those within X. Hence, the intra-X coercion and cooperation are "thicker" than those between X and Y citizens, and those between X and Y citizens are "thinner" than those inside X. Accepting the aforementioned rebuttal *arguendo*, I shall offer the following counterargument. In view of the thickness and thinness of coercion and cooperation, the relationship within X is thick while the colonial relationship between X and Y citizens was thin. Consequently, justice within X is thick, while justice between X and Y citizens is thin. Therefore, (1) contra nonrelationists, relationships matter: In this case, the colonial relationship between X and Y citizens—although thin—matters; (2) contra relationists, there is relationship outside the state: In this case, there is a relationship—although thin—between X and Y citizens; and (3) consequently, we need an intermediary position between the relational approach and the nonrelational approach to deal with the immigration from Y to X.

Right to Immigration as Rectification for Historical Injustice

In the preceding subsection, I explained that there are certain conditions that can create grounds of entry in cases of exception. The refugee case is the prominent one, but the case of colonial historical injustice is another one. Colonial historical relationships entail that states such as the United Kingdom, France, Belgium, Germany, the Netherlands, Spain, Portugal, and Italy should not be treated sui generis. They should be treated in relation to their former colonies. Moreover, through the process of acculturation, inculturation, assimilation, association, and/or socialization, the formerly colonized have become deeply entrenched in the culture of their former colonizers. As Edward Said (2003) says, the history of the colonized and the colonizers are intertwined, "one could not be written without taking the other into account" (s.p.).

Using the examples of the postcolonial relationships between the United Kingdom and India and between France and Algeria, Said (1993) asks, "Who in India or Algeria today can confidently separate out the British or French component of the past from the present actualities, and who in Britain or France can draw a clear circle around British London or French Paris that would exclude the impact of India and Algeria upon those two imperial cities?" (15). Said's postcolonial analysis of the relationship between former colonizers and their formerly colonized suggests that the formerly colonized's right of immigration to their former colonizers can be based on the grounds of culture.

> A major implication of colonialism . . . is that postcolonial migrants are already part of the "self" that determines the ex-colonizing nation, because they are essential contributors to its identity. This makes it the case that former

colonizers cannot justify the exclusion of immigrants they can regard as historically within the nation. Therefore, the exercise of the right to exclude is further constrained for nations that once were colonial powers. The obligation to let postcolonial migrants in is an addition to the constraints that liberal nationalists already accept, such as those stemming from humanitarian concerns . . . it is precisely on the basis of this obligation that an argument can be put forward in order to justify the right of postcolonial migrants to immigrate into a particular nation-state. (Amighetti and Nuti 2015, 12)

The formerly colonized's right of immigration to their former colonizers may not be based on the grounds of culture alone. It may also be based on the grounds of historical injustice. As Said (2003) says, "[T]he problem, then, is to keep in mind two ideas that are in many ways antithetical—the fact of the imperial divide, on the one hand, and the notion of shared experiences, on the other—without diminishing the force of either" (s.p.). In addition to the grounds of culture as discussed earlier, there is the grounds of historical injustice as discussed below.

Although there are other ways (reconciliation, apology, financial settlement, etc.) to rectify colonial historical injustice, the right to immigration may be one way. The push and pull factors—history and politics of contemporary migration from Africa to Europe—are no less historical injustice and rectificatory justice matters than they are freedom of movement and territorial sovereignty matters. Even as freedom of movement and territorial sovereignty matters, they are normative in both the ethical sense (the morally right thing to do) and the institutional sense (the acceptable norms, standards, or rules of behavior that are the order of the day). While the former is solely a matter for ideal and nonideal moral theory, the latter is simultaneously a matter for international history and international politics, on the one side, and ideal and nonideal moral theory, on the other side. Hence, the scope and content of the international historical and political relationship between, say, Africa and Europe have consequences for the global justice of migration, particularly migration from Africa to Europe. Therefore, given that historical injustice characterized the international historical and political relationship between, say, Africa and Europe—that is, the colonial and imperial domination of Africa by Europe—I will use insights from rectificatory justice to tease out why, on the one hand, contra relationists, X has an obligation to extend the right to immigration to its formerly colonized, in this case, Y citizens and, on the other hand, contra nonrelationists, X has no obligation to extend the right to immigration to others.

Ypi et al. (2009) aptly observes that the imposition of "alien rule on people, exploiting their persons and extracting their resources are historical wrongs crying out to be put right. That is the first thing that inevitably comes to mind when thinking about justice for former colonies, and rightly so" (103). Consequently, Ypi et al. assert that "[t]he legacy of colonialism poses huge issues of rectificatory justice" (ibid.). As a remedial principle of justice, rectificatory justice "applies when one person wrongly interferes with another's legitimate holdings" (Miller 2017, sec. 2.2). Rectificatory justice entails "a bilateral relationship between a wrongdoer and his victim, and demands that the fault be cancelled by restoring the victim to the position she would have been in had the wrongful behaviour not occurred; it may also require that the wrongdoer not benefit from his faulty behaviour" (Ibid.).

In addition to its original purpose of rectifying wrongful behavior, rectificatory justice can be used for instrumental purposes, as a means to rectify distributive injustice and ultimately to achieve distributive justice (Miller 2017, sec. 2.2). However, explaining the essence of rectificatory justice, Aristotle (1941) famously asserts that

> it makes no difference whether a good man has defrauded a bad man or a bad man a good one, nor whether it is a good or a bad man that has committed adultery; the law looks only to the distinctive character of the injury, and treats the parties as equal, if one is in the wrong and the other is being wronged, and if one inflicted injury and the other has received it. Therefore, this kind of injustice being an inequality, the judge tries to equalise it (Book V, ch. 4).

Miller's (2017) Alice and Bill case sheds light on Aristotle's (1941) assertion and clarifies the essence of rectificatory justice. In the case, Alice owns a computer that Bill dispossessed her of. Miller (2017) argues that "so long as Alice has a legitimate title to her computer, her claim of corrective justice against Bill does not depend on her having had, prior to the theft, the share of resources that distributive justice ideally demands. She might be richer than she deserves to be, yet corrective justice still requires that the computer be returned to her" (sec. 2.2).

In the X and Y citizens context, I am not advocating for corrective justice as a means to rectify the distributive inequality—perhaps one may be or may not be right to call it distributive injustice—between X and Y or between X citizens and Y citizens. In line with Aristotle's (1941) explanation of the essence of rectificatory justice and Miller's (2017) Alice and Bill case, whether X citizens are better off or worse off than Y citizens does not matter; what matters is the wrongful behavior of X citizens against Y citizens during colonialism. Therefore, rectificatory justice is a means to rectify X's historical injustice against Y citizens. In the X and Y citizens case, contra relationists, it does not matter that postcolonial Y citizens are not members, citizens, or subjects of X. What matters, taking a cue from relationists, is that colonial X had a relationship with colonized Y citizens. Since that relationship was characterized by historical injustice, rectificatory justice demands that X must rectify its wrongful behavior against Y citizens. As already mentioned, there are different ways to go about such rectification, and right to immigration is one way.

Given the essence of rectificatory justice as explained by Aristotle (1941), and in view of Miller's (2017) Alice and Bill case, the nature of rectificatory justice has two related requirements. First, it demands that it is Bill, and not any other person, who ought to compensate Alice. Second, it demands that it is Alice, and not any other person, who ought to be compensated by Bill. This is because rectificatory justice requires that it is the perpetrator himself, in this case Bill, who is to compensate the victim herself, in this case Alice, "even if the cause of distributive justice could be better served by transferring resources from a third party" (sec. 2.2). In view of the first requirement, it is X, and not any other state, that must compensate Y citizens. If right to immigration is the agreed form of compensation, then, contra nonrelationists, it is X—and not any other state—that must respect Y citizens' right to immigration. In view of the second requirement, it is Y citizens, and not any other people, that must be compensated by X. If right to immigration is the agreed form of compensation, then, contra non-relationists, it is Y citizens—and not any other people—whose right to immigration must be respected by X. Combing the first and second requirements, contra nonrelationists, X—not any other state—must respect Y citizens'—not any other people's—right to immigration.

The double requirements that X (the perpetrator) must be the state to compensate Y citizens (the victim)

> underlines the bilateral nature of corrective justice, and also the fact that it comes into play in response to faulty behaviour on someone's part. Its primary demand is that people should not lose out because others have behaved wrongfully or carelessly, but it also encompasses the idea that "no man should profit by his own wrong" . . . each person must take responsibility for his own conduct, and if he fails to respect the legitimate interests of others by causing injury, he must make good the harm. (Miller 2017, sec. 2.2)

On the one hand, the bilateral nature of rectificatory justice ties X and Y citizens together. Therefore, it nullifies the assumption of relationists that X does not owe Y citizens a duty of justice, specifically a duty to respect Y citizens' right to immigration (in the context of this article). To agree with the relationists that X does not owe Y citizens a duty to respect their right to immigration is simultaneously to accept that Y citizens should lose out because X has behaved wrongfully, and to accept that X should profit by its own wrong.

On the other hand, the bilateral nature of rectificatory justice does not tie X and other people together. Therefore, it nullifies the assumption of nonrelationists that X owes other people a duty of justice, specifically a duty to respect their right to immigration (in the context of this article). To agree with the nonrelationists that X owes every people a duty to respect their right to immigration and that every state owes Y citizens a duty to respect their right to immigration is to deny that X specially owes Y citizens a duty to respect their right to immigration. To deny that X specially owes Y citizens a duty to respect their right to immigration is to deny "that each person must take responsibility for his own conduct, and if he fails to respect the legitimate interests of others by causing injury, he must make good the harm" (Miller 2017, sec. 2.2).

The Significance of the Problem

The problem of migration is ubiquitous, and the problem of the influx of migrants from the Middle East and Africa to Europe and from South America to the United States is an important problem of global justice. Nevertheless, in the context of this book, the movement of migrants from some African countries to other African countries (e.g., from Zimbabwe to South Africa, and from Nigeria to South Africa and Ghana) is an important problem of regional relations. I think this problem is very important in this era of resurgent nationalism, populism, xenophobia (Afrophobia), anti-immigration wave, othering, and even securitization because some African countries (e.g., South Africa and Ghana) see the influx of migrants from other African countries (e.g., Nigeria in the case of Ghana, and Nigeria and Zimbabwe in the case of South Africa), exclusively, as a security threat and economic problem rather than also seeing it as a problem of justice.

Just as the relational approach and the nonrelationship cannot, sui generis, resolve the aforementioned cases of exception, so too neither the relational approach nor the nonrelational approach may be able to resolve the recent and current problem of migration, from some former colonies to other former colonies, that is partly conditioned by common colonial heritage—that is, the European colonization of Africa. By using the term *partly*, I acknowledge that such migration is not only colonialism induced; it is also induced by other factors such as economics, conflicts, climate change, and so on. For instance, due to their colonial historical relationships, Nigerians tend to migrate to Ghana while crossing Benin Republic and Togo rather than migrating to these two countries. So too, historically, Ghanaians tended to migrate to Nigeria while crossing Togo and Benin Republic rather than migrating to these two countries.

In the case of migration from a former colony to its former colonizer, as exemplified by the X and Y case, the dichotomy between the relational approach and the nonrelational approach is unhelpful because (1) there are rights and duties involved in the case; (2) the rights and duties in (1) are not only relational but also nonrelational; (3) hence, there are relational and nonrelational grounds on which the case is based; (4) there are advantages and disadvantages resulting from such grounds in (3); (5) the advantages and disadvantages in (3) are not only relationally divided but also nonrelationally divided; (6) the divisions in (5) are not only relationally determined, but also nonrelationally determined; and (7) in view of the stipulations from (1) to (6), neither the relational approach nor the nonrelational approach is sufficient to resolve the problem.

Like the case of refugees, the case of colonial historical relationships represents cases in which (1) contra the relational approach, insiders (citizens, compatriots, etc.) have duties of justice to certain outsiders (noncitizens, noncompatriots, etc.), and the latter have right claims against the former, and these duties and rights demand that the former should lift the restriction on the latter's right to immigration and (2) contra the nonrelational approach, the former owe only the latter (not all human beings) such duties of justice, and it is only the latter (not all human beings) that have such right claims against the former. This has a twofold significance. First, it signifies that there are cases of exception to the norms of the relational and nonrelational approaches. Second, it signifies that neither the relational approach nor the nonrelational approach is sufficient to resolve cases of exception.

To resolve cases of exception, we need to avoid the extremes of the two approaches by using the strength of the relational approach to compensate for the weakness of the nonrelational approach and vice versa. In other words, an intermediary approach between the relational and the nonrelational approaches is the best possible way to resolve cases of exception. An intermediary approach can be used to resolve cases of exception in the following way. There will be two interconnected levels, namely, the relational and the nonrelational levels. The relational level is the first, lower, and broader level, while the relational level is the second, higher, and narrower level. In architectural, structural, or Marxian terms, the nonrelational level is the substructure, while the relational level is the superstructure. The nonrelational level stipulates a universal, general, and "minimal moral threshold of immutable demands" (Dietzel n.d., 14) of justice that is based on nonrelational grounds. Then, the relational level stipulates a particular, specific, and maximal moral mutable demands of justice that are based on relational grounds (Ibid.).

On the one hand, the relational approach is practice dependent—that is, it accepts the status quo or relies on existing institutions and norms in spite of their arbitrariness. Consequently, it possesses practical force but lacks critical force. On the other hand, the nonrelational approach is practice independent—that is, it does not rely on existing institutions and norms. Consequently, it possesses critical force but lacks practical force (Sangiovanni 2008, 140).

On the one hand, the relational approach—because it lacks critical force— is unable to challenge many arbitrary grounds (Caney 2011, 526–27; Tan 2004, 156) on which formerly colonized people's right to immigration is restricted by their former colonizers. Therefore, it is questionable whether the approach is an appropriate approach to the problem of migration that is partly induced by colonial historical relations that were characterized by historical injustice. On the other hand, the nonrelational approach—because it lacks practical force—is unable to recognize the special relationship that resulted from practical historical encounters between formerly colonized people and their former colonizers. Consequently, it is unable to recognize that there is a qualitative and moral difference between (1) former colonizers restricting the right to immigration of their formerly colonized people and former colonizers restricting the right to immigration of other people and (2) formerly colonized people being denied their right to immigration by their former colonizers and formerly colonized people being denied the right to immigration by other states.

An intermediary approach uses the practical-force-strength of the relational approach to compensate for the lack-of-practical-force-weakness of the nonrelational approach and uses the critical-force-strength of the nonrelational approach to compensate for the lack-of-critical-force-weakness of the relational approach. Therefore, it can simultaneously challenge the arbitrary grounds on which formerly colonized people's right to immigration is restricted by their former colonizers and recognize the qualitative and moral difference between what former colonizers owe citizens of their former colonies and what the former owe other citizens who are not the latter, and between what citizens of former colonies are owed by their former colonizers and what the former are owed by other states who are not the latter.

An intermediary approach, using the relational approach to complement the nonrelational approach and vice versa, allows us to know what former colonial states owe their former colonies and why the former owe the latter what they owe them. As shown in the penultimate and preceding subsections, an intermediary approach allows us to know what exactly X owes Y citizens and why the former owe the latter what she owes them. While arguments for lifting restrictions on Y citizens' rights to enter X are usually based on cosmopolitan egalitarian grounds (the universal equality of persons) and humanitarian grounds, an intermediary approach bases the argument for lifting such restrictions on the grounds of, generally, the colonial historical relationship between former colonial states and their former colonies, specifically, the historical injustice that characterized the relationship. Note that an intermediary approach is not only applicable to migration, it can also be applied to other complex cases of global justice, such as international trade (which involves corporations, states, and the global institutional order) and resource curse, which involve complex and multifaceted agents, namely, interactional/micro agents (individuals and collectives) and institutional/macro agents (corporations, states, and the global institutional order), and domestic and global agents, which include individuals, collectives, corporations, states, and the global institutional order.

REFERENCES

Abizadeh, Arash. 2016. "The Special-Obligations Challenge to More Open Borders." In *Migration in Political Theory: The Ethics of Movement and Membership*, edited by Sara Fine and Lea Ypi, 105–24. Oxford: Oxford University Press.

Abumere, Frank Aragbonfoh. 2015. *Different Perspectives on Global Justice: A Fusion of Horizons*. Bielefeld: PUB—Publication at Bielefeld University.

Abumere, Frank Aragbonfoh. 2020. "Introducing Normativity in African International Politics." *Politikon: South African Journal of Political Studies* 47, no. 3: 342–60.

Amighetti, Sara, and Alasia Nuti. 2015. "A Nation's Right to Exclude and the Colonies." *Political Theory* 44: 1–26.

Aristotle. 1941. *Nicomachean Ethics*. In *The* Basic *Works of Aristotle.* Translated by W. D. Ross. New York: Random House.

Armstrong, Chris. 2012. *Global Distributive Justice: An Introduction.* Cambridge: Cambridge University Press.

Blake, Michael. 2003. "Immigration." In *A Companion to Applied Ethics*, edited by R. Frey and C. Wellman, 224–37. Malden, MA: Blackwell Publishing.

Black, Samuel. 1991. "Individualism at an Impasse." *Canadian Journal of Philosophy* 21, no. 3: 347–77.

Caney, Simon. 2005. *Justice beyond Borders: A Global Political Theory*. Oxford: Oxford University Press.

Caney, Simon. 2011. "Humanity, Associations and Global Justice: In Defence of Humanity-Centred Cosmopolitan Egalitarianism." *The Monist* 94: 505–34.

Carens, Joseph H. 2013. *The Ethics of Immigration*. Oxford: Oxford University Press.

Cole, Phillip. 2000. *Philosophies of Exclusion: Liberal Political Theory and Immigration*. Edinburgh: Edinburgh University Press.

Dietzel, Alix. n.d. "Relational vs Non-relational Climate Justice–The Case for a Mixed Approach." https://www.academia.edu/7514329/Relational_vs_Non_Relational_Climate_Justice_The_Case_for_a_Mixed_Approach Accessed: December 1, 2019.

Fine, Sarah. 2016. "Immigration and Discrimination." In *Migration in Political Theory: The Ethics of Movement and Membership*, edited by Sara Fine and Lea Ypi, 125–50. Oxford: Oxford University Press.

Krasner, Stephen. 1999. *Sovereignty: Organized Hypocrisy*. Princeton: Princeton University Press.

Kymlicka, Will. 1995. *Multicultural Citizenship*: *A Liberal Theory of Minority Rights*. Oxford: Oxford University Press.

Maffettone, Sebastiano. 2013. "Normative Approaches to Global Justice." In *Globalisation, Multilateralism, Europe*: *Towards a Better Global Governance?*, edited by Mario Telo, 125–43. Surrey: Ashgate.

Miller, David. 2016. *Strangers in Our Midst*: *The Political Philosophy of Immigration*. Cambridge, MA: Harvard University Press.

Miller, David. 2017. "Justice." *The Stanford Encyclopedia of Philosophy*, Fall edition. http://plato.stanford.edu/archives/fall2017/entries/justice/.

Oberman, Kieran. 2016. "Immigration as a Human Right." In *Migration in Political Theory*: *The Ethics of Movement and Membership*, edited by Sara Fine and lea Ypi, 32–56. Oxford: Oxford University Press.

Pettit, Philip. 1997. *Republicanism*: *A Theory of Freedom and Government*. Oxford: Oxford University Press.

Risse, Mathias. 2012. *On Global Justice*. Princeton, NJ: Princeton University Press.

Said, Edward. 1993. *Culture and Imperialism*. New York: Vintage Books.

Said, Edward. 2003. "Always on Top." *London Review of Books*. 25.

Sangiovanni, Andreas. 2007. "Global Justice, Reciprocity and the State." *Philosophy and Public Affairs* 35: 3–39.

Sangiovanni, Andreas. 2008. "Justice and the Priority of Politics to Morality." *The Journal of Political Philosophy* 16: 137–64.

Shachar, Ayelet. 2016. "Selecting by Merit: The Brave New World of Stratified Mobility." *Migration in Political Theory*: *The Ethics of Movement and Membership*, edited by Sara Fine and Lea Ypi, 175–204. Oxford: Oxford University Press.

Tan, Kok-Chor. 2004. *Justice without Borders: Cosmopolitanism, Nationalism and Patriotism*. Cambridge: Cambridge University Press.

UN (United Nations). 2010. "Minority Rights: International Standards and Guidance for Implementation." HR/PUB/10/3. Office of the High Commissioner for Human Rights, United Nations, New York. https://www.ohchr.org/Documents/Publications/MinorityRights_en.pdf. Accessed 19 June 2017.

Walzer, Michael. 1983. *Spheres of Justice*. New York: Basic Books.

Weber, Max. 1978. *Economy and Society*. Berkeley, CA: University of California Press.

Wellman, Christopher Heath. 2020. "Immigration." *The Stanford Encyclopedia of Philosophy*, Spring edition. https://plato.stanford.edu/archives/spr2020/entries/immigration/.

Ypi, Lea, Robert E. Goodin, and Christian Barry. 2009. "Associative Duties, Global Justice, and the Colonies." *Philosophy and Public Affairs* 37: 103–35.

1. Throughout this chapter and the entire book, I use the term *individual universal human rights* or *individual human rights* to signify the (universal) human rights of individuals in contradistinction to group rights or minority rights.

Chapter Three

Expected Migrant Minorities and Problematic Identities and Differences

In the second half of chapter 2, I explained that in the vast majority of political philosophy and political theory literature on migration, migration is mostly conceived as an issue of global justice in which the relational approach and the nonrelational approach are pitted against each other. I showed that both the relational approach and the nonrelational approach face a very important problem in common when one approach, without it being complemented by the other, is applied to cases of exception. Relying on my argument for cases of exception, I showed that rather than a dualistic application of either the relational approach or the nonrelational approach, an intermediary approach is the best fit for cases of exception. In view of the conclusion I reached in chapter 2, prima facie, there is nothing that negates the right of migrants to move from one African country to the other. While I looked at the concept of domination and migrants' right to immigration (*in theory*) in chapter 2, I shall look at the trajectory of immigration and the trend of discrimination against migrants (*in practice*) in this chapter.

MIGRATION AND GLOBALIZATION

The question or problem of identity and minorities discussed in chapter 7 are important to the trajectory of immigration and the trend of discrimination against migrants. In terms of philosophical and psychological worldview, one can look at the question or problem of identity in general and the question or problem of minorities in particular in different ways. One can be optimistic, pessimistic, or realist about them. From an angle of optimism, one can argue that even though there might be domination of, and discrimination against, minorities intranationally (e.g., Fulani and Hausa majority vs. Adara and Koro minority in Nigeria), such domination and discrimination may not necessarily apply to migrants internationally (e.g., South African majority vs. Zimbabwean minority in South Africa or Ghanaian majority vs. Nigerian minority in Ghana). This is because the local historical, sociological, cultural, and political factors that engender majorities such as Fulani and Hausa to dominate minorities such as Adara and Koro are different from the dynamics between majority South Africans and minority Zimbabweans or majority Ghanaians and minority Nigerians.

Concerning the dynamics between, for instance, host South Africans and migrant Zimbabweans or host Ghanaians and migrant Nigerians, the aforementioned optimistic view may deem domination and discrimination unlikely to occur regularly and less potent when it occurs because Africa and its subregions have devised mechanisms both at the regional level and at the subregional level to regulate regional and subregional relations. Notably,

> cooperation already exists in multilateral organisations such as the African Union (AU) at the regional level. Furthermore, at the subregional levels, cooperation already exists in multilateral organisations such as the Economic Community of West-African States (ECOWAS), Economic Community of Central African States (ECCAS), East African Community (EAC), Southern African Development Commission (SADC), Common Market for Eastern and Southern Africa (COMESA), Arab Maghreb Union (AMU), Community of Sahel-Saharan States (CEN-SAD) and Intergovernmental Authority on Development (IGAD). (Abumere 2020, 343; see Abumere 2015, 67)

Looking around the continent and its subregions from the optimistic angle, it is not too difficult to observe that "the emergence of sub-regional multilateral organisations . . . have been politically and economically beneficial to the subregions. These multilateral organizations include political and/or economic communities and/or unions such as AMU, COMESA, CEN-SAD, EAC, ECCAS, ECOWAS, IGAD, and SADC" (Abumere 2020, 343, 350; see Abumere 2015, 67).

Contrary to the above optimism, from an angle of pessimism, one can argue that just as there is domination of, and discrimination against, minorities intranationally (e.g., Fulani and Hausa majority vs. Adara and Koro minority in Nigeria), such domination and discrimination may apply to migrants internationally (e.g., South African majority vs. Zimbabwean minority in South Africa or Ghanaian majority vs. Nigerian minority in Ghana). This is in spite of the fact that the local historical, sociological, cultural, and political factors that engender majorities such as Fulani and Hausa to dominate minorities such as Adara and Koro are different from the dynamics between majority South Africans and minority Zimbabweans or majority Ghanaians and minority Nigerians. Concerning the dynamics between, for instance, host South Africans and migrant Zimbabweans or host Ghanaians and migrant Nigerians, the aforementioned pessimistic view may deem domination and discrimination likely to occur regularly and even potent when it occurs because although Africa and it its subregions have devised mechanisms both at the regional level and at the subregional level to regulate regional and subregional relations, regional and subregional "normative fabrics have been neglected in Africa" (Tieku 2013, 17).

On the one hand, while looking around the continent and its subregions from the optimistic angle reveals that the emergence of subregional multi-lateral organizations—including political and/or economic communities and/ or unions such as AMU, COMESA, CEN-SAD, EAC, ECCAS, ECOWAS, IGAD and SADC—have been politically and economically beneficial to the subregions. From the pessimistic angle, looking around the continent and its subregions reveals that borders and margins have caused both tractable and intractable crises and conflicts on the African continent. Mentioning some of the crises and conflicts will suffice to show how deadly the consequences of the arbitrary imperialist balkanization of the continent have been. From 1961 to 1991, Eritrean separatists fought a war of independence against the Ethiopian government. While from 1998 to 2000, the independent Eritrea fought a border war against Ethiopia. And from 2008 to 2018, the two countries would again engage in a standoff. In 2008, Eritrea was once more engaged in a border conflict, but this time around with Djibouti. On its part, from 1977 to 1978, Ethiopia fought a border war against Somalia. While earlier on, from 1963 to 1967, Somalia fought a border war against Kenya (Aremu 2010, 550).

Furthermore, from 1978 to 1979, Tanzania fought a border war against Uganda. A year before this war, in 1977, Kenya, Tanzania, and Uganda had political disagreements that resulted in the collapse of the East African Community (EAC). From 1971 to 2002, Cameroon and Nigeria were engaged in a border disputation. Algeria was engaged in a confrontation with Morocco in 1963 when the two countries laid claim to the Atlas Mountain area (Aremu 2010, 550). Morocco again, from 1975 to 1991, fought a war against the Polisario Front over claims to Western Sahara. Since 1970, Morocco and the Polisario Front have been engaged in the ongoing Western Sahara Conflict. In 1977, Egypt fought a border war against Libya. While Libya, again, from 1978 to 1987, fought a war against Chad (Abumere 2020, 351–52).

Contrary to both the optimistic and pessimistic views, I look at the question or problem of identity in general and the question or problem of minorities in particular from a realistic view. The realistic view neglects neither the observation of the optimistic view nor the observation of the pessimistic view. However, it accepts that domination and discrimination are rife on the continent but at the same time pan-Africanism is the order of the day on the continent. Since pan-Africanism has greatly affected African international politics, any theorization about domination and discrimination in African international politics and how they can be resolved must take pan-Africanism into consideration. "Pan-Africanism is a description of African political elites' internalisation of the norm that Africans are one, and as such, Africans ought to support, and cooperate, with one another. In other words, unity ought to be the right kind of relationship among Africans, and African leaders must always act harmoniously, seeking compromise rather than confrontation" (Abumere 2020, 347; see Tieku 2013, 7). On regional matters such as discrimination against migrants, pan-Africanism simultaneously discourages disagreements among African leaders, encourages consensus among them, and pressurizes them to align with the consensus (Clapham 1996).

In conformity with the norm of pan-Africanism, African governments go as far as often sacrificing the interests and preferences of their states. Setting the normative standard of behavior for African states, governments, and their representatives, pan-Africanism does

> not only encourage African political elites to show loyalty in public to continental unity; it also makes it hard for those elites to oppose openly an issue that commands broad support. Decision-making is often made easy by the self-regulation of the norm. It is the powerful effect of the norm that allows African states to develop common positions on crucial international issues. It often encourages African governments to engage in block voting in international forums. Indeed, it dictates actions of African governments in international politics especially in the absence of obvious material concerns. (Tieku 2013, 7–8)

In face of the discrimination against migrants, and in spite of the pessimistic view on the fate of migrants, what pan-Africanism shows is that even though the optimistic view might be far-fetched, the discrimination against migrants can still be resolved, and this is what gives rise to the realistic view. After all,

> the central referent of international politics in Africa are group preferences formation, consensual decision-making procedures and the solidarity principle . . . except these three collective traits are taken into consideration, we will not be able to explain international politics in Africa. In other words, any African international relations theory that fails to consider the three collective traits in its explanation of international politics in Africa is bound to fail. Consequently, to employ norms at the African regional level, one must rely on the three collective traits. In sum, to employ norms at the African regional level, one must rely on pan-Africanism. (See Abumere 2020, 347; Tieku 2013, 1)

It is important whether one adopts the optimistic view, the pessimistic view, or the realistic view because, on the one hand, "[m]igration has become a continuous phenomenon in the history of human societies. The migration of individuals and groups over time is associated with the emergence of cultures and of civilizations throughout the world" (Usman and Falola 2009, 1). On the other hand, "[m]igration is synonymous with the history of Africa itself" (ibid.). Migrations and movements of people are central "in the historical evolution of African peoples and societies" (ibid.). As Toyin Falola (2006) says, "Africans have always been on the move, ever since the time they created civilization and scattered it around the continent and elsewhere" (1). Usually, among African migrants, the continent remains their number one destination. In other words, among the migrant population, more people migrate to other African countries, while less people migrate to other continents. This fact is not only historical, but it is still the current situation. Presently, in comparative terms, there are more Africans migrating to other African countries than there are Africans migrating to other continents including Europe. The UN says that recently, within the space of ten years, from the year 2010 to the year 2020, the number of migrants from sub-Saharan Africa who migrated to other African countries rose to nineteen million, a figure that the UN says represents more than 40 percent increment in the number of Africans who migrate to other African countries. Even this nineteen million figure or 40 percent increment given by the UN is seen as an inaccurate representation of reality because it seems it is below the actual figure. The UN's more-than-40 percent-increment or nineteen million figure is "a figure many experts call an underestimate" (The Economist 2021, s.p.).

At different epochs and at different places globalization has always played a role in the migrations and movements of people, sometimes to a lesser extent and at other times to a larger extent. But the extensity, intensity, and velocity of the current form of global movement amplified the role of globalization in the migrations and movements of people, and consequently amplified the centrality of the migrations and movements of people in the contemporary evolution of African societies and peoples. This contemporary development is a linear progression from the historical phenomenon.

V. Y. Mudimbe's (2003) describes globalization as "a general unification of economic with scientific projects, and a certain dimension of the cultural (e.g., in dance, foods, music, beliefs, etc.)" (211–12). Then, he argues for "three different models as frameworks for a good understanding of types of collaboration between politics of globalization and politics of identities" (210). These models consist of what he refers to as the Western model or the Western space (model one), the Japanese model or the Japanese experience (model two), and the African model or the sub-Saharan space (model three), which refers to the African experience of globalization. First, in terms of the Western model, he argues that

> the Western space would incarnate a perfect homogenization of economic and cultural capital. In actuality, it could be said, on the one hand, that globalization would play back and forth the saga of European geographical and imperial expansion that began at the end of the fifteenth century; on the other hand, globalization or the institution of a new Order might seem to be the last moment of a historical genealogy that includes theories of wealth in the seventeenth century, mercantilism in the eighteenth century, the genesis of capitalism and its development in the nineteenth and twentieth centuries. (210–11)

Second, in terms of the Japanese model and in contradistinction to the Western space, he argues that

> at the other extreme, a different model is well signified by the Japanese experience. In this case, one notes the great deviation existing between economic capital and space on the one hand, and cultural capital on the other. In effect, the economic organization and its superstructural appendages proceed as consequence and result of an internal discontinuity, the nineteenth-century Meiji reformation; on the other hand, the politics of cultural identities . . . are predicated by clearly autonomous traditional grids of values and meanings. (210–11)

Finally, in terms of the African model and in contradistinction to both the Western space and the Japanese experience, he argues that the African experience of globalization sits middle-of-the-road between the extremes of the Western experience on one side and the Japanese experience on the other side. He argues that

> if globalization indicates the imperativeness of an inscription in model one, the validity of politics of identity would demand, as in the Japanese case, a relative autonomy. . . . There is a difference: the Japanese prise de conscience was induced internationally, but really thematized and expressed in Japanese conceptual and linguistic categories, whereas the African could be described as a response to external constraints represented by the colonial mission civilisatrice. (210–11)

Until recently, that is before the resurgence of nationalism and the ascendancy of populism, (political) globalization seemed to be unstoppable and irreversible. Nevertheless, global political phenomena such as the surge or resurgence of nationalism in Europe, BREXIT in the United Kingdom, xenophobia in South Africa, the emergence of Donald Trump as the president of the United States and his unrestricted America First nationalism and populism, and the rhetoric and actions of populists all over the world contradict the claim that the future of world history and global politics is a more globalized and cosmopolitan world. Based on current realities, globalization is receding and the world is becoming less cosmopolitan. More importantly, the current nationalist and populist wave has amplified othering in both domestic and international politics—othering is in ascendance in both domestic and international politics. This current global political phenomenon has ramifications for African migrants both within and outside the continent as can be seen in places such as the United States, the United Kingdom, France, Hungary, Poland, Brazil, South Africa, so on and so forth.

Resurgent nationalism, populism, and xenophobia are catastrophic especially for migrants because they are a special kind of minority; they seem to be more vulnerable than regular or national minorities. Capotorti's and Deschênes' definitions in chapter 2 refer to national minorities but do not sufficiently capture the condition of migrants. Within the context of the AfCFTA, one may argue that in contradistinction to national minorities, migrants are a special kind of minority because: (1) they relocate from their states to other states as a positive effect of AfCFTA; (2) they may suffer domination, and discrimination, due to the AfCFTA-induced regional integration; and (3) the domination, and discrimination, they may suffer will be due to certain identities and differences that they have in contradistinction to their host states, groups in the states, or nationals of the states. The condition of these migrants "captures the essential paradox inherent in African migration. On the one hand, the migrant's hopes and aspirations call for some celebrative 'smiling,' but on the other, the harsh realities of adjustment in a new but enchanting setting turns 'smiling' into a necessary mask, a disguise or even therapy to cope with the nightmarish 'suffering' engendered by displacement" (Falola and Afolabi 2007, xix).

The fate of migrants may be the same as the fate of already-existing national minorities. The current slave trade in Libya (Arab Africans selling Black Africans) and xenophobia in South Africa (South Africans murdering other Africans) show that in Africa identities and differences are very consequential. More important, they show that in Africa migrants need protection against domination and discrimination. In view of pan-Africanism as discussed above, one would expect that the condition of migrants will attract attention even if the condition of already-existing national minorities does not. Consequently, among regional policymakers, one would expect that there will be a focus on the resolution of the condition of migrants even if there is no similar focus on the resolution of the condition of national minorities. This focus would be good for migrants even though it may not make any practical difference in the condition of already-existing national minorities. Nevertheless, a mere focus on the plight of migrants will not guarantee their minority rights. To ensure that migrants do not suffer the same fate as the already-existing national minorities, there must be normative international relations on the continent. I shall explain what such normative international relations entail and then argue for such normative international relations in chapters 7 and 8. For now, I shall continue teasing out the trajectory of immigration and trend of discrimination against migrants.

FUTURE POSSIBILITY

The African Union (AU) has been moving toward the free movement of goods, services, capital, and persons in a bid to achieve a comprehensive regional integration. In January 2018, the AU introduced both the AfCFTA and the FMP. Recently, in April 2019, the establishment of the AfCFTA came into effect. In addition to AfCFTA, building on similar arrangements at the subregions such as the Economic Community of West African States (ECOWAS), the Southern African Development Community (SADC), East African Community (EAC), and so on, in early 2018 the AU's "Assembly of Heads of State and Government adopted the Protocol to the Treaty Establishing the African Economic Community Relating to the Free Movement of Persons, Right of Residence and Right of Establishment (the Free Movement Protocol)" (Sharpe 2020, s.p.).

The above shows that the AU is committed to a comprehensive regional integration and has taken important steps to realize it. Moreover, in 2016, the AU "decided to move towards a 'borderless' Africa with seamless intracontinental migration. The bloc created a single continental passport and gave it first to national leaders, with a plan to distribute it more widely and enable Africans to move around the continent without a visa. Two years later, the effort was codified in the AU Protocol on Free Movement of Persons" (Okunade 2021, s.p.). In late 2019, the AU assessed the implementation progress of the FMP Protocol and reported that thirty-three states have signed the FMP Protocol—"[m]issing among the signatories to the FMP were all the North African countries; nearly half of the SADC countries, including Namibia, Botswana, South Africa and Zambia; Ethiopia in the horn of Africa; Nigeria in West Africa; and Cameroon in Central Africa" (Hirsh 2020, 3).

Since the FMP is required to be ratified by fifteen states for it to come into force, the AU still has a long way to go to get the required ratifications because only four states have as yet ratified it—namely, Mali, Niger, and Sao Tome and Principe in West Africa and Rwanda in East Africa.

The hesitance to commit to the FMP Protocol points to a range of concerns about giving up sovereign protections regarding the movement of people and about the implementation plan for the Protocol. There are concerns about the impact of higher levels of immigration on the domestic economic and security environments. In general terms, because of the design of the Protocol and its accompanying "Roadmap", ratification of the treaty could be interpreted to entail the virtually immediate implementation of Phase One, "the right of entry and abolition of visa requirements" in regard to all countries which have concluded the ratification process. (Hirsh 2020, 3)

The above hesitation to commit to the FMP Protocol shows that boundaries and borders are still a problematic phenomenon on the continent in spite of the FMP, AfCFTA, even the AU itself and the subregional multilateral organizations. At its 25th World Congress, "Borders and Margin," in 2018, the International Political Science Association (IPSA) stated that

[b]orders are more than territorial lines demarcated by road signs, official checkpoints, even barbed-wire fences and fortified walls, but institutions in themselves. They have a dynamic character arising from their formal or informal functions and impacts. At a time when entire regions have been destabilized by the implosion of borders—often imposed by former and current imperialisms rather than arising through freely negotiated or democratic means—these margins are now conflict zones and flash points in national and international politics. (IPSA/AISP 2018, s.p.)

Borders and margins have caused both tractable and intractable crises and conflicts on the African continent. Mentioning some of the crises and conflicts will suffice to show how deadly the consequences of the arbitrary imperialist balkanization of the continent have been. From 1961 to 1991, Eritrean separatists fought a war of independence against the Ethiopian government. While from 1998 to 2000, the independent Eritrea fought a border war against Ethiopia. And from 2008 to 2018, the two countries would again engage in a standoff. In 2008, Eritrea was once more engaged in a border conflict, but this time around with Djibouti. On its part, from 1977 to 1978, Djibouti fought a border war against Somalia. While earlier on, from 1963 to 1967, Somalia fought a border war against Kenya (Aremu 2010, 550).

From 1978 to 1979, Tanzania fought a border war against Uganda. A year before this war, in 1977, Kenya, Tanzania, and Uganda had political disagreements that resulted in the collapse of the East African Community (EAC). From 1971 to 2002, Cameroon and Nigeria were engaged in a border disputation. Algeria was engaged in a confrontation with Morocco in 1963 when the two countries laid claim to the Atlas Mountain area (Aremu 2010, 550). Morocco again, from 1975 to 1991, fought a war against the Polisario Front over claims to Western Sahara. Since 1970, Morocco and the Polisario Front have been engaged in the ongoing Western Sahara Conflict. In 1977, Egypt fought a border war against Libya. While Libya again, from 1978 to 1987, fought a war against Chad (Abumere 2020, 351–52).

Apart from the aforementioned crises and conflicts, borders and margins have also created a situation whereby migrants from one African country are discriminated against in another African country. The Ghanaian sociologist, Kwasi Kwaa Prah (2012), says:

> In Africa, in my lifetime, I have seen Ghanaians thrown out Nigerians and other West Africans, under provisions of a so-called Aliens Compliance Act, during the Busia era, only for Ghanaians and other West Africans in turn, at a later stage, to be kicked out of Nigeria. Xenophobia against Somalis in Kenya has been well within the notice of my experience. Angolans are not loved in Namibia. In Botswana, since the 1970s, anti-makwerekwere language has been common. Eritreans, during the period of their war of independence were, as refugees, despised in the Sudan. Basuto, from what I know from the years I was there, sometimes treated other Africans, particularly with contempt. . . . Rwandans are not loved in the Congo. There was a time, in the 1980s, when Zimbabweans became in wider Africa circles infamous for their ill-regard for other Africans. (116)

To investigate the above phenomenon, in 2020, I conducted an omnibus survey of politicians, businesspersons, students, farmers, civil servants, professionals, and others. Africa is estimated to have a population of 1,240,000,000. Roughly, an Africa country has an average population of 30,000,000. So the baseline criterion for selecting which countries to include in the survey is a country that has a population of at least 30,000,000. Other minimal criteria for selecting which countries to include in the survey are the following. While any country that is included in the survey must meet the aforementioned baseline criterion, it only has to meet at least one of the following minimal criteria: First, the country must be one of the largest economies in Africa, or in a sub-region; second, the country must be very attractive economically or in terms of soft power (e.g., education—universities) to other Africans or at least to citizens of other countries in the same subregion and; third, the country must be a country whose citizens tend to migrate (in comparative terms, more than other countries) to other countries.

In view of the aforementioned baseline criterion and minimal criteria, alongside additional considerations, I included Nigeria, South Africa, and Ghana in the survey. Being the largest economy and most populous country in Africa, I chose Nigeria because the country can affect AfCFTA in a way that no any other country can. Moreover, Nigerians are notorious for migrating to, residing in, and doing business in other African countries across the continent in a way that is unrivalled (in terms of number of persons) by other Africans from other countries. I chose South Africa because it is the second largest economy in Africa and arguably the most sophisticated economy on the continent. In its own way (different from the Nigerian way), South Africa can affect AfCFTA in a way that no other country on the continent can. For instance, South African MNCs across different economic sectors, such as MTN, Multichoice, Shoprite, and so on are dominant not only in South Africa but also across the continent. I chose Ghana because it competes with Ivory Coast as the second largest economy in West Africa, and although it lacks the ability to affect AfCFTA or the continent in the way Nigeria and South Africa respectively can, it offers insight into how a nondominant country on the continent and even in the West African subregion, but more powerful than most other countries in its subregion, can affect AfCFTA and the continent.

In the survey in Nigeria, South Africa, and Ghana, the survey instrument included the following wide-ranging items. The first part surveyed citizens (nationals) in terms of their experience with foreigners residing in their country and their view on the arrival of more foreigners and departure of existing foreigners, while the second part surveyed foreigners in terms of their experience with citizens and their country of residence. Then, the third part surveyed citizens on the likelihood that they would want to migrate to another African country for economic reasons. I drew my sample from residents in political and/or economic capitals since these are likely to be more in tune with the developments of AfCFTA.

To both citizens and foreigners, I asked a mixture of closed questions and open-ended questions. The questions without asterisk are universal questions for both citizens and foreigners. The questions with a single asterisk are particular questions for citizens, while the questions with double asterisks are particular questions for foreigners. The questions are as follows. First, do you think AfCFTA will enable more mobility of persons across the continent? (*a borderless continent*). Second, would you like to relocate to another country in Africa for economic, educational, or professional reasons if AfCFTA makes mobility easier? (*possible AfCFTA-induced mobility*). *Third, do you share the perception that foreigners are net negative—that is, foreigners take citizens' jobs, foreigners commit crimes? (*the question of foreigners*). Or **do you share the perception that foreigners are treated badly in your country of residence? (*the condition of foreigners*). *Fourth, do you share the belief that more foreigners should not come to your country? (*willingness to accept more foreigners*). Or **do you think if there are more foreigners in your country, the perceived bad treatment will increase? (*better off or worse off*). *Fifth, do you think the foreigners in your country should leave? (*repatriation 1*). Or ** do you think the government and citizens want you to leave? (*repatriation 2*).

In total, I asked citizens five questions and asked foreigners five questions. My sample of persons who received the survey is 1,001 in Nigeria (including

902 citizens and 99 foreigners), 297 in South Africa (including 254 citizens and 43 foreigners), and 155 in Ghana (including 126 citizens and 29 foreigners). Evidently, the surveys were distributed to approximately 1/200,000 of the population of each country. And I target around 10 percent of the surveys to go to foreigners in each country. The total sample was 1,454. The response I received was 310 from Nigeria (31 percent response rate), 62 from South Africa (21 percent response rate), and 39 from Ghana (25 percent response rate). This yielded a final sample size of 411 and a total response rate of 28 percent. After testing for the representativeness of the sample, the difference between respondents and nonrespondents is insignificant. I coded three responses to each question: positive/yes, neutral/not sure, and negative/no. I asked respondents to choose only one option among the three options rather than choosing preferences in a ranked order. Hence, there was no need to create any weighted total or assign points to the options since there were no ranked preferences.

Table 3.1 The Future of Migration in Africa

	Positive/Yes	Neutral/Not Sure	Negative/No
A Borderless Continent	161	184	66
Possible AfCTA-induced Mobility	201	119	91
*The Question of Foreigners	154	78	89
**The Condition of Foreigners	51	19	20
*Willingness to accept more foreigners	32	112	206
**Better-off or Worse-off	9	20	61
*Repatriation 1	199	101	21
**Repatriation 2	73	11	6
Total	880	644	560

The positive/yes responses indicate the probability of having higher interstate mobility and discrimination, the negative/no responses indicate the probability of having lesser interstate mobility and discrimination, while the neutral/not sure responses are middle-of-the-road between the positive/yes and the negative/no responses. The ratio of the positive/yes responses to the negative/no responses is 1.57 to 1. The ratio of the positive/yes responses to the neutral/not sure responses is 1.37 to 1. While the ratio of the neutral/not sure responses to the negative/no responses is 1.15 to 1.

The above responses show that, on the one hand, due to AfCFTA, there may be (this is an expression of probability rather than certainty) more movement from some African countries (that are less economically attractive) to other African countries (that are more economically attractive). On the other hand, the responses show that there may be (again this is an expression of probability rather than certainty) discrimination against migrants who move from less economically attractive countries to more economically attractive countries due to AfCFTA. While the responses represent present sentiments, to understand the causal and constitutive factors for this phenomenon, we must decipher "the pattern of the past which explained the present" (Watt et al. 1988, 135).

Deciphering the pattern of the past and explaining the present helps us make an educated guess about what the future is likely to be. Nevertheless, this educated guess is not a precise prediction of the future in the realm of physics, and it is not a mathematical forecast for the future with certainty (Abumere 2019, 27)—even in physics and mathematics, there is margin of error. Rather, this is an interpretation of the trajectory of reactions to economic migrants on the continent. Without appealing to historical determinism, the interpretation sees the present to be correlated with the past and sees the future to be a consequence of the present. Since the present resembles the past, it is probable that the consequences of the present will resemble the consequences of the past.

The discrimination against migrants has its origin in colonialism. For instance, in 1958, the French colonialists expelled West Africans of mostly Nigerian, Beninois (Dahomeyan), and Togolese origins from Ivory Coast. Before then, the British colonialists expelled West Africans of mostly Nigerian origin from Ghana in 1954. Xenophobic expulsions of migrants by host country governments occurred in both the colonial (pre-independence) and the post-colonial (postindependence) history of the continent. For instance, postindependence West Africa is notorious for such expulsions. "West Africa has experienced a variety of migrations caused by population pressure, poverty, poor economic performances and endemic conflicts. Historically, migrants regarded the sub-region as an economic unit within which trade in goods and services flowed, and people moved freely" (Adepoju 2005, 1). While West African migrants see the subregion as an economic unit within which trade in goods and services flowed and people moved freely, host country governments and citizens tend to see migrants as an economic, and sometimes security, threat.

The aforementioned negative stereotyping of, and discrimination against, migrants did not only happen before the ECOWAS Treaty; it is still happening many years after the treaty came into effect. In other words, the negative stereotyping of, and discrimination against, migrants happens in spite of the aims and objectives of the ECOWAS Treaty, which include the promotion of cooperation and integration in the subregion. Article 3 (Aims and Objectives) of the 1993 ECOWAS Revised Treaty stipulates that "[t]he aims of the Community are to promote co-operation and integration, leading to the establishment of an economic union in West Africa in order to raise the living standards of its peoples, and to maintain and enhance economic stability, foster relations-among Member States and contribute to the progress and development of the African Continent" (ECOWAS Commission 1993).

Article 59, Paragraph 1 of the 1993 ECOWAS Revised Treaty stipulates that "[c]itizens of the Community shall have the right of entry, residence and establishment and Member States undertake to recognize these rights of Community citizens in their territories in accordance with the provisions of the Protocols relating thereto" (ECOWAS Commission 1993). Paragraph 2 of the same Article stipulates that "[m]ember States undertake to adopt all appropriate measures to ensure that Community citizens enjoy fully the rights referred to in paragraph 1 of this Article" (ECOWAS Commission 1993). While paragraph 3 stipulates that "[m]ember States undertake to adopt, at national level, all measures necessary for the effective implementation of the provisions of this Article" (ECOWAS Commission 1993). However, as already mentioned, negative stereotyping of, and discrimination against, migrants by both host country governments and citizens is still happening in the subregion.

To reiterate the negative stereotyping of, and discrimination against, migrants by both host country governments and citizens in postindependence West Africa predate ECOWAS, which was founded in 1975, and goes all the way back to colonial pre-independence West Africa. To illustrate my point, I shall briefly present a trajectory of expulsions of migrants in West Africa, starting from colonial pre-independence West Africa, going through pre-ECOWAS postindependence West Africa, to postindependence ECOWAS West Africa. In 1958, Ivory Coast expelled over 1,000 Beninois and Togolese, while Chad also expelled thousands of Beninois who were classified as illegal migrants and deemed to be not law abiding. In 1964, Ivory Coast, resuming its expulsion mission, this time around expelled around 16,000 Beninois. In 1967, Senegal embarked on its own expulsion by expelling Guineans. A year later, in 1968, Ivory Coast, Guinea, and Sierra Leone simultaneously expelled Ghanaian fishermen. Then, in 1978, the Gabonese government ordered the expulsion of all Beninois. While, in early 1979, Ivory Coast and Ghana simultaneously expelled Togolese farmers (Adepoju 2005, 4).

In 2008, the South African Human Sciences Research Council (HSRC) empirically showed that xenophobic scapegoating in Ghana has two characteristics (HSRC 2008). First, fellow Africans, rather than non-Africans, were the targets of xenophobic resentment and scapegoating. Second, "the violence was largely restricted to urban informal settlements in major cities" (Brobbey 2018, 71) such as Kumasi (the second most important city in Ghana) and Accra (the capital and the most important city in Ghana). Earlier, in 1969, the Ghanaian government used its Aliens Compliance Order to expel other West Africans, especially Nigerians. The Ghanaian government expelled "all illegal aliens without valid residence permit as from 2 December 1969" (Adepoju 2005, 4). Nigerians did not only suffer expulsion from Ghana, but Nigerian traders also suffered expulsion from another fellow West African country Ivory Coast, and two Central African countries—namely, neighboring Cameroon and Zaire (present-day DRC; Ibid.).

The Nigerian government too would join the bandwagon of African governments that resort to the expulsion of African migrants by blaming the economic malaise of the host country on African migrants who are most poor. From early 1970s to early 1980s, Nigeria experienced an oil boom "and the prosperity that followed was a major factor that attracted other nationals into Nigeria, particularly Ghanaians who took up menial jobs and occupied the small and medium enterprises sector in Nigeria" (Oni and Okunade 2018, 43). Then, from early 1980s, Nigeria experienced a series of economic recessions that would plunge the country into an economic depression. Resorting to scapegoating African migrants (who are mostly poor) for the economic malaise of the country, in 1983 and 1985, the Nigerian government expelled West Africans' mostly of Ghanaian origin (43).

In recent times, around 100, 000 Congolese (most of them either fled the conflict in their country or migrated to Angola for economic reasons) were expelled by Angola in 2004 (Siegel 2009, 23). A few years later, within the space of one year (from December 2008 to December 2009), Angola expelled more than 160, 000 Congolese (Adebajo 2011, 91). In defense of the expulsions, the Angola government accused the Congolese of engaging in criminal activities particularly illegal mining. The then Angola foreign minister claimed that the Angolan government "will never give up its right to protect its natural resources and its right to repatriate citizens who are acting in a way which do not benefit the country" (Siegel 2009, 23). Congolese back home "amid a rising wave of popular anger over the humiliating treatment of those expelled by Angola" (Human Rights Watch 2012, 11) demanded for retaliation. Then, in a retaliatory act, the government of the Democratic Republic of Congo invoked the principle of reciprocity in international relations and diplomacy and consequently expelled an estimated 50, 000 Angolans in 2009 (Oni and Okunade 2018, 42; Siegel 2009, 23).

Around 2017–2018, "thousands of Rwandans were expelled from Tanzania where, as minorities, they have lived in accord with locals since the 1930s" (Akinola 2018a, 27). In Tanzania, to stir up or engender anti-immigrant sentiments, the popular nationwide newspaper, The Tanzanian Daily News, published an editorial in which it alarmingly claimed that "[t]he tide of illegal immigrant arrivals is so huge the immigration officers have virtually failed to control them. Some come into this country to pursue economic prosperity. Others are smugglers of counterfeit goods. . . . In some cases the aliens collude with locals including corrupt immigration officers and members of the Police Force" (Editorial, Tanzania Daily News 2017).

In Africa, what all the above instances of negative stereotyping of, and discrimination against, migrants signify is that "xenophobic violence has become part of the African story. . . . From Ghana to Nigeria and Zambia to South Africa hostility has been directed against 'the others' and non-nationals of African descent" (Akinola 2018b, 1). In Africa, just like in other parts of the where xenophobia is rife, xenophobia "is located within the economic, social, political systems and exists like the dark matter of physics but is the motive force of what otherwise seem to be irrational explosions of subjective violence" (Ndlovu-Gatsheni 2013, 127).

Xenophobia takes different forms in different African countries—that is, xenophobia exists and xenophobic scapegoating is carried out for different reasons in different countries in Africa (Romola 2015). For instance, in South Africa and Angola, in Southern Africa, and in Nigeria and Ghana, in West Africa, migrants suffered xenophobic scapegoating due to economic reasons—that is, protectionism by the governments, high rate of unemployment among the citizens, and so on. Whereas

> in Chad and Kenya, xenophobic prejudices were informed by the war on terror. In Cote d'Ivoire, Gabon and Equatorial Guinea, politics as well as economic considerations triggered xenophobic expulsions. In Tanzania, Burundi and Congo Brazzaville, xenophobic actions were largely spurred by the rhetoric that foreigners were committing crime. In Congo Kinshasa, the expulsion of Angolans was political. Although, xenophobia takes different dimensions, they all have a unified goal; hatred for foreigners. (Oni and Okunade 2018, 40)

Whether in Nigeria, Ghana, South Africa, Botswana, or elsewhere on the continent, citizens think foreigners are responsible for the former's economic woes, which may be unemployment, underemployment, or unprofitable or less profitable business. Furthermore, in some cases, the latter are seen as the perpetrators of criminal activities that strain the social and moral fabric of the society. Hostilities (Afrophobia) against African migrants are now very pervasive all over the continent, especially in Southern Africa (Akinola 2018a, 23). Empirical study shows that governments in Southern African have weaponized immigration by exaggerating the volume of immigration they allow entry to and the population of immigrants they host. The purpose of the weaponization or exaggeration is to create resentment in the citizens against migrants, which in turn leads to scapegoating (Crush and Pendleton 2007), victimization, xenophobic attacks, and expulsion.

Adeoye Akinola (2018a) observes that "subtle forms of xenophobia have been a consistent feature of Botswana's policymaking and social reality for decades" (23). In Botswana, Zimbabweans have been the main target of such xenophobic discrimination. While in Zambia, Rwandese have been the main target of violence against African migrants (23). On their part, South Africans "seem to accommodate citizens from Ghana and Senegal, while displaying acute hostility to those from Nigeria, Zimbabwe and Somalia" (Akinola 2018b, 1–2). Black South Africans in postapartheid South Africa are notorious for xenophobia, specifically Afrophobia. Jean Pierre Misago (2017) notes that in postapartheid South Africa the incidence of violence perpetrated by Black South Africans against Africa migrants has not decreased (40). This is alarming to the extent that "there is a growing recognition, even among some government officials, that violent attacks on foreign nationals have taken on disturbing proportions. Since May 2008, attacks against outsiders—most notably foreign shopkeepers and workers—have resulted in an ever-growing number of murders and injuries at the hands of members of their host communities" (41).

THE CASE OF SOUTH AFRICA

Xenophobic or Afrophobic attacks against other Africans are not a new phenomenon in South Africa. Xenowatch, the most reliable platform that tracks incidents of xenophobic attacks in South Africa, reveals that "more than 500 attacks occurred between 1994 and 2018. The attacks seem to spike periodically; more than 100 attacks in 2008 left more than 60 people dead, and more than 70 attacks occurred in 2015. This year [2019] is on track to be another violent one, with more than 40 incidents recorded. More than half of the incidents unfolded in Johannesburg, the country's largest city" (Solomon 2019, s.p.).

The aforementioned attacks include the killing of persons, injuring of persons, looting of shops, and vandalization of properties. In retaliation against the 2019 South African xenophobic (Afrophobic) attacks against Nigerians, Nigerians looted South African–owned telecommunication company MTN and retailers such as Shoprite and PEP in Lagos, the commercial capital of Nigeria.

Defending the 2015 xenophobic (Afrophobic) attacks in South Africa, President Jacob Zuma said:

Our brother countries contribute to this. Why are their citizens not in their countries? It is not useful to criticise South Africa as if we mushroom these foreign
nationals and then ill-treat them. . . . Everybody criticises South Africa as if
we have manufactured the problem. Even if people who are xenophobic are a
minority, but what prompts these refugees to be in South Africa? It's a matter we
cannot shy away from discussing. (quoted in ANA 2015, s.p.)

Four years later, following in the footsteps of Jacob Zuma, Bongani
Mkongi—South African deputy minister of police—justified the 2019 xenophobic (Afrophobic) attacks. He said, "You won't find South Africans in
other countries dominating a city up to 80% . . . we cannot surrender South
Africa to foreign nationals" (quoted. in Signal 2019, s.p.). Although the claim
that African foreigners dominate 80 percent of Johannesburg is evidently
false, such claims fuel the resentment Black South Africans have for other
Africans such as Nigerians, Zimbabweans, Mozambicans, Somalis, and other
nationalities with significant presence in South Africa.

Table 3.2 Threats, attacks and killings against foreigners in South Africa from 2007 to 2019

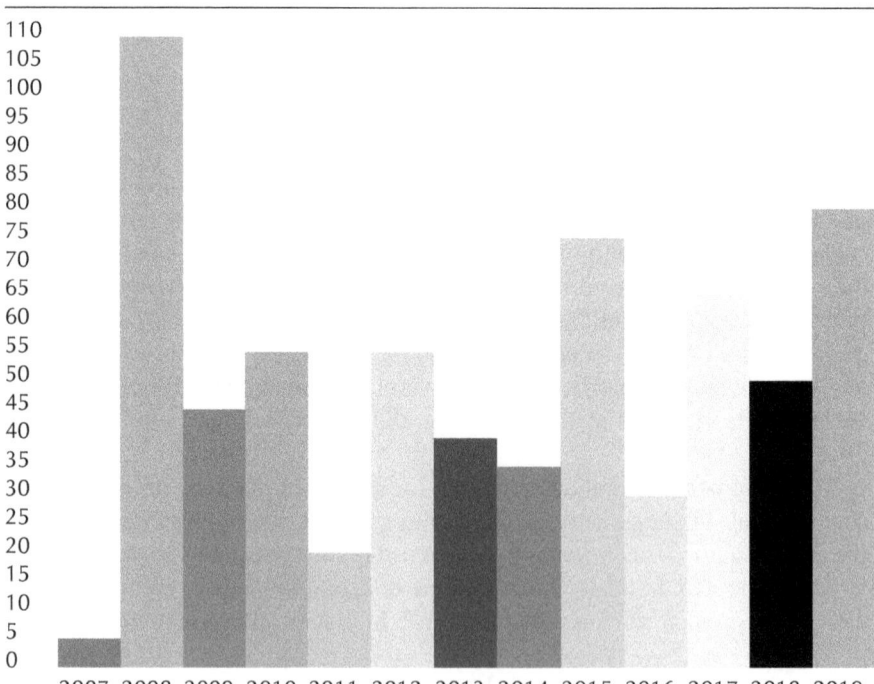

Source: Adapted from: (i) Xenowatch African Centre for Migration and Society; (ii) "South Africa: How
Common are Xenophobic Attacks?", BBC News, 02 October 2019, https://www.bbc.com/news/
world-africa-47800718

Table 3.3 Xenophobic Attacks in South African Provinces from 1994 to 2018

Northern Cape Province	5
Free State Province	19
North West Province	20
Mpumalanga Province	22
Eastern Cape Province	33
Limpopo Province	40
Kwazulu-Natal Province	67
Western Cape Province	111
Gauteng Province	212

(Listed in ascending order starting from the province with the lowest number of attacks and ending with the province with the highest number of attacks)

Source: Adapted from: (i) Xenowatch African Centre for Migration and Society; (ii) "South Africa: How Common are Xenophobic Attacks?", BBC News, 02 October 2019, https://www.bbc.com/news/world-africa-47800718

According to Achille Mbembe (2015), "South Africa is fast approaching its Fanonian moment. A mass of structurally disenfranchised people have the feeling of being treated as 'foreigners' on their own land. Convinced that the doors of opportunity are closing, they are asking for firmer demarcations between 'citizens' (those who belong) and 'foreigners' (those who must be excluded)" (s.p.). Mbembe's claim is supported by the fact that members of the South African parliament received very forceful "complaints from their constituents about the presence of foreign citizens in their neighborhoods. Studies of media coverage of immigration issues and the public utterances of elected officials from all of South Africa's political parties suggested that the view on the streets was more than a grassroots phenomenon" (Crush 2000, 107).

Private citizens are not alone in demanding for the "othering" of African migrants in South Africa. Even public institutions and government officials at the highest levels of government are part of this politics of othering. Unfortunately, for African migrants, "government departments, parliamentarians, the police . . . and the law itself have all been reinforcing a one-way message since the 1990s: We are being invaded by illegal immigrants who are a threat to national stability . . . our development, our social services, and the very fabric of our society" (Neocosmos 2008, 588). In this vein, South Africa's "Human Sciences Research Council (HSRC) used derogatory terms such as 'hordes' and 'floods' to describe undocumented migrants" (Steenkamp 2009, 441) (emphasis in original). Prima facie, that South Africa's popular and respected HSRC described African migrants as "hordes" and "floods" might be surprising. But it is only surprising to those who are not familiar with the situation in South Africa. For those who are familiar with the situation, this is just part and parcel of normal proceedings in the country. Moreover,

> [t]he focus of the state on what it sees as the parasitical relationship of non-South Africans to the nation's resources, and the way that the state criminalizes them, suggests that the state sees immigrants, and particularly undocumented migrants, as a threat to the nation and the post-1994 nation building process. The language of the state, which rarely attaches the prefix African, shows that it conceptualizes most immigrants as Africans, and Africans as potentially the most dangerous of all "aliens." (Peberdy 2009, 296)

Having been told or shown categorically that they are not welcome in South Africa, the psychological pressure of having been made to feel unwelcome has driven some African migrants to the point of considering departing the country. One African foreign student in South Africa says, "I came here just to study and after my degree I am going home. The way this South African people treat us, I can't stay here even during holidays; I want to be with my family. I only call or WhatsApp them during school time and before the university closes, I [have] already bought air-ticket to travel home and I am always going home. . . . I know it is expensive but my parents understand because they see the xenophobia on TV and they know we are not safe here" (Pineteh and Mulu 2016, 390).

While another African foreign student in South Africa says:

> When the lecturers give group work, South African students do not want to work with us. When we ask them they will say it is because they want to talk their local language and we are not going to understand. But I think it is because South Africans don't like foreigners . . . they think we are going to take their jobs when we finish studying. Like they are always asking us when are we going back home? "Are you going back home after you finish?" You can see that they don't like us here. (Pineteh and Mulu 2016, 395)

Xenophobic, or specifically Afrophobic, arguments in South Africa are based on neither reality nor fact, but on myth and falsehood. Merchants of xenophobia or Afrophobia in South Africa rely "heavily on the circulation of myths and stereotypes about foreigners. Foreigners in South Africa are typically accused of committing crimes; bringing disease (particularly HIV/ Aids), 'stealing' employment and swamping social services. Foreigners have quickly become the scapegoats for the continuing social and economic ills facing many South Africans" (Steenkamp 2009, 439–440). For instance, there is "widespread stereotype that all Nigerians in Johannesburg's inner city are drug-dealers and crooks" (Morris 1998, 1126). This Afrophobic stereotyping of Nigerians "is not surprising, since it is constantly voiced in the media and by those in positions of power. The information disseminated by the media and those in influential positions has undoubtedly had a significant impact" (ibid.).

In view of the foregoing discussion, it should be apparent that negative stereotyping of, and discrimination against, migrants by host countries and their citizens takes place in the context of an asymmetrical relationship between migrants and their host countries. In these asymmetrical relationships, the host countries negatively relate with—that is, discriminate against—migrants to the detriment of migrants and sometimes or even to the detriment of both parties since, as numerous econometrics and development economics research have shown empirically, migrants make net-positive economic contributions to their host countries. When discrimination against migrants is formal—that is, ingrained in laws and procedures—the situation becomes more precarious and alarming, but we know exactly what we are dealing with. However, when it is informal—that is, when it takes the form of systemic biases—the situation may be less precarious and alarming but becomes complex in the sense that we may not even know exactly what we are dealing with. Given that states may not want to be seen as violating international law, African regional law, subregional law, and even national law, the discrimination against migrants is often informal and seldom formal.

DOUBLE JEOPARDY

As the preceding and penultimate sections show, Africa is littered with a plethora of cases of discrimination and domination against African migrants. In these cases, even children from migrant groups are treated unjustly because of their status as migrants. When migrant families are discriminated against in their host country, the perpetrators of the discrimination—be it the state, government and its agencies, groups, or persons—do not make any distinction between the adult members of the families and the children of the families. For instance, when Nigerian migrants were expelled from Ghana (as discussed in the first section), the Ghanaian government did not spare Nigerian children; everyone including father, mother, brother, and sister whether adult or minor was expelled. So too, when Ghanaian migrants were expelled from Nigeria (as discussed in the first section), the Nigerian government did not spare Ghanaian children; everyone including father, mother, brother, and sister whether adult or minor was expelled.

In the above examples of the expulsion of Nigerian migrants from Ghana and the expulsion of Ghanaian migrants from Nigeria, even if the Ghanaian government made exceptions for Nigerian children or the Nigerian government made exceptions for Ghanaian children—that is even if children were not *directly* expelled—they may still be *indirectly* expelled. This is because as dependents, children are likely to follow their parents or their guardians whom they depend on. Outside these cases of expulsions, even when children are not directly discriminated against, as long as their parents or guardians or adult siblings or close relatives whom they depend on are discriminated against, children are indirectly discriminated against because what affects the family members who children depend on invariably affects the children. The unemployment of a father might result in lack of education for a child, the loss of job by mother might mean undernourishment for a child. In the case of South Africa discussed in the preceding section, when migrant parents are killed in xenophobic or Afrophobic violence, the lives of the children are turned upside down in every way imaginable.

Alarmingly, discrimination against, and domination of, children from migrant groups are a double jeopardy because they simultaneously violate two group rights—namely, minority rights and children's rights. The United Nations Convention on the Rights of the Child (UNCRC), Article 1, defines children as human beings who are yet to attain the age of eighteen years, unless in certain jurisdictions the age of majority is attainable before the age of eighteen years under the law applicable to children. Children are a special category of human beings; this assertion is not contentious. What makes children special or agreeing on what makes children special might be a bit contentious. We may not agree on whether a certain characteristic makes children special or not. We may agree that a certain characteristic makes children special but disagree on what extent—larger or lesser—the characteristic makes children special. Yet, it is apt to claim that the common denominator of what makes children special include the following. Generally, "children are not able to fully understand their situation . . . they are limited in their ability to make reasonable decisions about themselves and their actions . . . they do not always act in their best interest . . . they need the help and guidance of adults, and . . . they need special protection from various harms and from making wrong choices" (Graf and Schweiger 2015, X).

The age and developmental stage of a child determine to what extent the child is more like an adult or less like an adult in terms of vulnerability, competence, and dependence. For instance, toddlers are more vulnerable, less competent, and more dependent than are adolescents. In other words, generally, the younger a child, the more vulnerable, less competent, and more dependent he or she is. While, generally, the older a child, the less vulnerable, the more competent, and the less dependent he or she is. Nevertheless, generally, children are more vulnerable, less competent, and more dependent than are adults. In terms of vulnerability, "[T]he bodies and minds of children are 'weaker' and less robust" (Graf and Schweiger 2015, 7). In terms of competence, they "have limited capacities in comparison to adults. They have fewer abilities and opportunities to shape their lives—if they are very young this is nearly impossible for them" (Ibid.). In terms of dependence, they depend "on adults for their well-being and well-becoming and they are [more] limited in their capacities to protect themselves" (ibid.).

The condition of the child as described in the preceding paragraph is not only biological but also social. Children are not only inherently vulnerable but also situationally vulnerable (Schweiger and Graf 2017, 250). "They are in danger of being exploited by others because they have weaker capacities than adults (or older children) and because there is a certain way the institution of childhood is framed in society" (Ibid.). The condition of the starving children in the barbaric war in Yemen unfortunately shows how children, compared with adults, are more vulnerable to physical and social adversities.

It should not be very contentious to claim that as a special category of human beings, children require special care: "Children are special subjects of justice and this care for children is driven by such interrelated concepts as vulnerability, innocence and incompetence. They justify a particular concern for children's well-being and well-becoming and why paternalism—in a more comprehensive way than it is justified towards adults—is the right way to fashion the relationship between children, adults and institutions" (Graf and Schweiger 2015, 6–7). Thus, it is indisputable that children require special protection. This special protection is a twofold interactional and institutional protection: (1) the negative duty to refrain from harming children and (2) the positive duty to (a) remedy any harm that has been done to children, (b) prevent children from being harmed, and (c) provide the material means required for their well-being and well-becoming.

Ultimately, the protection of children is aimed at fostering the well-being of children and, equally important, the "well-becoming" (Schweiger 2015, 84) of children. "Well-being refers to the actual state of a child, while well-becoming is concerned with the transition from one state of being to another" (Graf and Schweiger 2015, 5). The well-being of children is not only valuable in itself because of the special characteristics of children, but it also has an instrumental value because the "well-being during childhood has a significant influence on the entirety of a child's future life and adulthood" (Graf and Schweiger 2015, X). In other words, while the well-being of children has a present value because of the state of children, it also has a future-value because, largely, it shapes the well-becoming of children and, to a large extent, accounts for the positive or negative result of the well-becoming.

Therefore, fostering the well-being and well-becoming of children is necessary because the well-being and well-becoming of children serve as "ultimate goals of justice" (Schweiger 2015, 84) in both our interactional and institutional relationships with children. As ultimate goals of justice, the well-being and well-becoming of children play two critical roles. First, they enable "us to better understand the specific needs of children as agents of justice and their embededness in certain social contexts" (Ibid.). Second, they "guide the selection of the currency of justice and the rule of their distribution" (Ibid.).

Rights, alongside needs and capabilities, are the major perspectives from which the well-being and well-becoming of children can be looked at (Axford 2012; Graf and Schweiger 2015, 1). Certain fundamental rights are very important for the well-being and well-becoming of children. It is for this reason that the UNCRC seeks to protect, among other rights, the following rights. Article 6, paragraph 1 of the UNCRC stipulates that "[s]tate Parties recognise that every child has the inherent right to life," and paragraph 2 stipulates that "[s]tate Parties shall ensure to the maximum extent possible the survival and development of the child." Furthermore, the UNCRC stipulates that children have the right to protection from "all forms of physical or mental violence, injury or abuse, neglect or negligent treatment, maltreatment or exploitation, including sexual abuse" (Article 19, para. 1); right not to "be subjected to torture or other cruel, inhuman or degrading treatment or punishment" (Article 37, para. "a"); right to be protected from economic exploitation and hazardous work (Article 32), right to healthcare (Article 24), right to education (Article 28), and so on.

Essentially, the aforementioned negative and positive rights, and the negative, positive, and republican freedoms of children, are to be respected because they are necessary for the well-being and well-becoming of children. Protecting the individual human rights of children is necessary for the well-being and well-becoming of children. But when children from migrant groups are discriminated against or dominated because of their status as migrants, the protection of their individual human rights is insufficient. In such cases, minority rights are needed to protect the children. But as I shall show in subsequent chapters, even minorities are not a realistic resolution to the problem of domination and discrimination on the continent.

REFERENCES

Abumere, Frank Aragbonfoh. 2015. "Context as the Principal Determinant of the Behaviour of States in Global Politics." *International Journal of Peace and Conflict Studies* 2, no. 3: 57–68.

Abumere, Frank Aragbonfoh. 2019. "World Government, Social Contract and Legitimacy." *Philosophical Papers* 48, no. 1: 9–30.

Abumere, Frank Aragbonfoh. 2020. "Introducing Normativity in African International Politics." *Politikon: South African Journal of Political Studies* 47, no. 3: 342–60.

Adebajo, A. 2011. *UN Peacekeeping in Africa: From the Suez Canal to the Sudan Conflicts*. Colorado: Lynne Rienner Publishers.

Adepoju, A. 2005. "Migration in West Africa." A Paper Prepared for the Policy Analysis and Research Programme of the Global Commission on International Migration, Global Commission on International Migration. Available online: http: //iom.ch/jahia/webdav/site/ myjahiasite/shared/shared/mainsite/policy_and_resear ch/gcim/rs/RS8.pd

Akinola, Adeoye O. 2018a. "The Scourge of Xenophobia: From Botswana to Zambia." In *The Political Economy of Xenophobia in Africa,* edited by Adeoye O. Akinola, 23–36. Cham: Springer.

Akinola, Adeoye O. 2018b. "Introduction: Understanding Xenophobia in Africa." In *The Political Economy of Xenophobia in Africa,* edited by Adeoye O. Akinola, 1–8. Cham: Springer.

ANA. 2015. "Jacob Zuma asks Africa: Why are Their Citizens Not in Their Countries and are in South Africa?," April 28, 2015. https://www.lusakatimes.com/2015/04 /28/ acob-zuma-asks-africa-why-are-their-citizens-not-in-their-countries-and-are-in-south-africa/)

Aremu, Johnson Olaosebikan. 2010. "Conflicts in Africa: Meaning, Causes, Impact and Solution." *African Research Review* 4, no. 4: 549–60.

Axford, Nick. 2012. *Exploring Concepts of Child Well-Being: Implications for Children's Services*. Bristol: Policy.

Brobbey, Collins Adu-Bempah. 2018. "Democratisation and Legitimisation of Zenophobia in Ghana." In *The Political Economy of Xenophobia in Africa,* edited by Adeoye O. Akinola, 69–80. Cham: Springer.

Clapham, Christopher S. 1996. *Africa and the International System: The Politics of State Survival*. Cambridge: Cambridge University Press.

Crush, Jonathan. 2000. "The Dark Side of Democracy: Migration, Human Rights and Xenophobia in South Africa." *International Migration* 38, no. 6: 103–34.

Crush, Jonathan, and W. Pendleton. 2007. "Mapping Hostilities: The Geography of Xenophobia in Southern Africa." *The South African Geographical Journal* 89, no. 1: 64–82.

The Economist. 2021. "Many More Africans Are Migrating within Africa than to Europe." *The Economist*.

ECOWAS Commission. 1993. Economic Community of West African States (ECOWAS), Revised Treaty, ECOWAS Commission, Abuja, Nigeria.

Falola, Toyin. 2006. "Welcome." Conference Program, Movements, Migrations, and Displacements in Africa, Africa Conference 2006, The University of Texas at Austin, March 25–27, 2006.

Falola, Toyin, and Niyi Afolabi. 2007. "Preface." In *The Human Cost of African Migrations*, edited by Toyin Falola and Niyi Afolabi, xix–xx. New York and London: Routledge.

Graf, Gunter, and Gottfried Schweiger. 2015. "Introduction: Conceptualizing Children's Well-Being." In *The Well-Being of Children: Philosophical and Social Approaches,* edited by Gottfried Schweiger and Gunter Graf, 1–17. Berlin: De Gruyter Open.

Hirsh, Alan. 2020. "A Strategic Consideration of the African Union Free Movement of Persons Protocol and Other Initiatives Towards the Freer Movement of People in Africa." South African Institute of International Affairs, University of the Witwatersrand, Johannesburg.

HSRC (Human Sciences Research Council). (2008). "Violence and Xenophobia in South Africa: Developing Consensus, Moving to Action." edited by A. Hadland. http://hdl.handle.net/20.500.11910/5188

Human Rights Watch. 2012. "If You Come Back We Will Kill You": Sexual violence and otherabuses against congolese migrants during expulsions from Angola (p. 81). New York: HumanRights Watch Publications.

Human Rights Watch. 2012. *Prohibited Persons*: *Abuse of Undocumented Migrants, Asylum-seekers, and Refugees in South Africa*. New York: Human Rights Watch.

IPSA/AISP (International Political Science Association). 2018. "IPSA Congress Theme: Borders and Margin." https://wc2018.ipsa.org/events/congress/wc2018/congress-theme-borders-and-margins.

Mbembe, Achille. 2015. "The State of South African Political Life." *African is a Country*. September 19, 2015. https://africasacountry.com/2015/09/achille-mbembe-on-the-state-of-south-african-politics

Misago, Jean Pierre. 2017. "Politics by Other Means? The Political Economy of Xenophobic Violence in Post-Apartheid South Africa." *The Black Scholar*: *Journal of Black Studies and Research* 47, no. 2: 40–53.

Morris, A. 1998. "Our Fellow Africans Make Our Lives Hell: The Lives of Congolese and Nigerians living in Johannesburg." *Ethnic and Racial Studies* 21, no. 6: 1116–36.

Mudimbe, V. Y. 2003. "Globalization and African Identity." *CR: The New Centennial Review* 3, no. 2: 205–18.

Ndlovu-Gatsheni, S. J. 2013. "Coloniality of Power in Postcolonial Africa. Myths of Decolonization." CODESRIA, Dakar.

Neocosmos, M. 2008. "The Politics of Fear and the Fear of Politics: Reflections on Xenophobic Violence in South Africa." *Journal of Asian and African Studies*, 43, no. 6: 586–94.

Okunade, Samuel. 2021. "Africa Moves towards Intracontinental Free Movement for Its Booming Population." Migration Information Source, Migration Policy Institute, January 21, 2021. https://www.migrationpolicy.org/article/africa-intracontinental-free-movement

Oni, Ebenezer O., and Samuel K. Okunade. 2018. "The Context of Xenophobia in Africa." In *The Political Economy of Xenophobia in Africa*, edited by Adeoye O. Akinola, 37–52. Cham: Springer.

Peberdy, S. 2009. *Selecting Immigrants: National Identity and South Africa's Immigration Policies, 1910–2008.* Johannesburg: Wits University Press.

Pineteh, E., and T. Mulu. 2016. "Francophone Transnational Students, Social Exclusion and the Challenges of Adaptation at a South African University of Technology." *African Human Mobility Review* 2, no. 1: 383–403.

Prah, Kwasi Kwaa. 2010. Soundings: Studies on African Transformation. CASAS Book Series, no. 79. Cape Town,: Centre for Advanced Study of African Society. NOtE: The correct reference year is 2010 rather than 2012

Romola, A. 2015. "Preventing Xenophobia in Africa: What must the African Union Do?." *AHMR* 1, no. 3: 254–59.

Schweiger, Gottfried. 2015. "Justice and Children's Well-Being and Well-Becoming." In *The Well-Being of Children: Philosophical and Social Approaches*, edited by Gottfried Schweiger and Gunter Graf, 84–96. Berlin: De Gruyter Open.

Schweiger, Gottfried, and Gunter Graf. 2017. "Ethics and the Dynamic Vulnerability of Children." *Les Ateliers des l'Éthique* 12, no. 2–3: 243–61.

Sharpe, Marina. 2020. "The Free Movement of Persons with the African Union and Refugee Protection." *RefLaw*, May 25, 2020. https://reflaw.org/the-free-movement -of-persons-within-the-african-union-and-refugee-protection/

Siegel, D. 2009. *The Mazzel Ritual: Culture, Customs and Crime in the Diamond Trade.* Dordrecht: Springer.

Signal, September 2,ignalingignalng.com

Solomon, Salem. 2019. "After a Week of Xenophobic Attacks, South Africa Grapples for Answers." VOA, September 6, 2019. https://www.voanews.com/africa/after -week-xenophobic-attacks-south-africa-grapples-answers.

Steenkamp, C. 2009. "Xenophobia in South Africa: What Does It Say about Trust?." *The Round Table* 98, no. 403: 439–47.

Tanzania Daily News. 2017. "Tanzania: Illegal Immigrants Must Pay for Unlawful Stay." Editorial, Dar es Salaam, April 20, 2017. http://www.dailynews.co.tz/index .php/

Tieku, Thomas Kwasi. 2013. "Theoretical Approaches to Africa's International Relations." In *Handbook of Africa's International Relations*, edited by Tim Muruthi, 11–20. New York: Routledge.

UNCRC (United Nations Convention on the Rights of the Child). Adopted and Opened for Signature, Ratification and Accession by General Assembly Resolution 44/25 of 20 November 1989, Entry into Force 2 September 1990 in Accordance with Article 49. Office of the High Commissioner for Human Rights, United Nations, New York. https://www.ohchr.org/en/professionalinterest/pages/crc.aspx. Accessed: 17 November 2018.

Usman, Aribidesi, and Toyin Falola. 2009. "Introduction: Migrations in African History—An Introduction." In *Movements, Borders, and Identities in Africa*, edited by Toyin Falola and Aribidesi Usman, 1–34. Rochester: University of Rochester Press.

Watt, D. C., Simon Adams, Roger Bullen, Kinley Brauer, and Akira Irayee. 1988. "What Is Diplomatic History?" In *What Is History Today*? edited by Juliet Gardiner, 131–42. London: Macmillan.

Xenowatch. 2019. "Incidents of Xenophobic Violence in South Africa: 1994 - 28 June 2022", Xenowatch Dashboard, Xenowatch, African Centre for Migration and Society (ACMS), University of the Witwatersrand, Johanesburg, South Africa. https://www.xenowatch.ac.za/statistics-dashboard/.

Chapter Four

Problems With Minority Rights Approach

In this chapter, I shall discuss the legal and political approach to addressing the question of minority—that is, the problem of the domination of, and discrimination against, minorities. The basic point of the discussion is to weigh the strengths and weaknesses of the legal and political approach on a scale and see which one outweighs the other. Based on the result that the scale shows, the remainder of the book (i.e., chapters 5, 7, and 8, except chapter 6) will extrapolate or deduce whether such a legal and political approach (notably minority rights) will result in a realistic resolution to the discrimination against migrants. While my concern is with Africa as a whole, I shall focus on Nigeria for the purpose of contextualizing the discussion in the chapter. This contextualization is important because being the most populous country in Africa, Nigeria represents a microcosm of Africa. Therefore, understanding the Nigerian case will probably give us insights into the other cases, or at least to some of the other cases, on the continent.

THE NIGERIAN EXAMPLE OF DOMINATION AND DISCRIMINATION (PART 1)

The term *minority rights* rarely appears in Nigerian discourses. Whether at the national or local levels, or whether formally or informally, this term is not one of the familiar or popular terms one will readily come across in official documents, newspapers, the airwaves of television stations and radio stations, or the social media. In short, both de jure and de facto, this term has been, whether intentionally or unintentionally, alienated, or at least relegated, from national discourse. Nevertheless, "minority discrimination" and "minority domination" are part of everyday life in Nigeria. Therefore, while explicitly Nigeria does not seem to be concerned with the term *minority rights*, the country is continuously dealing with problems, and it can be argued that the country is at least implicitly concerned with the term because the term is the one side of a coin whose other side is minority discrimination and minority domination.

I shall proceed with the discussion by giving an overview of the composition of majorities and minorities in Nigeria, which will serve as a prelude to the substantive discussion in the chapter. My focus is on ethnic groups in Nigeria, specifically ethnic domination in Nigeria. I proceed by describing the composition of ethnic groups in Nigeria. Based on the description of what a minority is in chapter 1, there are a few hundreds of ethnic minorities in Nigeria. There are different speculations, estimates, and approximations about the number of ethnic groups in Nigeria. There is no one agreed-on number, and there is not even any average number with any reasonable margin for error that may be deemed reliable. Some put the number at 400, some put it at 250, and some put it at 350, and so on and so forth. The statistical discrepancies among the figures that have been bandied around by the "experts" on the subject do not even allow for an arithmetic mean, not even to mention reasonable estimation or reliable approximation. For instance, the United States' Central Intelligence Agency (CIA; 2017) says that Nigeria is composed of more than 250 ethnic groups.

Renate Wente-Lukas puts the number of ethnic groups between 550 and 619, Hoffman puts the number at 394, Onigu Otite (1991) says it is 374 (35–36), while Yusuf Bangura says the accurate number is 470. At school, pupils are taught that the accurate number is 250; hence, most of the general population grows up to believe that the accurate number is 250. However, as one commentator succinctly puts it, the common myth is that Nigeria has 250 ethnic groups; but the simple fact, as Abdul Raufu Mustapha (2003) says, is that there is no one who actually knows the exact figure, and depending on the singular criterion or the plural criteria one uses, one's estimate will vary widely from another person's estimate or other peoples' estimates.

In Nigeria's population of around 200 million, numerically no single ethnic group constitutes 50 percent plus one. The most populous and politically influential among the ethnic groups are the Hausa/Fulani—29 percent, the Yoruba—21 percent, the Igbo—18 percent, the Ijaw—10 percent, the Kanuri—4 percent, the Ibibio—3.5 percent, and the Tiv—2.5 percent (CIA 2017). Apparently, the Hausa/Fulani, the Yoruba, and the Igbo are the three largest ethnic groups. They are considered to be the majority, not just collectively but also separately, because although none of them separately constitutes 50 percent plus one of the total population, their separate populations far outnumber the separate populations of the minorities. Their ethnic numerical advantage translates to political advantage; consequently, these so-called majority ethnic groups also dominate the minority ethnic groups politically.

On the numerical scale, the separate populations of the so-called majority ethnic groups far outnumber the separate populations of the so-called minority ethnic groups to the extent that the former are able to capitalize on it to the detriment of the latter. In other words, the vast disparities between the numerical superiority of the so-called majority ethnic groups and the numerical inferiority of the so-called minority ethnic groups lead to the domination of the latter by the former.

Any other ethnic group apart from the three mentioned earlier is considered to be a minority group. Among the minorities, on the one hand, there are the large or major minority groups such as Ijaw, Kanuri, Ibibio, Tiv, Edo, Nupe, Urhobo, and Igala. On the other hand, there are the small or minor minority groups such as Efik, Igede, Yala, Itsekiri, Isoko, Ishan (Esan), Etsako, Anetuno, Ebira, Idoma, Gwandara, Gbagi (Gwari), Kadara, and so on. Since in Nigeria ethnic numerical advantage and disadvantage determine the political strength and consequently the dominant or nondominant status of a group, comparatively the small or minor minority groups suffer more discrimination than the large or major minority groups, while the large or major minority groups have more political strength than the small or minor minority groups. Succinctly put, there are different degrees of "minoritiness" in Nigeria; some minorities are of a lesser degree while others are of a higher degree, and these degrees have political and economic consequences (Otite 1991, 26).

In summary, just as the ethnic numerical advantage of the majority groups translates to political advantage and the consequent political domination of the minority groups, the ethnic numerical disadvantage of the minority groups translates to political disadvantage and consequently the political domination by the majority groups. For instance, since the return to democracy in 1999, the majority ethnic groups have produced three presidents, while the minority ethnic groups have only produced one president (Olusegun Obasanjo—ethnic majority Yoruba (29 May 1999–29 May 2007); Umar Yar'Adua—ethnic majority Hausa/Fulani (29 May 2007–9 February 2010); Goodluck Jonathan—ethnic minority Ijaw (9 February 2010–29 May 2015); and Mohammadu Buhari—ethnic majority Hausa/Fulani (29 May 2015—present). The ethnicity of a president matters because it is a measurement of the just representation of the minority ethnic groups and the unjust representation of the majority ethnic groups.

Nigeria is not alone in having a multitude of ethnicities. Berman et al. (2004) correctly say:

> Despite the media stereotype that Africa is uniquely afflicted by ethnic and tribal conflicts, the fact is that many other countries around the world have faced comparative problems. Very few countries are united by common descent, language,

religion and culture. . . . In every other country, the sense that there is one united people inhabiting one connected country has had to be constructed. (13)

Nevertheless, the question is, what are the conditions under which ethnic domination is manifested in Nigeria? In other words, what are the conditions that result in the very specific kinds of ethnic domination in Nigeria? The task of this section of the chapter is to provide an answer to the above questions by preliminarily describing certain conditions that make the kinds of ethnic domination we have in Nigeria possible. There are certain conditions that make the domination, as described in the previous section, possible in Nigeria. These conditions do not only make the domination mentioned earlier possible; they are also the source and origin of ethnic domination in Nigeria as described in the previous section. I will refer to these conditions as (1) the multiple majorities condition; (2) the multiple minorities condition; (3) the major majority condition; (4) the minor majority condition; (5) the major minorities condition; and (6) the minor minorities condition.

Usually, when ethnic domination is discussed, there is often one behemoth majority that does the domination—that is, there is often one dominant majority that the minority or minorities that are being dominated have to deal with. But in Nigeria, there is no singular majority; there are rather three majorities. Hence, the minorities have not only one majority to contend with but rather three majorities. This condition is what I refer to as the multiple majorities condition. But among the three majorities, one is the most dominant, and another is the least dominant; the former condition is what I refer to as the major majority condition, while the latter condition is what I refer to as the minor majority condition.

Also, usually, when ethnic domination is discussed, there is often one or few minorities that are being dominated. But in Nigeria, there are not just a few minorities; rather, there are a few hundreds of minorities. So an ethnic minority that is being dominated is neither the only minority that is being dominated nor one of the few minorities that are being dominated; rather, it is just one of the few hundreds of minorities that have to contend with the multiple majorities that are dominating the minorities. This condition is what I refer to as the multiple minorities condition.

While there are three ethnic majority groups and a few hundreds of ethnic minority groups in Nigeria, there are ethnic groups that are not part of the majorities, are part of the minorities, but are somewhat middle-of-the-road between the majorities and the rest of the minorities. Their middle-of-the-road character is derived from their numerical inferiority to the majorities and their numerical superiority to the rest of the minorities. Hence, they are called major minorities. Unlike the majorities, their numerical advantage over the rest of the minorities is not huge enough for them to be one of the dominant groups in the country. Put differently, they do not equal the majorities in numerical strength, and they do not have the capacity to contend or compete with the majorities in terms of dominance.

On the one hand, due to their numerical inferiority to the majorities, they are susceptible to being dominated by the majorities. Nevertheless, their ability to resist the majorities, and the extent or degree to which they can resist the majorities, is greater than that of other minorities. On the other hand, given the numerical advantage they have over the rest of the minorities, the rest of the minorities are susceptible to being dominated by them. In other words, due to their numerical inferiority to the majorities, they are susceptible to, and in fact suffer, domination by the majorities and are dominated by the majorities. While, due to their numerical superiority to the rest of the minorities, they in turn dominate other minorities, especially in the geographical territories where the former has numerical superiority or enjoy a substantial numerical advantage—that is, in their areas of dominance or spheres of influence. This condition is what I refer to as the major minorities condition. While the condition of the rest of the minorities who can be dominated by both the majorities and these major minorities is what I refer to as the minor minorities condition.

Note that it is not my claim that any of the conditions described in the preceding paragraphs is necessary or sufficient for ethnic domination in its current form in Nigeria—for ethnic domination could well exist in Nigeria even if one or some of these conditions were not in place. Rather, my claim is that it is a combination of all these conditions that has made ethnic domination possible in Nigeria, and that this combination is the source and origin of ethnic domination in Nigeria. It is not that absent these conditions there could not have been ethnic domination in Nigeria. Absent these conditions, perhaps there might have been ethnic domination or there might have not been ethnic domination. Also absent these conditions, if there were ethnic domination, it would not be the specific kinds of ethnic domination that currently exist in Nigeria. For it is those conditions that make the specific kinds of domination we have in Nigeria possible.

Therefore, understanding the conditions described in the preceding paragraphs is important for two reasons. First, they are important for understanding the nature of ethnic domination in Nigeria; in other words, they are important for diagnosing the problem. Second, they are important for prescribing a realistic resolution to the problem—that is, prescribing a remedy in view of the diagnosis. In this section, having preliminarily described what the conditions of ethnic domination in Nigeria are, my next task is to explain in detail how these conditions make the specific kinds of ethnic domination we have in Nigeria possible and how they are the source and origin of ethnic domination in Nigeria.

(1) The Multiple Majorities Condition

There is no one single majority vying for dominance or that is actually dominating the minorities. There are three majorities vying for domination and
actually dominating the minorities. Although not acting in concert—that is,
although acting separately, together these three majorities make it difficult for
minorities to have a sustainable and viable opposition to domination. Given
that minorities have to contend with the dominance impulses of these majorities simultaneously, the resistance resources of these minorities are easily
exhausted, their resistance capacities become stretched, and they become
weakened in the face of domination.

(2) The Multiple Minorities Condition

As already mentioned, there are not just a few minorities, but rather a few
hundreds of minorities in Nigeria. When a single minority or a few minorities
are dominated, the situation of the minority or minorities is clear and distinct,
and as such they distinctly feel how they have been isolated, how different they are from the majority or majorities, and how disadvantaged such
domination has rendered them. But when a few hundreds of minorities are
dominated, their plight becomes somewhat fuzzy, since it is difficult to tell to
what degree and to extent each group has been dominated, and the situation
of one out of a few hundred groups suffering the same plight will hardly ring
alarm bells in our ears. The situation of the one group, at best, will be con-
flated with the situation of the rest. Even ironically, some groups might have
false consolation knowing that they are not alone in their suffering; they may
even think that they are doing relatively well since their situation is better or
at least not worse than that of another group or those of other groups.

(3) The Major Majority Condition

Dominating the other yields advantages to the majorities. So any majority
that persists with domination accumulates advantages over time, while any
majority that desists from domination may over time lose ground to the one
that persists with domination. If majority *A* desists from dominating minorities, while majorities *B* and *C* continue with dominating minorities, majority
A may even in the long run become a victim of majorities *B* and *C*. Majority
A does not only have to count the losses of the illegitimate gains from dominating minorities, but it also has to fear being dominated by majorities *B* and
C. So the incentive to continue with domination is high, while the price of
desisting may be very costly.

The majorities are always vying to be ahead of one another in the domination race. While on the eve of independence the Hausa/Fulani feared that the Yoruba and the Igbo were dominant due to Yoruba's and Igbo's educational advantage over the Hausa/Fulani, in the present era—and since independence—the Hausa/Fulani have capitalized on their numerical advantage to dominate the political sphere. The fear that the Yoruba and the Igbo will be the dominant majorities led the Hausa/Fulani to oppose the first independence motion in 1953. For the Hausa/Fulani, they needed time to bridge the educational gap between them and the Yoruba and the Igbo in order to prevent the Yoruba and the Igbo from leveraging educational advantage to become dominant.

After the January 1966 coup led by mostly Igbo officers in which many Hausa/Fulani civilian and military heavyweights were killed, few Yoruba civilian and military heavyweights were killed, and no Igbo civilian and military heavyweight was killed, the Hausa/Fulani felt that they had lost their dominance to the Igbo. In the coup the most prominent Hausa/Fulani politician was killed, and the most prominent Igbo politician was spared; the most senior-ranking Hausa/Fulani politician was killed, and the most senior-ranking Igbo politician was spared; and the most senior-ranking Hausa/Fulani military officer was killed, and the most senior-ranking Igbo military officer was spared. Above all, the prime minister, a northerner from the Hausa/Fulani region, was killed, while an Igbo took over as the head of state. This sense of loss of dominance by the Hausa/Fulani to the Igbo led the former to embark on the July 1966 countercoup in which prominent Igbo military officers, including the head of state, were killed and a northerner from the Hausa/Fulani region replaced the assassinated Igbo military officer as head of state.

Cumulatively, these events led to the secession attempt by the Igbo and the consequent civil war. While, prima facie, this can be seen as a mere fatal struggle for dominance by two major ethnic groups, minorities had a lot to lose—including numerous lives—during the crises. Even in the present era, minorities still have a lot to lose in the struggle for dominance among the majorities. As the saying goes, "[W]hen elephants fight, it is the grass that suffers."

(4) The Minor Majority Condition

Among the majorities, the Hausa/Fulani are currently seen as the major majority, and they subjectively identify as the major majority. The Yoruba are seen as the middle-of-the-road between the Hausa/Fulani and the Igbo. While the Igbo are seen, and they subjectively identify, as the minor majority. Having already attempted a failed secession between 1967 and 1970, a large number of the Igbo are again agitating for secession. The grievance is that they feel they have been marginalized, and are being marginalized, by the other majority groups, especially the Hausa/Fulani.

As the biblical saying goes, "For if they do these things to the green wood, what will be done to the dried woods?" (Luke 23: 31). In other words, if the green woods can be set ablaze, what is the fate of the dried woods? Without any attempt at scriptural exegesis, the significance of the question leads one to imagine, in our case, if the Igbo are suffering domination from fellow majorities, what is the fate of the minorities? If one majority can dominate another majority, then surely minorities are in grave danger. For if a major majority can dominate a minor majority, then it will be too easy for that major majority to dominate a minority. However, if a major majority focuses all its effort on dominating a minor majority, the major majority may not have time and stamina to dominate minorities, and may even think it is unnecessary to do so, as the minor majority is considered the main threat to be contained, not the far weaker minorities.

(5) The Major Minorities Condition

While the major minorities suffer domination by the majorities because of their different identities, so also members of the minor minorities suffer domination by the major minorities because of their different identities. This is not to say that domination is an inherent element of there being different groups of different sizes and identities. There can be a number of identity groups in a society and yet they may have no interest in dominating one another. Nevertheless, this is not the case in Nigeria.

In Nigeria, on the one hand, due to different identities, the major minorities do not enjoy inclusion or an adequate level of inclusion in affairs and schemes of the polity nationally; they unjustly and unfairly suffer exclusion, or at least a substantial degree of exclusion, from affairs and schemes of the polity by the majority groups at the federal level. On the other hand, in their areas of dominance or spheres of influence, the major minorities too, in terms of inclusion and exclusion, fail to treat the minor minorities fairly and justly. As already mentioned, the minor minorities do not only suffer domination at the hands of the majorities, but they also suffer domination at the hands of the major minorities in the areas where the major minorities have numerical advantage—that is, in their areas of dominance or spheres of influence. So a group can be both a victim and a perpetrator or a prey and a predator.

(6) The Minor Minorities Condition

The minor minorities are so numerically disadvantaged that none of them as a single unit has the capacity to fend off domination from the majorities and the major minorities. The plight of these minor minorities are rarely on the front burner because individually (as single groups) these groups do not have the wherewithal whether in numerical strength or otherwise to effectively challenge their dominators. As individual groups, they cannot force the dominant groups to rein in the latter's dominant instinct or at least to force the latter to check their impulsive excesses of domination.

THE NIGERIAN EXAMPLE OF ETHNIC DOMINATION AND DISCRIMINATION (PART 2)

The intractability of the problem of ethnic domination is something only a few people can genuinely elide from their "knowledge" of Nigeria. This problem is distinctive because it renders millions of Nigerians second class citizens even in their own country. However, there is an institutional failure—the attempt to resolve ethnic domination—which although not glaring to the world, is a grave failure because it has failed to prevent or stop the rendering of millions of Nigerians second class citizens in their own country. In the attempt to resolve the problem, Nigeria employs certain constitutional devices—namely, the creation of new states and local government areas, and the adoption of a federal character as a constitutional principle and a quota system as an administrative principle. I contend that the attempt to resolve the problem is a failure. Employing theoretical and historical analysis, I show that the problem remains unresolved because the constitutional devices are not based on the systemic, pervasive, historical, and consistent nature of the ethnic domination they are intended to regulate.

Using various constitutional devices in an attempt to resolve the intractable problem of ethnic domination in the country is a commendable legal and political policy because it simultaneously acknowledges that minorities are dominated and they have group rights. But these devices have not resolved the problem; if anything, they have only changed "the constitutional and institutional context, if not the substance, of minority discrimination" (Mustapha 2003, 8–9). Recently, the case of the Ijaw ethnic group has generated a debate on whether the Ijaw suffer domination at the hands of the dominant groups or whether the Ijaw are actually one of the dominant groups perpetrating domination. The Ijaw case is important for two reasons. The first reason is minor, while the second reason is major.

First, the status of the Ijaw needs to be clarified in order to ascertain whether they are a prey, a predator, or both a prey and a predator in the domination wildlife. Unless we ascertain whether they are one of the preys or one of the predators, they will be as good as excluded from the attempt to resolve ethnic domination in Nigeria because uninformed recommendations may make them either more vulnerable (if they are a prey) or abet their destructive capacity (if they are a predator). Second, comparatively, the Ijaw are more powerful than almost every other ethnic minority group, because they are numerically superior to almost every other minority group and numerical superiority is a source of power in Nigeria. Therefore, if the Ijaw are dominated by the majority ethnic groups, then the case will serve as an illustration of the extent to which ethnic domination in Nigeria is systemic, pervasive, historical, and consistent.

It is argued that the Ijaw (1) being the fourth largest ethnic group, behind only the three major ethnic groups; and (2) having been in power; (3) are to be seen as one of the dominant groups (Gilead 2015). First, this article contends that the first premise of the aforementioned argument may be correct or may be wrong. There are no definitive facts to support the claim that the Ijaw are the fourth largest ethnic group. Therefore, we cannot be certain that they are the fourth largest ethnic group. Even if they are the fourth largest ethnic group, the conclusion of the argument does not necessary follow from this first premise and the second premise. Second, the article contends that given the nature of ethnic domination in Nigeria, just because certain members of the Ijaw ethnic group were in power does not necessarily make the Ijaw dominant. Then, third, the article disagrees that the Ijaw are one of the dominant ethnic groups.

Nigeria is currently estimated to have around 180 million population, and the Ijaw with an estimated population of between five and six million are said to make up between 9 and 10 percent of the Nigerian population. For this reason, the Ijaw are seen as the fourth largest ethnic group in the country only behind the three major ethnic groups—in other words, the Ijaw are seen as the largest minority group in the country. However, this perception or speculation might be wrong, and it is likely to be wrong, if we look at reliable figures from the past. In 1963, the Ijaw were the eighth largest ethnic group and the fifth largest minority group, but since the Ijaw neither procreate more nor do they live longer than the other minority groups that were larger than them in 1963, one wonders how the Ijaw dramatically became the fourth largest group and the largest minority group in the country. The following table (Table 4.1) shows the largest ethnic groups in Nigeria and the position of the Ijaw. Unfortunately, we must rely only on these old numbers and projections. Because, since the past three or four decades, censuses have been deemed inaccurate; consequently, many people and states have rejected them. For instance, many people and states in the South reject the most recent census (the 2006 census) on the basis that numbers were inflated to favor the North (Ahemba 2007).

Table 4.1 *Population of the Twelve Largest Ethnic Groups in Nigeria*

Ethnic Group	1963 Population	1986 Population (estimated)
Hausa	11,653,000	23,233,000
Yoruba	11,321,000	22,571,000
Igbo	9,246,000	18,434,000
Fulfulde	4,784,000	9,538,000
Kanuri	2,256,000	4,498,000
Ibibio	2,006,000	3,999,000
Tiv	1,394,000	2,779,000
Ijaw	1,089,000	2,171,000
Edo	955,000	1,904,000
Nupe	656,000	1,314,000
Urhobo	639,000	1,274,000
Igala	582,000	1,160,000

Source: Jibril 1991, 111.

Jibril, Munzali. "Minority-Languages and Lingua Francas in Nigerian Education." In *Multilingualism, Minority Languages and Language Policy in Nigeria,* edited by Emmanuel Nwanolue Emenanjo. Agbor: Central Books, 1991.

In sum, the Ijaw are not part of the majorities, they are part of the minorities, but unlike the rest of the minorities they are not just ordinary minorities. They are part of a group of minorities that is referred to as "major minorities," while the rest of the minorities are referred to as "minor minorities." There are nine (plus or minus) of these major minorities in Nigeria, and the Ijaw are one of them. Depending on the census you deem credible, or the estimate you deem credible, or the expert or commentator (e.g., Muzali Jibril, Abdul Raufu Mustapha, Onigu Otite, etc.; Jibril 1991, 111) you deem reliable, at least numerically the Ijaw are the most powerful, the second, the third, the fourth, or even the fifth most powerful among the major minorities.

Although there are various subethnic groups (e.g., the Kalabari in Rivers State is one subethnic group, while the Arogbo in Ondo State is another subethnic group), they subjectively self-identify or group-identify as one holistic Ijaw people, and they are in turn objectively identified as such. They share a common culture that includes a common language. Although they are from six different states and two different geopolitical zones, to the extent that they are all from the Niger Delta it can be said that they share one geographical territory. Altogether, they are from six of the thirty-six states in Nigeria—all in the Niger Delta of Nigeria. Geopolitically within Nigeria, they are mainly from the south-south (one of the six geopolitical zones) and to a lesser extent from the south-west (another geopolitical zone). In the south-south, they are from Bayelsa, Delta, Rivers, Akwa-Ibom, and Edo States, while in the south-west they are from Ondo State. The Ijaw are the majority in Bayelsa State, and one of the majority groups in Rivers State and Delta State. The map of Nigeria shows the locations of the geographical territories mentioned earlier.

The ethnic status of the Ijaw means that they are characterized by three conditions; in the ethnic domination game the first and second conditions are disadvantages while the third condition is an advantage. First, the Ijaw do not compete only with the majority ethnic groups; they also have to compete with fellow minority ethnic groups. Put differently, the Ijaw do not only have to fear being dominated by the majority ethnic groups, but they also have to fear being dominated by minority ethnic groups. Second, due to the multiplicity of states and local government areas, the Ijaw are no longer "united" with fellow minority ethnic groups in opposing their domination by the majority ethnic groups. They, like other minority groups, are now forced to stand alone as they wage separate oppositions to the domination by the majority ethnic groups. By standing alone, the Ijaw, like other minority groups, are now weaker to oppose the majority groups. Consequently, the dominant status of the majority groups becomes even more entrenched. However, third, having become a "major" minority in some states, the Ijaw too have assumed a dominant status in those states (but not nationally) and are in turn accused of dominating ethnic minority groups in those states.

The foregoing explanation has shown why we cannot be certain, given current information and facts, that the Ijaw are the fourth largest ethnic group in Nigeria and that this should be used as one of the two premises to argue that they are one of the dominant ethnic groups in Nigeria. Now, the chapter will turn to refuting the other premise on which the alleged dominant status of the Ijaw is based. In this refutation, the chapter argues that having been in power does not grant any dominant status to the Ijaw. A series of questions will help start the explanation of why although certain members of Ijaw were in power, the Ijaw had no dominant status. Thus, the following familiar questions. Is it possible for members of a minority group to be in power and yet be deemed nondominant? Is it possible for members of majority groups not to be in power and yet be deemed dominant? Or is it possible for members of majority groups not to be in power and yet be accused of dominating a minority group whose members are in power? How can a minority group be said to be dominated when a member of the minority is actually the president of the country?

From 5th May 2010 to 29th May 2015 (a period of five years), a member of the Ijaw ethnic group—Goodluck Jonathan—was the president of Nigeria. Before that he had been acting president from 9th February 2010 to 5th May 2010. The fact that an Ijaw was president is seen as sufficient evidence that the Ijaw are part of the dominant ethnic groups because, according to Nkolika Obianyo and Miriam Clark (n.d.), the introduction of the elective principle in Nigeria within the tripod structure (of the Hausa/Fulani in the north, the Yoruba in the West and the Igbo in the East) brought about the hegemonic control enjoyed by these three ethnic groups in Nigerian politics and their supposed superiority complex and belief that because of their numerical strength they have an unquestionable right to control the number one position in the country. (1).

The reasoning is that the dominant group is always in power, and the group in power is always the dominant group. Following this reasoning, what it means, or at least part of what it means, to be dominant is to be in power; and what it means, or at least part of what it means, to be in power is to be dominant.

History and reality tell us that the aforementioned reasoning is not always right. In fact, we can mention a very recent prominent situation or case where and when the reasoning was wrong. From 20th January 2009 to 20th January 2017 (a period of eight years) an African American—Barack Obama—was the president of the United States of America. Following the above reasoning, one would argue that during that eight-year period, African Americans were in power and as such were the dominant group in the United States of America; consequently, they were not dominated during that period. As we know, there has never been a time when African Americans were the dominant group in the United States of America, whether before Obama, during Obama, or after Obama. As it is with African Americans in the United States, so also it is with the Ijaw in Nigeria.

The UN Committee on the Elimination of Racial Discrimination (CERD)—which tackles racism, ethnicism, religious discrimination, and related discriminations—had issued statements warning against discrimination in Nigeria and the United States. According to Malik Nesrine (2017), "Those countries that receive rebuke from the UN over human rights . . . don't tend to be ones that developed problems overnight" (s.p.). For instance, in August 2017, Nesrine argued:

What the Trump era is graphically exposing is that America's very public meltdown is an unravelling of issues that were suppressed, deflected or denied for many years. This didn't all happen in the eight months since Trump became president. The pertinent fact here is that it took only eight months. It took only eight months to go from a nation that voted for a black president two times in a row to one that is suffering from race riots and killings, with officials having to send troops out onto the streets and declare a state of emergency. The speed with which it happened is the clue that it was in fact happening all along, unseen. . . . The foundations were there and continued to be laid even during Obama's leadership. (s.p.)

Even if for the sake of argument we accept that the Ijaw were the dominant group during the presidency of one of their members, it does not also follow that they were the dominant group before his presidency and they are the dominant group after his presidency. The history of domination and discrimination in Nigeria neither started in 2010 when a member of the Ijaw ethnic group became president nor ended in 2015 when that member of the Ijaw ethnic group stopped being president. Certain individuals—Goodluck Jonathan (the president), Edwin Clark (the president's political godfather), Diezanni Alison-Madueke (minister of petroleum), and so on—from the Ijaw ethnic group were very influential during the presidency of Jonathan. Nevertheless, to take their influence to mean the dominance of the Ijaw ethnic group is to do the following two things. First, it is to commit the fallacy of composition: The assumption that something is true of a part or every single part necessarily means that it is also true of the whole as a unit. Second, it is to miss the fact that ethnic domination in Nigeria, as explained earlier, neither started during the presidency of an Ijaw nor ended with that presidency.

That a member of the Ijaw ethnic group became president was not by design, it was by accident. Goodluck Jonathan (Ijaw—minority) was picked as a vice presidential candidate (running mate) to Umaru Musa Yar'Adua (Hausa/Fulani—majority) to appease the minorities of the south-south geopolitical region in light of their agitations due to the losses they suffer without any meaningful development in the Niger Delta. The Niger Delta is the oil-producing hub of Nigeria, and oil is the main source of revenue for the government. The agitations are directly linked to the expropriation of "gains" (oil revenues) by government and oil companies and the bearing of "losses" (negative externalities from oil exploitation) by the people of the Niger Delta. The agitations had earlier led to a very short-lived secession attempt in 1966, and recently it led to militant groups such as the Niger Delta People's Volunteer Force (NDPVF), the Movement for the Emancipation of the Niger Delta (MEND), and so on.

Jonathan only became president as a successor to Yar'Adua due to the latter's death while still in office. As vice president, and later acting president (due to Yar'Adua's illness), Jonathan was constitutionally recognized as the legitimate successor to Yar'Adua when the latter died in office. Those who are familiar with Nigerian history and politics will remember that the transition from Yar'Adua to Jonathan was nothing close to seamless. While I will not recount the history and politics here, I will mention the crux of the history and politics that is relevant to our subject matter. The majority Hausa/Fulani did not want power transferred from one of their members to a member of a minority group. When at his inauguration Jonathan said he became president under "very sad and unusual circumstances" (Al Jazeera 2010, s.p.), he was obviously, prima facie, referring to the death of his principal and his

(Jonathan's) succession of his principal. However, the statement readily brings home to mind what is already known; without the death of Yar'Adua (a member of one of the majority groups), Jonathan (a member of one of the minority groups) would not have been president. The sole purpose here is to discern the nature of ethnic domination in Nigeria. Therefore, the explanation provided earlier does not endorse the presidency of Jonathan.

MIGHT MAKES RIGHT

The argument in the previous sections explained the domination of ethnic minorities by ethnic majorities in Nigeria. If we take the previous sections as premises, we can conclude that in Nigeria, between majorities and minorities, "might makes right." In the Nigerian "might makes right" arena, where "the strong do what they can and the weak suffer what they must" (Thucydides 1972, Book Five), in essence the nature of ethnic domination can be described as (1) systemic; (2) pervasive; (3) historical; and (4) consistent. The term *systemic* rather than the term *institutional* or the term *structural* is preferred in this article. Adopting and adapting The Aspen Institute's (n.d.) definitions of institutional racism, structural racism, and systemic racism, we can define institutional ethnic domination, structural ethnic domination, and systemic ethnic domination in the context of Nigerian ethnic domination in the following ways. First, institutional ethnic domination "refers to the policies and practices within and across institutions that, intentionally or not, produce outcomes that chronically favour, or put [. . . an ethnic] group at a disadvantage" (Ibid.). An example of institutional ethnic domination in Nigeria can be found in the political system in which members of the majority ethnic groups are more likely to get political offices.

Second, structural ethnic domination refers to a situation and an arrangement "in which public policies, institutional practices, cultural representations, and other norms work in various, often reinforcing ways to perpetuate [. . . ethnic] group inequality" (Aspen Institute, n.d.). Structural ethnic domination "is not something that a few people or institutions choose to practice. Instead, it has been a feature of the social, economic and political systems in which" (Ibid.) Nigerians live. Therefore, an analysis of structural ethnic domination identifies dimensions of Nigerian "history and culture that have allowed privileges associated with" majority ethnic groups "and disadvantages associated with" minority ethnic groups "to endure and adapt over time" (Ibid.). An example of structural ethnic domination in Nigeria can be found in the political system in which since the return to democracy in 1999 the majority ethnic groups have been producing the presidents of the country except on one occasion when the minority groups produced a president. The emergence of a member of a minority as a president, in the first instance, was an accident rather than by design.

Third, systemic ethnic domination is almost the same thing as structural ethnic domination except that, comparatively, systemic ethnic domination is less institutional while structural ethnic domination is more institutional (the former is likely to be noninstitutional, while the latter is likely to be institutional) and, comparatively, systemic ethnic domination is less intentional while structural ethnic domination is more intentional (the former is likely to be nonintentional, while the latter is likely to be intentional). Nevertheless, both systemic and structural ethnic domination may be institutional, noninstitutional, or partly institutional and partly non-institutional, and they may be intentional, nonintentional, or partly intentional and partly nonintentional.

Constitutionally, minority discrimination is outlawed in Nigeria. At independence, it was enshrined in the Nigeria (Independence) 1960 constitution that it is unlawful to discriminate against "a particular community, tribe, place of origin, religion or political opinion" (Bach 1997, 338). Consequently, de jure, there were no constitutional restrictions on the political and civil rights of minorities (Mustapha 2003, 8). But, de facto, minorities have been suffering discrimination since the creation of Nigeria. For this reason, ethnic domination in Nigeria is systemic in the sense that in theory, in law, and directly the majority groups are not allowed to dominate the minority groups, the former are not allowed to discriminate against the latter, both the former and the latter are equal. But in practice, in reality, and indirectly, the majority groups dominate the minority groups, the former discriminate against the latter, and the former and the latter are not equal.

In terms of its pervasive nature, ethnic domination in Nigeria is pervasive in the sense that ethnic domination and ethnic discrimination in Nigeria are not restricted to a few individuals in certain places, at certain times, and holding certain offices, or to a few individuals in certain places, at certain times, and not holding certain offices. It is about the majority groups dominating the minority groups nationally across the many institutions and facets of the federation. The pervasiveness of ethnic domination in Nigeria is aided by the fact that there is a high degree of negative stereotyping in Nigeria. Because of negative stereotyping, members of one ethnic group perceive members of another ethnic group in certain negative ways and, consequently, treat them accordingly. According to Lawrence Blum (2004):

> When we say that group X is stereotyped in a certain way, or that "there is a stereotype of group X", we generally refer to the recognizable presence in a certain sociocultural context of salient images of that group—more precisely, of associations between a group label and a set of characteristics. In this sense, stereotypes are cultural entities, widely held by persons in the culture or society

in question, and widely recognized by persons who may not themselves hold the stereotype. (252)

In addition, the nature of ethnic domination in Nigeria is described as historical due to the following reasons. The fears of minorities that they will be dominated by the majority groups were a major concern even on the eve of Nigeria's independence. But,

> [t]he departing British colonial authorities, in collusion with aspirant hegemonic politicians from the majority ethno-regional blocs, rejected any attempt to restructure the federation to take account of the legitimate fears of the minority ethnic groups. Instead, sops were offered in the form of a Bill of Rights and the Willink Commission which sat in 1958 to investigate "minority fears". Its report and the resulting recommendations did not depart from the framework already agreed upon by the British and the hegemonic nationalist politicians. (Mustapha 2003, 8)

Ethnic domination in Nigeria is historical in the sense that the history of ethnic domination in Nigeria neither started recently with the reemergence of democracy nor in 1963 when Nigeria became a republic and severed the remnants of its colonial bondage to Britain, and it did not even start in 1960 when Nigeria became independent from British colonial rule. It started in 1914 when the Southern Protectorate and the Northern Protectorate were amalgamated by Lord Fredrick Lugard (the British Colonial Governor General) to form Nigeria. Moreover, as Jean-François Bayart (2005) says, "The political importance of ethnicity proceeds precisely from the fact that it is an eminently modern phenomenon connected to the 'imported state'" (29–30). This is why shortly before independence the British colonial government set up the Willink Commission to resolve the problems of majority domination and minority discrimination so that minorities might be "safe" after independence. But as already mentioned, the commission was no way a success.

The above description of the historical nature of ethnic domination in Nigeria leads us to its consistency nature. Ethnic domination in Nigeria is consistent in the sense that the three majority groups that have been dominant since 1914 have remained dominant through 1960, and 1963, to current day. Moreover, the greatest calamity in the history of Nigeria, the civil war, is attributed not only to "the competition between the three dominant ethno-regional blocs" but also to its "attendant suppression of minority rights" (Mustapha 2003, 8). To avoid such ethnic domination calamities, Nigeria employed certain constitutional devices to regulate ethnic domination, but the plethora of ethnic domination calamities in the country show that such devices have been a failure. The contention of this chapter is that the failure of the devices is a consequence of the devices not being based, or at least only insufficiently and incorrectly being based, on the systemic, pervasive, historical, and consistent nature of ethnic domination in Nigeria. The following section will tease out this failure.

CONSTITUTIONAL DEVICES

The argument in the preceding section was concluded by mentioning that Nigeria employs certain constitutional devices to resolve the intractable problem of ethnic domination in the country. Then, it was asserted that the constitutional devices failed because they are not based, or are only insufficiently and incorrectly based, on the nature of ethnic domination in Nigeria. These devices are the creation of new states and local government areas; the adoption of federal character as a constitutional principle and quota system as an administrative principle; and the adoption of the doctrine or principle of indigeneity. But these devices have not resolved the problem; if anything, they have only changed "the constitutional and institutional context, if not the substance, of minority discrimination" (Mustapha 2003, 8–9). In teasing out the failure of the devices, this section will begin with an analysis of the creation of new states and local government areas and end with an analysis of the adoption of federal character and quota system as constitutional and administrative principles, respectively.

To resolve the problem of ethnic domination, Nigeria embarked on the creation of states in order to cater to the needs of minorities. From the creation of four regions in 1964 to the present day thirty-six states and the Federal Capital Territory, and even with the multiplication of local government areas at the third and lowest level of government,[1] fears of ethnic minorities have not been successfully allayed (Mustapha 2003, 8–9) and the problem of ethnic domination has not been resolved. As Mustapha says, "Some states are ethnically homogeneous, with sub-ethnic divisions being politically salient at the local level. Others contain a majority group with some minority groups. Yet some others contain a 'major' minority group with some smaller minority groups. Finally, others . . . contain two or three 'major' minority groups in uneasy balance" (5).

Rather than catering to the needs of minorities, allaying minority fears, and resolving the problem of minority discrimination, the creation of new states and local government areas merely meant that although "many ethnic minority groups came to control their own state or local government" (Mustapha 2003, 8–9) other problems were added to the domination of ethnic minorities by ethnic majorities. These "additional problems" are as follows: (1) the creation of new states and local government areas meant that "in many cases, a number of ethnic minorities were lumped together in a state or local government, thereby unleashing intra-minority competition" (Ibid); (2) the creation of new states and local government areas led to "the fragmentation of the generic 'minority' identities built up in the previous era" (Ibid); and (3) the creation of new states and local government areas led to the emergence of "major" minority groups in some states (5).

The creation of new states was aimed at remedying ethnic domination. However, such remedy has not worked because given their numerical inferiority, minority groups have fewer states, while given their numerical superiority, majority groups have more states. Moreover, since every state and every local government area is entitled to revenue allocation from the federal government, the more states and local government areas a particular ethnic group controls, the more revenue that group is entitled to. The "Allocation of Revenue (Federation Account, etc.) Act" [1992 No. 106. S.I.9 of 2002] stipulates:

> The amount standing to the credit of the Federation Account, less the sum equivalent to [. . . thirteen] percent of the revenue accruing to the Federation Account directly from any natural resources as a first line charge for distribution to the beneficiaries of the derivation funds in accordance with the Constitution, shall be distributed among the Federal and State Governments and the Local Government Councils in each State of the Federation on the following basis: (a) the Federal Government—[fifty-six] percent; (b) the State Governments—[twenty-four] percent; (c) the Local Government Councils (Areas)—[twenty] percent. (Nigerian Law Intellectual Property Watch n.d., s.p.)

Given that the sharing of national revenues is based on natural resource derivation, federal government, and "territorially defined states and local governments, the ethnic majority groups who control the preponderant numbers of these units continue to enjoy a preponderant share, and this is coming on top of their already accumulated advantages." (Mustapha 2003, 10). Consequently, the dominant ethnic groups are prone to use their dominant status to ensure that they have more states compared with the nondominant minority groups, which can only get more states from the rare benevolence of the dominant groups.

The division of Nigeria into thirty-six states is economically unviable because many of the states either lack revenue-generation capacity or lack the political will to be self-reliant. Nevertheless, the economic motive mentioned in the preceding paragraphs is part of the main reason why there are numerous states in Nigeria and why people are still clamoring for more. According to Mustapha (2003), this important

> reason why the ethnic minorities continue to suffer from disadvantages relates to the distributive logic of the rentier state in Nigeria, particularly after its coffers

were filled with oil revenues from 1970. . . . the new states and local governments were in no position to finance their own operations and all depended
on federal handouts. Indeed, ethnic majority groups also demanded additional
states and local governments because such territorial units were vital for access
to federal funds. The reliance on grants controlled by a federal centre still dominated by ethnic majority interests meant that the new ethnic minority states were
severely constrained in their ability to fully represent their local constituency,
even if . . . they wanted to do so. (10–11)

In addition to the economic motive is the political motive. Since every state
is entitled to political representation at the federal level, the number of states
an ethnic group controls determines the amount of political representation
the ethnic group will have at the federal level, and this will in turn determine
the amount of political influence such ethnic groups can wield in the country.
As already mentioned, minority groups get less number of states due to their
numerical disadvantage, while majority groups get more number of states due
to their numerical advantage. The consequence is that the dominant status
of the majority groups becomes more entrenched while the non-dominant
status of the minority groups becomes more entrenched too. The three majority groups control two-thirds of the states, while all the minority groups
combined control only one-third of the states. Consequently, although the
creation of states was meant to ensure "equality between the majority and
minority ethnic groups, in practice it has reproduced the extant inequalities
that have been historically structured into the construction of the Nigerian
state" (Mustapha 2003, 10).

Realizing that the creation of new states and local government areas was
not enough to allay minority fears and deal with minority discrimination,
Nigeria adopted "'federal character' as a constitutional principle, and 'quota
system' as an administrative principle" (Mustapha 2003, 9). This was not
only meant to allay minority fears and deal with minority discrimination, but
it was equally meant to ensure that no one of the three major ethnic groups
dominates the other major ethnic groups or no one of the major ethnic groups
is dominated by the other two. To achieve this twofold aim, the 1979 constitution stipulated that at the first tier of government,

> [t]he composition of the Government of the Federation or any of its agencies
> and the conduct of its affairs shall be carried out in such manner as to reflect the
> federal character of Nigeria and the need to promote national unity, and also to
> command national loyalty thereby ensuring that there shall be no predominance
> of persons from a few States or from a few ethnic or other sectional groups in
> that government or in any of its agencies. (Constitution of the Federal Republic
> of Nigeria, 1979, Sec. 15.3).

Furthermore, the 1979 constitution stipulated that at the second and third tiers of government,

[t]he composition of the Government of a State, a Local Government or any of the agencies of such Governments, and the conduct of the affairs of the Governments or such agencies shall be carried out in such manner as to recognize the diversity of the people within its area of authority and the need to promote a sense of belonging and loyalty among all the people of the Federation (Constitution of the Federal Republic of Nigeria, 1979, Sec. 15.4).

The federal character and quota system formulae that have been retained and strengthened in the latest constitution—the 1999 Constitution—are not restricted to the holding of public offices and civil service; the formulae are applicable to the armed forces and political parties (Mustapha 2003, 10). For instance, it is not enough for the executives of political parties to reflect the federal character, but political parties must also not limit their presence to a certain part or certain parts of the country; they must be present nationwide before they can be qualified to be registered and allowed to contest elections (Ibid.). Furthermore, the 1999 Constitution stipulates that for "a candidate for an election to the office of President [. . . to] be deemed to have been duly elected," it is not enough that the candidate "has the majority of votes cast at the election," or that the candidate "has the highest number of votes cast at the election," but the candidate must also have "not less than one-quarter of the votes cast at the election in each of at least two-thirds of all the States in the Federation and the Federal Capital Territory" (Constitution of the Federal Republic of Nigeria, 1999, Secs. 133, 133(b), 134.1, 134.1(b), 134.2., 134.2(b)).

To ensure that the principles of the federal character and quota system are adhered to, the 1999 Constitution, Section 153.1(c), created the Federal Character Commission, and "the Commission has since generated two extensive surveys of the ethnic composition of various federal bureaucracies" (Mustapha 2003, 9). However, "quotas and concessions given to a territorially defined state or local government could still be distributed with an ethnic bias within the state or local government. And this is more the case when different ethnic groups within a given territory have accumulated different historical advantages and opportunities" (15). In Nigeria, "[E]ven within the context of an open and competitive political system, and explicit constitutional provisions, the ethnic minorities suffer from different degrees of discrimination and neglect, largely because of the majoritarian tendencies of a political and social system with scarce economic and political resources" (8). Moreover, in developing countries like Nigeria where sharp ethnic cleavages are coupled with religious cleavages and the condition of poverty, the consequence is that "almost invariably the rights of subordinate groups are insufficiently respected, the institutions of government are insufficiently inclusive and the allocation of society's resources favours the dominant faction[s] over others" (United Nations 2000, 45).

The last factor responsible for the continual suffering of disadvantages by minorities is the doctrine or principle of "'indigeneity' which arose as a consequence of the adoption of the federal character principle. Nigeria is a country of high human spatial mobility. Even by the 1950s, 5 million of the 55 million population of the country were living in areas other than the ones to which they ethnically belonged" (Mustapha 2003, 11; see Eleazu 1977). To support his claim, he goes on to argue that in precolonial era, in the place now known as Nigeria, those involved in the aforementioned high spatial mobility "might ultimately be absorbed into their host communities as full members; but in the colonial and post-colonial periods, boundaries of community membership became more tightly drawn, and such resident 'strangers' were often denied full community membership. Even the British colonial administration encouraged this attitude through its concept of the 'native foreigner'" (Mustapha 2003, 11; see Bach 1997; Mustapha 1998; Nnoli 1978).

In view of the aforementioned high human spatial mobility "and the effective division into 'citizens and strangers,' it became important to specify who was to benefit from the share of resources allocated to a state or local government area" (Mustapha 2003, 11). To resolve the benefit-sharing problem that resulted from resource allocation to states and local government areas, the government adopted the doctrine or principle of indigeneity, which stipulates that "such resources should go to 'true indigenes' determined by blood ties and ethnicity, and not just to anybody living there, no matter how long they may have been resident there" (Ibid.). Consequently, Section 329, subsection 1, of the Constitution of the Federal Republic of Nigeria (1979); Section 329, subsection 1, of the Constitution of the Federal Republic of Nigeria (1979); and Section 318, subsection 1, of the Constitution of the Federal Republic of Nigeria (1999) defined at both the state level (the second tier of government) and the local government level (the third tier of government) as "a person either of whose parents or any of whose grandparents was a member of a community indigenous to that State" (see Mustapha 2003, 11).

As Mustapha (2003) succinctly and correctly argues, the aforementioned constitutional provision, that is the doctoring or principle of indigeneity, should ideally "strengthen the access of ethnic minorities to resources allocated to their states or local government areas; in reality, it has only fueled conflict and violence in many ethnic minority areas" (11). Examples of areas where such conflicts and violence have occurred include the Southern Kaduna State in North Western Nigeria, Nassarawa State in North Central Nigeria, and Taraba State and Adamawa State in North Eastern Nigeria (Ibid.).

The doctrine or principle of indigeneity is meant to protect indigenes or state citizens from domination by nonindigenes or state foreigners. Unwittingly, this also means that indigenes of state A who are protected in state A will automatically be nonindegenes in state B and will not be protected in state B if they move to state B. Since Nigeria has thirty-six states and a federal capital territory—in sum thirty-seven geographical territories—a Nigerian, by virtue of indigeneity, can only be an indigene of one geographical territory and can only be guaranteed protection in that geographical territory. Unfortunately, such a Nigerian is a foreigner—that is, nonindigene, in the remaining thirty-six geographical territories and thus lacks protection in those geographical territories.

So in spite of the creation of new states and local government areas, the adoption of federal character and quota system, and the adoption of the doctrine or principle of indigeneity, Nigeria is still plagued by ethnic domination; consequently, "ethnic minorities in Nigeria continue to face major disadvantages in their access to political and economic resources" (Mustapha 2003, 10). In summary, the forgoing argument shows that what the framers of the constitutional devices fail to realize is that unless attempts to resolve the intractable problem of ethnic domination in Nigeria are sufficiently and correctly based on the systemic, pervasive, historical, and consistent nature of the phenomenon, the dominant groups will remain dominant and the dominated groups will remain dominated.

REFERENCES

Ahemba, Tume. 2007. "Lagos Rejects Nigeria's Census, Says Has 17.5 Million." *Reuters*, February 6, 2007. https://uk.reuters.com/article/nigeria-lagos-idUKL0674057420070206.

Al Jazeera. 2010. "Nigeria Swears in New President: Goodluck Jonathan Assumes Power as Thousands Attend Funeral of Umaru Yar'Adua." May 8, 2010. http://www.aljazeera.com/news/africa/2010/05/20105681641917266.html?xif=Wforum.

The Aspen Institute. n.d. "Glossary for Understanding the Dismantling Structural Racism/Promoting Racial Equity Analysis." Roundtable on Community Change. file:///C:/Users/fab005/Desktop/RCC-Structural-Racism-Glossary.pdf. Accessed: January 19, 2018.

Bach, Daniel C. 1997. "Indigeneity, Ethnicity, and Federalism." In *Transition without End: Nigerian Politics and Civil Society under Babangida*, edited by Larry Diamond, Anthony Kirk-Greene and Oloyele Oyediran. Boulder: Lynne Rienner.

Bayart, Jean-François. 2005. *The Illusion of Cultural Identity*. London: Hurst and Company.

Berman, B. et al. 2004. "Introduction: Ethnicity and the Politics of Democratic Nation-Building in Africa." In *Ethnicity and Democracy in Africa,* edited by B. Berman, D. Eyoh and W. Kymlicka. Athens, Ohio: Ohio University Press.

Blum, Lawrence. 2004. "Stereotypes and Stereotyping: A Moral Analysis." *Philosophical Papers* 33, no. 3. 251–289.

CIA (Central Intelligence Agency). 2017. "Africa: Nigeria." *The World Factbook,* August 2017. https://www.cia.gov/library/publications/the-world-factbook/geos/ni .html. Accessed: August 21, 2017.

Constitution of the Federal Republic of Nigeria, 1979. http://www.lawnigeria.com/ CONSTITUTIONHUB/Constitution/1979ConstitutionofNigeria.html.

Constitution of the Federal Republic of Nigeria, 1999. http://www.nigeria-law.org/ ConstitutionOfTheFederalRepublicOfNigeria.htm

Eleazu, Uma O. 1977. *Federalism and Nation-Building: The Nigerian Experience, 1954–1964.* Ilfracombe: Arthur H. Stockwell.

Gilead, Ekomeko. 2015. "Ijaw Marginalizing Other Niger Delta Ethnic Groups." *The Nigerian Voice,* July 2, 2015. https://www.thenigerianvoice.com/news/184327/ijaw -margainalising-other-niger-delta-ethnic-groups.html. Accessed: January 14, 2018.

Jibril, Munzali. 1991. "Minority-Languages and Lingua Francas in Nigerian Education." In *Multilingualism, Minority Languages and Language Policy in Nigeria,* edited by Emmanuel Nwanolue Emenanjo. Agbor: Central Books.

Mustapha, Abdul Raufu. 1998. "Identity Boundaries, Ethnicity and National Integration in Africa." In *Ethnic Conflicts in Africa,* edited by Okwudibe Nnoli, 27–52. Dakar: CODESRIA.

Mustapha, Abdul Raufu. 2003. "Ethnic Minority Groups in Nigeria—Current Situation and Major Problems." UN Commission on Human Rights, Sub-Commission on Promotion and Protection of Human Rights, Working Group on Minorities, Ninth Session. E/CN.4/Sub.2/AC.5/2003/WP.10, May 2003. http://www.nigerianmuse .com/20101205024305zg/sections/general-articles/ethnic-minority-groups -in-nigeria-current-situation-and-major-problems-by-abdul-raufu-mustapha/. Accessed: August 10, 2017.

Nesrine, Malik. 2017. "After a UN Warning over Racism, America's Self-Image begins to Crack." *The Guardian,* London, August 25, 2017.

Nigerian Law Intellectual Property Watch. n.d. "Allocation of Revenue (Federation Account, etc.) Act." https://nlipw.com/allocation-revenue-federation-account-etc -act/. Accessed: January 28, 2018.

Nnoli, Okwudiba. 1978. *Ethnic Politics in Nigeria.* Enugu: Fourth Dimension Publishers.

Obianyo, Nkolika E., and Miriam Ikejiani Clark. n.d. "Negotiating Political Power in a Federal State: The Minorities and Electoral Democracy in Nigeria's Fourth Republic.," http://paperroom.ipsa.org/papers/paper_9691.pdf. Accessed: July 16, 2018.

Otite, Onigu. 1991. *Ethnic Pluralism and Ethnicity in Nigeria.* Ibadan: Shaneson, 1991.

Thucydides. 1972. *History of the Peloponnesian War.* London: Penguin Books.

United Nations. 2000. *We the Peoples*: *The Role of the United Nations in the 21st Century*. New York: United Nations, Department of Public Information.

NOTE

1. Nigeria has three tiers of government: the first tier is the federal government, the second tier is the state governments, and the third tier is the local government areas.

Chapter Five

A Preliminary Discourse on a Realistic Resolution to Domination and Discrimination

In chapter 3, I explained that apart from certain notorious crises and conflicts, borders and margins have also created a situation whereby migrants from one African country are discriminated against in another African country. This phenomenon of discrimination against migrants deserves the maximum effort that is required to resolve it because the current trend of migration shows that there is likely going to be more and more of migrants rather than less and less of migrants on the African continent. As I explained in chapter 2, usually, among African migrants, the continent remains their number one destination. In other words, among the migrant population, more people migrate to other African countries while less people migrate to other continents. This fact is not only historical; it is still the current situation. Presently, in comparative terms, there are more Africans migrating to other African countries than there are Africans migrating to other continents including Europe. The UN says that recently, within the space of ten years, from the year 2010 to the year 2020, the number of migrants from sub-Saharan Africa who migrated to other African countries rose to nineteen million, a figure which the UN says represents more than a 40 percent increment in the number of Africans who migrate to other African countries. Even this nineteen million figure or 40 percent increment given by the UN is seen as an inaccurate representation of reality because it seems that it is below the actual figure. The UN's more-than-40-percent-increment or nineteen million figure is "a figure many experts call an underestimate" (The Economist 2021, s.p.).

As I explained in chapter 3, the responses to the survey questions in the same chapter show that, on the one hand, due to AfCFTA, there may be (this is an expression of probability rather than certainty) more movement from some African countries (that are less economically attractive) to other

African countries (that are more economically attractive). On the other hand, the responses show that there may be (again this is an expression of probability rather than certainty) discrimination against migrants who move from less economically attractive countries to more economically attractive countries due to AfCFTA. While the responses represent present conditions, to understand the causal and constitutive factors for this phenomenon we must decipher "the pattern of the past which explained the present" (Watt et al. 1988, 135). Moreover, deciphering the pattern of the past and explaining the present helps us make an educated guess about what the future is likely to be. Nevertheless, this educated guess is not a precise prediction of the future in the realm of physics, and it is not a mathematical forecast for the future with certainty (Abumere 2019, 27)—even in physics and mathematics, there is margin of error. Rather, this is an interpretation of the trajectory of reactions to economic migrants on the continent. Without appealing to historical determinism, the interpretation sees the present to be correlated with the past and sees the future to be a consequence of the present. Since the present resembles the past, it is probable that the consequences of the present will resemble the consequences of the past.

Given this explanation, I aver that negative stereotyping of, and discrimination against, migrants by host countries and their citizens takes place in the context of an asymmetrical relationship between migrants and their host countries. In these asymmetrical relationships, the host countries negatively relate with—that is, discriminate against—migrants to the detriment of migrants and sometimes even to the detriment of both parties since, as numerous econometrics and development economics research have shown empirically, migrants make net-positive economic contributions to their host countries. When discrimination against migrants is formal—that is, ingrained in laws and procedures—the situation becomes more precarious and alarming, but we know exactly what we are dealing with. However, when it is informal—that is, when it takes the form of systemic biases—the situation may be less precarious and alarming but becomes complex, in the sense that we may not even know exactly what we are dealing with. Given that states may not want to be seen as violating international law, African regional law, subregional law, and even national law, the discrimination against migrants is often informal and seldom formal.

In essence, in chapter 3, I showed that Africa is littered with a plethora of cases of discrimination and domination against African migrants. I also pointed out that in these cases even children from migrant groups are treated unjustly because of their status as migrants. When migrant families are discriminated against in their host country, the perpetrators of the discrimination—be it the state, government and its agencies, groups, or persons—do not make any distinction between the adult members of the families and the children of the families. Using the histories of Ghana and Nigeria, I illustrated that when Nigerian migrants were expelled from Ghana (as discussed in the first section), the Ghanaian government did not spare Nigerian children—everyone including father, mother, brother, and sister whether adult or minor was expelled. So too, when Ghanaian migrants were expelled from Nigeria (as discussed in the first section), the Nigerian government did not spare Ghanaian children—everyone including father, mother, brother, and sister whether adult or minor was expelled.

In the examples of the expulsion of Nigerian migrants from Ghana and the expulsion of Ghanaian migrants from Nigeria, even if the Ghanaian government made exceptions for Nigerian children or the Nigerian government made exceptions for Ghanaian children—that is, even if children were not directly expelled—they may still be indirectly expelled. This is because as dependents children are likely to follow their parents or their guardians whom they depend on. Besides these cases of expulsions, even when children are not directly discriminated against, as long as their parents or guardians or adult siblings or close relatives whom they depend on are discriminated against, children are indirectly discriminated against because what affects the family members children depend on invariably affects the children. The unemployment of a father might result in lack of education for a child, the loss of job by a mother might mean undernourishment for a child. In the case of South Africa, as discussed in chapter 3, when migrant parents are killed in xenophobic or Afrophobic violence, the lives of the children are turned upside down in every way imaginable. Alarmingly, discrimination against, and domination of, children from migrant groups are a double jeopardy because they simultaneously violate two group rights—namely, minority rights and children's rights.

Then, I explained that, essentially, the negative and positive rights, and the negative, positive, and republican freedoms of children, are to be respected because they are necessary for the well-being and well-becoming of children. Protecting the individual human rights of children is necessary for the well-being and well-becoming of children. But when children from migrant groups are discriminated against or dominated because of their status as migrants, the protection of their individual human rights is insufficient. In such cases, minority rights are needed to protect the children. But as I showed in chapter 4, even minority rights are not a realistic resolution to the problem of domination and discrimination on the continent. In the chapter, using Nigerian as an example, I discussed the legal and political approach to addressing the question of minority—that is, the problem of the domination of, and discrimination against, minorities. The basic point of the discussion was to weigh the strengths and weaknesses of the legal and political approach on a scale and see which one outweighs the other. Based on the result that

the scale showed, my extrapolation or deduction, which I shall discuss in
the remainder of this book (this chapter and the subsequent chapters), is that
such a legal and political approach (notably, minority rights) is not a realistic
resolution to the discrimination against migrants.

In chapter 4, while my concern was with Africa as a whole, I focused on
Nigeria for the purpose of contextualizing the discussion in the chapter. I
explained that the contextualization is important because being the most populous country in Africa, Nigeria represents a microcosm of Africa. Therefore,
understanding the Nigerian case would probably give us insights into the
other cases, or at least some of the other cases, on the continent. Following
this same trend of contextualization, my aim in this chapter is to proffer ways
to resolve the problem of discrimination discussed previously.

SOME PERTINENT QUESTIONS

Article 27 of the International Covenant on Civil and Political Rights
(ICCPR) states that "in those states in which ethnic, religious or linguistic
minorities exist, persons belonging to such minorities shall not be denied
the right, in community with the other members of their group, to enjoy
their own culture, to profess and practice their own religion, or to use their
own language." In short, Article 27 of ICCPR does not condone "the sys-
tematic oppression and domination of the members of one group by those of
another" (Wheatley 2005, 23). Furthermore, according to Article 4(1) of the
UN "Declaration on the Rights of Persons belonging to National or Ethnic,
Religious and Linguistic Minorities," states have an obligation to "ensure that
persons belonging to minorities may exercise fully and effectively all their
human rights and fundamental freedoms without any discrimination and in
full equality before the law."

There is no question that the domination mentioned in chapter 4violates
the aforementioned articles. But the question is how do we get groups to
refrain from domination? Whatever resolution we proffer for the problem
will have an appropriate, or at least an adequate, response to the following
pertinent questions. Firstly, beginning with the general relationship between
the majorities and the minorities, we ask, (1) "Do the majorities have any just
and fair grounds to dominate the minorities?" (2) "Do the majorities have any
moral obligations (duties of justice and rights) toward the minorities?" and
(3) conversely, "Do the minorities have any rights and justice claims against
the majorities?" Second, ending with the specific relationship between the
major minorities and the minor minorities, we also ask, (1) "Do the major
minorities have any just and fair grounds to dominate the minor minorities?"
(2) "Do the major minorities have any moral obligations (duties of justice

and rights) toward the minor minorities?" and (3) conversely, "Do the minor minorities have any justice and right claims against the major minorities?"

To answer the sets of questions, we can appeal to the relational and the nonrelational approaches to justice. The relational approach is associative—that is, it is member based; it emphasizes the common relationships that bind together subjects and agents of justice; it is a member-based approach—that is, it is associative. For the relational approach, if you are not part of a particular relationship, then you do not have any obligation to the members of that relationship and they do not have any right claims against them (Abumere 2021). In contrast, the nonrelational approach to justice "does not see justice to be dependent on such relationship or any relationship other than common humanity and its variants. Justice, the non-relational approach claims, is not based on any special relationship and its variants such as citizenship, compatriotism, etc., but on common humanity and its variants such as basic human needs, natural prerogatives and sufferance, etc." (Maffettone 2013, 127).

Using the relational and the nonrelational approaches to provide responses to our first and second sets of questions, respectively, in the two instances, although the premises are different the conclusions are the same. Regardless of whether we think of justice in relational or in nonrelational terms, there does not seem to be any morally reasonable justification to argue that a dominant group has just or fair grounds to dominate another group, unless, arbitrarily, we further constrain the scope of justice to apply it only within a particular ethnic group. In a country of around 400 ethnic groups, constraining the scope of justice to apply only within a particular ethnic group is not merely arbitrary, it is also unjust and unfair.

On the one hand, we can answer the first set of questions by arguing that based on the fact that the majorities and the minorities share a common humanity, the former have no just and fair grounds to dominate the latter, the former owe the latter moral obligations (duties of justice and rights), and, conversely, the latter have justice and right claims against the former. When we answer the first set of questions in this way, we are appealing to the nonrelational approach to justice. On the other hand, we can answer the first set of questions by arguing that based on the fact that the majorities and the minorities are members of Nigeria and participants in the Nigerian polity, the former have no just and fair grounds to dominate the latter, the former owe the latter moral obligations (duties of justice and rights), and, conversely, the latter have justice and right claims against the former. When we answer the first set of questions in this way, we are appealing to the relational approach to justice.

If we turn to our second set of questions, we will have something similar to what we had when dealing with the first set of questions. On the one hand, we can answer the second set of questions by arguing that based on the fact that the major minorities and the minor minorities share a common humanity, the former have no just and fair grounds to dominate the latter, the former owes the latter moral obligations (duties of justice and rights), and, conversely, the latter have justice and right claims against the former. When we answer the second set of questions in this way, we are appealing to the nonrelational approach to justice. On the other hand, we can answer the second set of questions by arguing that based on the fact that the major minorities and the minor minorities are members of Nigeria and participants in the Nigerian polity, the former have no just and fair grounds to dominate the latter, the former owe the latter moral obligations (duties of justice and rights), and, conversely, the latter have justice and right claims against the former. When we answer the second set of questions in this way, we are appealing to the relational approach to justice.

Here we see that while the relational and the nonrelational approaches to justice started from different premises, they reached the same conclusion. Given that, we can assume that the conclusion is right, but the question is are both premises right, or wrong, or is one right and the other wrong? Nevertheless, since what I am in search of is a resolution, I will accept the congruence of the two conclusions reached by the two approaches rather than concern myself with their different premises.

These approaches have clarified that neither the domination of minorities by the majorities nor the domination of minor minorities by the major minorities is right. But, again, the question is how do we get ethnic groups in Nigeria to refrain from domination? In cases like this that manifest the combination of poverty and ethnic discrimination, "[T]he solution is clear, even if difficult to achieve in practice: to promote human rights, to protect minority rights and to institute political arrangements in which all groups are represented" (United Nations 2000, 45). After all, nondiscrimination against minorities and the recognition of the rights of the minority reduce cases of ethnopolitical conflicts (Gurr 2000, 211). To this effect, the following admonition of the Organization for Security and Cooperation in Europe (OSCE) is useful.

The OSCE advises that the "effective participation of national minorities in public life is an essential component of a peaceful and democratic society. Experience in Europe and elsewhere has shown that, in order to promote such participation, governments often need to establish specific arrangements for national minorities" (OSCE High Commissioner on National Minorities 1999). Part of the problem with Nigeria is not that ethnic minorities do not participate in public life but that they do not participate effectively. By this I mean that the historical, consistent, pervasive, and systemic nature of ethnic domination in Nigeria does not allow minorities to have meaningful participation in national public life. Another part of the problem with Nigeria is that though the government has established specific arrangements for ethnic minorities, the arrangements are not effective.

There are "approaches that have been adopted by democratic states to reconcile ethnic diversity and common citizenship, and that have been adopted or recommended in the African context" (Berman et al. 2004, 13). Prominent among these approaches are neutral or blind state, Jacobin republicanism or nation building from above, civil society or nation building from below, federalism or decentralization, and consociationalism (14). While these approaches have their merits, they also have their demerits. Hence, while these approaches have worked in some countries, they have failed in others. And while one or a combination of the approaches may be appropriate for certain contexts given certain spatiotemporal circumstances, they may not be appropriate for other contexts given certain spatiotemporal circumstances. Nigeria has already tried all sorts of approaches, which include confederationalism, unitarism, and federalism. It has also oscillated between civilian and military rule, and has even exchanged a parliamentary system of government for a presidential system of government. Yet the country has not come any closer to getting a reprieve from ethnic rivalries.

The reality of our case is that "wounds that have festered for a long time will not heal overnight. Nor can confidence be built or dialogues develop while fresh wounds are being inflicted. There are no quick fixes, no shortcuts. Every group needs to become convinced that the State belongs to all people" (United Nations 2000, 45). In light of this, Kymlicka (2007) argues that "any sensible approach to the governing of ethnic diversity will need to combine both long-term ideals and short-term pragmatic recommendations" (9). In our case, my proposed realistic resolution will not be a set of policies or recommendations that are actionable. Nevertheless, the realistic resolution will tell us where to start from if we are to have a set of policies that are actionable. To arrive at the realistic resolution, I will take a cue from Rousseau and Rawls. Although the Nigerian context is very different from the contexts Rousseau and Rawls were concerned with, I think the two thinkers are relevant to, and their ideas are useful in, the Nigerian context because of how the thinkers theorize about justice—namely, their ideal theory.

THE STARTING POSITION OF A
REALISTIC RESOLUTION (PART 1)

Having ended the last section with an allusion to the importance of Rousseau's and Rawls' ideal theory to my proposed realistic resolution, I shall begin this section with an explication of their ideal theory. The ideal theory, first of all, "assumes strict compliance and works out the principles that characterize a well-ordered society under favourable circumstances" (Rawls 1971, 245). Then, it prescribes for us "a conception of a just society that we are to achieve if we can" (246). Finally, it posits that we are to judge our existing institutions in accordance with the prescribed conception (Ibid.). A key characteristic of the ideal theory is that it is a realistic utopia. It is realistic in that it accommodates the real situation of our world; it deals with people, institutions, and the world as they are; and it is actually practicable or can be applied to the political structures of our world. It is also utopian because it points to what political arrangements ought to be (Rawls 1999, 7).

To formulate the principles of the ideal theory, like Jean-Jacques Rousseau, we take "men as they are and laws as they might be" (7) and then "we ask what could come into existence as a result of our choices, given the limits set by our moral and psychological natures and by facts about social institutions and how humans can live under them" (Simmons 2010, 7). Consequently, relying on conjectures and speculations to determine what is practically possible, we use the ideal theory to explore boundaries of "practicable political possibility" (Rawls 2001, 4, 13), although bearing in mind that "what counts as practically possible may be in certain respects historically relative" (Simmons 2010, 8). Nevertheless, to avoid unrealistic utopia, our aim in the ideal theory is to make assumptions that are realistic (Ibid.).

At the beginning of *The Social Contract*, Rousseau says, "My purpose is to consider if, in political society, there can be any legitimate and sure principle of government, taking men as they are and laws as they might be. In this inquiry, I shall try always to bring together what right permits with what interest requires so that justice and utility are in no way divided" (quoted in Rawls 1999, 13; Rousseau 1997 [1762], 41), but all the while conscious that "the limits of the possible in moral matters are less narrow than we think. It is our weaknesses, our vices, our prejudices, that shrink them" (Rousseau quoted in Rawls 1999, 7). Following Rousseau, Rawls says for a conception of justice to be realistic, it needs to meet two necessary conditions. The first condition is that the conception of justice "must rely on the actual laws of nature and achieve the kind of stability those laws allow, that is stability for the right reason" (13). In this first condition, for a liberal conception of justice to be realistic, "it takes people as they are (by the laws of nature), and constitutional and civil laws as they might be, that is, as they would be in a reasonably just and well-ordered democratic society" (Ibid.). The second condition is that the first principles and precepts of the conception of justice must "be workable and applicable to ongoing political and social arrangements" (Ibid.).

Rawls says, "[B]y showing how the social world may realize the features of a realistic utopia, political philosophy provides a long-term goal of political endeavor, and in working toward it gives meaning to what we can do today" (128). In our case, by showing the conditions of a realistic resolution to the problem of ethnic domination in Nigeria, my proposition puts us on the track to finding a long-term resolution to ethnic domination in Nigeria, and on this track my proposition shows us where our starting point should be in the race to reach an ethnic domination-free Nigeria, or at least a relatively just and fair society or a relatively ethnic domination-free society. Our starting point—as will be elaborated in the remainder of this section—should be the conditions of ethnic domination in Nigeria—namely, (1) the multiple majorities condition, (2) the multiple minorities condition, (3) the major majority condition, (4) the minor majority condition, (5) the major minorities condition, and (6) the minor minorities condition.

The resolution I prescribe in view of these conditions is strategic alliances and balance of power. In subsequent paragraphs, I will describe how different groups may ally with one another in the struggles for power. Ultimately, normatively, a human rights framework and a minority rights framework should be the long run possible resolution because they are more sustainable and more acceptable than strategic alliances and balance of power. However, I am prescribing strategic alliances and balance of power as the short run realistic resolution because pragmatically they are easier to adhere to than a human rights and minority rights framework. Therefore, adopting strategic alliances and balance of power in the short run creates space and time for us to work toward a rights framework in the long run.

In his *Law of Peoples*, Rawls (1999) "call(s) a world in which . . . great evils have been eliminated and just (or at least decent) basic institutions established by both liberal and decent peoples who honor the Law of Peoples a 'realistic utopia'" (126). But what I refer to as a realistic utopia in this chapter is a Nigeria that may not be totally free from ethnic domination, but also is not characterized by ethnic domination; a Nigeria that is at least relatively free from ethnic domination. My envisaged society is realistic because it takes the conditions of ethnic domination in Nigeria as they are, and it is utopian because it shows how these same conditions can actually be used as the starting point of a realistic resolution to the problem of ethnic domination that originated from the conditions.

In spite of the society I envisage we may have may be merely relatively just and fair or relatively free, it may still be seen as a realistic utopia. Not an "ideal" realistic utopia as Rawls (1999) would have it but a "non-ideal" realistic utopia. The scenario I am dealing with is realistic, not merely because "it could and may exist" (7) but also because it actually exists as described in this chapter. And it is utopian not in the negative sense of the word but in the sense that "it joins reasonableness and justice with conditions enabling citizens (and especially minorities) to realize their fundamental interests" (Ibid.).

Dialectically, we will derive our realistic resolution from the same sources from where the problem is generated. In this sense, we can see the conditions of domination as dialectical conditions. In this struggle between the problem and the realistic resolution, the problem may not win outright and the realistic resolution may not win outright, but, at least, in the end, even if we do not have a society that is totally free from domination, we will not also have a society that is totally dominated. In other words, even if we do not have a utopia, we will not have a dystopia. What we will have may be a relatively just and fair society, a society that is relatively free from domination. The next section will tease out the workings of this dialectics in detail.

THE STARTING POSITION OF A
REALISTIC RESOLUTION (PART 2)

While the previous section was devoted to the preliminary explanation of the starting position of a realistic resolution to the case mentioned in chapter 4, this section is devoted to a detailed explanation of that starting position. Therefore, in this section, I explain how the conditions of the domination, which are the source and origin of the problem, can also be the starting position of a realistic resolution to the problem. Any actionable set of policies or recommendations that aims to resolve the problem will do well to take the following strategic alliances and balance of power into consideration.

(1) The Multiple Majorities Condition

The fact of having three major ethnic groups vying for dominance serves as checks and balances. No one single group has the luxury to act on its whims and caprices without the other dominant groups trying to check it and balance against it. It is this fact of one dominant group serving as a counterweight to another dominant group that has partly contributed to ensuring that the Nigerian polity has not been totally hijacked by any one majority group. To use an analogy from economics, the market of domination we have is not a monopoly but an oligopoly. If it were a monopoly, one single major group will exclusively control the affairs of the polity, whereas everyone else will be at its mercy. Since it is an oligopoly, the limited competition among the majority ethnic groups ensures that at least there is a bit of respite for the minorities.

(2) The Multiple Minorities Condition

Since there are a few hundreds of minorities, if they are able to act as a unit or come together under one umbrella to fight their cause, the dominant status of the majorities will be significantly weakened. There have been episodic attempts by some minorities in the middle belt (North Central) and the Niger Delta (especially in the south-south), respectively, to act as a unit. If attempts of this sort are enlarged to include most minorities, if not all minorities, and if the attempts are sustained, then minorities are likely to see their situation improve.

(3) and (4) The Major Majority Condition and The Minor Majority Condition

In a situation when and where the major majority is oppressing or dominating the minor majority, the minor majority might be inclined to identify with minority groups or join them in their resistance against the major majority that also oppresses the minorities. With the minor majority—albeit for enlightened self-interest—identifying with and joining the minorities, their capacity to reduce the dominant status of the major majority becomes greater and their resistance becomes more effective.

(5) The Major Minorities Condition

Although the major minorities are dominated by the majorities, the major minorities have a relatively greater capacity than the minor minorities to resist the majorities. Therefore, the plight of the major minorities is not as bad as that of the minor minorities. But, more importantly, while the majorities dominate major minorities nationally at the national or federal level, the major minorities are "free" in the geopolitical zones or states in which they reside, have numerical advantage, and run the state, regional, or zonal affairs. Thus, while the majorities are able to dominate the minorities successfully at the national or federal level, the major minorities have succor at the state, regional, or zonal level. If every major minority succeeds in preventing the majorities from extending the majorities' domination tendencies to the areas controlled by the major minority, then, cumulatively, the major minorities would have succeeded in reducing the domination power of the majorities.

(6) The Minor Minorities Condition

On the one hand, the minor minorities need to ally with the major minorities in order to resist the domination tendencies of the majorities. On the other hand, the minor minorities also need to form an alliance among themselves in order to resist the domination tendencies of the major minorities. The minor minorities are the worst off in the domination cycle. Focusing on their plight, alleviating their suffering, and eliminating discrimination against them should be priority for the country. In terms of dealing with the problem of domination in the country, the situation of this group serves as a barometer by which we can gauge the progress or lack of progress in the struggle against domination. When they become worse off than they were, we know that the domination situation is tragically deteriorating. When their situation remains the same, we know that in the struggle against domination we have not yet begun the race, we are still barely on our marks. But if they become better-off than they were, then we know that progress is being made in the struggle against domination.

Nevertheless, the aforementioned is not necessarily always the case because there can be a situation where it is in the interest of the most dominant group to level down the advantages of other groups. In this case, the situation of the worst off may become better due to the level down effect, but the situation of many others will be worsened by the level down effect. In this case, we will not say that the struggle against domination has been successful; rather, we will say that the heterogeneity in the struggle has been replaced by homogeneity. Therefore, a luta continua!

LONG RUN AND SHORT RUN

To conclude the discussion in this chapter, I will reiterate the following claims. First, although, ultimately, normatively a human rights and minority rights framework should be the long run possible resolution, the realistic resolution I prescribe in the short run is strategic alliances and balance of power. Second, although a rights framework is more sustainable and more acceptable than strategic alliances and balance of power, I am prescribing strategic alliances and balance of power as the short run realistic resolution because pragmatically they are easier to adhere to than a human rights and minority rights framework. Third, therefore, adopting strategic alliances and balance of power in the short run creates space and time for us to work toward a rights framework in the long run.

If we seek a realistic resolution, starting with a rights framework might be possible in theory but not in practice. Due to the historical, consistent, pervasive, and systemic nature of ethnic domination, we need to reach a certain threshold in order for a rights framework to be effective. A successful resolution to the problem is analogous to a reservoir. In the "resolution-reservoir," when water reaches or goes beyond a certain threshold, then we can apply a rights framework. But when water does not reach a certain threshold, that is when water is below a certain threshold or when the "resolution-reservoir" is empty; then, we need strategic alliances and balance of power. Nevertheless, the question is "What is the threshold?" The threshold is that point when and where the dominant groups will lose much of their capacity to dominate others and when and where they will be amenable to being persuaded to respect human rights and minority rights. Therefore, the adoption of strategic alliances and balance of power is not a negation of a rights framework; rather, the adoption of the former in the short run paves the way for the adoption of the latter in the long run.

As shown in chapter 4, the dominant groups do not respect human rights and minority rights; it is for this reason that we need a prior mechanism as our starting position before we appeal to a rights framework. When dealing with a disaster, it is not always plausible or practicable to start with, or only focus on, the long run. In our case, those who think the only term plan is the long run and the only ideal resolution is a rights framework might be in danger of setting themselves "too useless a task if in tempestuous seasons they can only tell us that when the storm is long past the ocean is flat again" (Keynes 1924, 80). Although not always the case, sometimes the "long-run is a misleading guide to current affairs" (Ibid.) and sometimes to historical affairs. Also, if we neglect the short run, perhaps as John Maynard Keynes quips, although not always the case, sometimes "in the long-run we are all dead" (Ibid.).

The above approaches are not mutually exclusive. Exclusively relying on rights and justice without any consideration of security may in extreme cases lead to anarchy, thereby paradoxically further undermining right and justice claims. So, it is important that security is considered. Nevertheless, disregarding right and justice concerns due to "false" security, which is aimed at protecting not the entire population but the illegitimate advantages that accrue from the dominant status of the dominant ethnic groups, is unacceptable. There is a biblical saying that "the Sabbath was made for man, not man for the Sabbath" (Mark 2: 27). Without sermonizing or basing my argument on Christian morality, we can take a cue from the biblical saying and likewise say that national security is meant to safeguard the entire people of a state; the people are not meant to be sacrificed at the altar of "false" security. "But too often, security fears have driven out considerations of justice . . . with results that are detrimental not only to justice, but also, paradoxically, for security" (Kymlicka 2007, 9).

In the literature on minority rights, there is an assumption, and even a naiveté, that enshrining minority rights in constitutions and staking a legal claim to minority rights will save minority groups from the domination of a majority group—the idealistic framework. Ceteris paribus, the institutionalization of minority rights should protect minority groups from the domination of the majority group. However, this is mere de jure minority rights. Unless minority rights are equally de facto, minority groups will remain unprotected from the majority group. After all, even in democracies (more accurately, quasi-democracies), in cases of domination, the majority group controls the legislature (it makes the laws), controls the executive (it implements the laws), and controls the judiciary (it interprets the laws). The prejudices of the majority group will usually reflect in the justice system. Minority groups may get procedural justice sometimes, but substantive justice will often elude them. While the idealistic framework meets the conditions of theoretical plausibility and moral reasonableness, it fails to meet the condition of practical possibility. It is for reasons such as this that I argue for a realistic resolution to the problem of discrimination against minorities and migrants (see chapters 7 and 8).

REFERENCES

Abumere, Frank Aragbonfoh. 2019. "World Government, Social Contract and Legitimacy." *Philosophical Papers* 48, no. 1: 9–30.

Abumere, Frank Aragbonfoh. 2021. *Global Justice and Resource Curse*: *Combining Statism and Cosmopolitanism*. London: Routledge.

Article 4(1). "Declaration on the Rights of Persons belonging to National or Ethnic, Religious and Linguistic Minorities." GA Res. 47/135, adopted 18 December 1992. http://www.un.org/documents/ga/res/47/a47r135.htm. Accessed: August 10, 2017.

Article 27. "International Covenant on Civil and Political Rights." Adopted and Opened for Signature, Ratification and Accession by General Assembly Resolution 2200A (XXI) of 16 December 1966 entry into force 23 March 1976, in accordance with Article 49, Office of the High Commissioner for Human Rights, United Nations. http://www.ohchr.org/EN/ProfessionalInterest/Pages/CCPR.aspx Accessed: August 10, 2017.

Berman, B. et al. 2004. "Introduction: Ethnicity and the Politics of Democratic Nation-Building in Africa." In *Ethnicity and Democracy in Africa*, edited by B. Berman, D. Eyoh and W. Kymlicka. Athens, OH: Ohio University Press.

The Economist. 2021. "Many more Africans are Migrating within Africa than to Europe." *The Economist*.

Gurr, T. 2000. *Peoples Versus States*: *Minorities at Risk in the New Century*. Washington, DC: United States Institute of Peace Press.

Keynes, John Maynard. 1924. *A Tract on Monetary Reform*. London: Macmillan.

Kymlicka, Will. 2007. *Multicultural Odysseys*: *Navigating the New International Politics of Diversity*. Oxford: Oxford University Press.

Maffettone, Sebastiano. 2013. "Normative Approaches to Global Justice." In *Globalisation, Multilateralism, Europe: Towards a Better Global Governance?*, edited by Mario Telo, 125–43. Surrey: Ashgate.

OSCE High Commissioner on National Minorities. 1999. "The Lund Recommendations on the Effective Participation of National Minorities in Public Life." September 1999. http://www.osce.org/hcnm/32240. Accessed: August 19, 2017.

Rawls, John. 1971. *A Theory of Justice*. Cambridge, MA: Harvard University Press.

Rawls, John. 1999. *The Law of Peoples: With the Idea of Public Reason Revisited.* Cambridge, MA: Harvard University Press.

Rawls, John. 2001. *Justice as Fairness: A Restatement*. Cambridge, MA: Harvard University Press.

Rousseau, Jean-Jacques. 1997 [1762]. *The Social Contract*. In *Rousseau: The Social Contract and Other Later Political Writings*, edited by V. Gourevitch. Cambridge, MA: Cambridge University Press.

Simmons, John. A. 2010. "Ideal and Non-ideal Theory." *Philosophy and Public Affairs*, 38, no. 1: 5–36.

United Nations. 2000. *We the Peoples: The Role of the United Nations in the 21st Century.* New York: United Nations, Department of Public Information.

Watt, D. C., Simon Adams, Roger Bullen, Kinley Brauer, and Akira Iriyee. 1988. "What is Diplomatic History?." In *What is History Today?*, edited by Juliet Gardiner, 131–42. London: Macmillan.

Wheatley, Steven. 2005. *Democracy, Minorities and International Law*. Cambridge: Cambridge University Press.

Chapter Six

The Status of Minority
Rights in Africa

In chapters 4 and 5, using Nigeria to contextualize my argument, I discussed how and why the minority rights framework has not worked very well in Africa. A major reason why proponents of the minority rights framework tend to simultaneously overestimate the framework and underestimate its lack of practicability is their failure to recognize that African states have widely rejected the framework, and this rejection of the framework in turn compounds and exacerbates an already bad situation. This does not mean that the framework is wholly rejected. What it means is that the framework is neither dominant nor pervasive. Consequently, any attempt to comprehend the problem of domination and discrimination on the continent must take into consideration the compound nature of the problem.

I have a twofold aim in this chapter. First, I will contend that—at the theoretical and methodological level—unless we look at two kinds of explanations, we will not have a robust explanation for why African states *widely* reject minority rights. Second, I will contend that—at the practical and policy level—when dealing with minority rights, unless African states disregard the internal and external dynamics, they may not "value" minority rights. To defend this second contention, I will argue that by virtue of the features and functionality of minority rights, African states can see the protection of minority rights as a categorical imperative or as a hypothetical imperative and see minority rights as a universal human and helpful phenomenon rather, or as a particular and harmful Western phenomenon—that is, a harmful source of disunity.

I divide the discussion in this chapter into two parts. In the first, I present the internal and external explanations of the rejection of minority rights in Africa. Then in the second part, I explain why neither the internal explanation nor the external explanation constitutes a robust explanation of the rejection of minority rights in Africa. Based on this premise, I argue that we need to focus on the two kinds of explanations in order to have a robust explanation for the rejection of minority rights in Africa. Since African states reject minority rights and the West seems or pretends to be concerned about minority rights, the latter employs some strategies to get the former to accept minority rights. Therefore, I explore the consequences of these strategies. I conclude the discussion by reiterating the need to focus on both the internal and the external explanations and then explain what African states may make of minority rights in spite of the internal and external dynamics.

INTERNAL AND EXTERNAL EXPLANATIONS

Minority rights, as explained in chapter 1, are "legal provisions that have two key features: first, they are intended to recognise or accommodate the distinctive needs of non-dominant . . . groups; and second, they do so by adopting minority-specific measures, above and beyond the non-discriminatory enforcement of universal individual rights that apply regardless of group membership" (Kymlicka n.d.). In addition, minority rights perform two theoretical functions. First, they describe a normatively wrong, unjust, or immoral situation—that is, they describe the situation of a set of people who are normatively wrongly, unjustly or immorally marginalized, discriminated against, or dominated by another set of people. Second, they prescribe a normatively right, just, or moral resolution to the situation.

Historically, and generally, African states are politically skeptical about minority rights, and consequently juridical obscurity characterizes their approach to minority rights (Gilbert 2013, 415). "Africa's modern constitutions typically do no more than guarantee all citizens equal rights before the law and protection against official discrimination on the basis of ethnicity, among others. Minority or group-specific rights receive no explicit or special recognition or protection" (Prempeh 2013, 440). At the constitutional level, the main problem with African states is the absence of minority-specific rights—both positive and negative rights specifically meant for minorities. As individual citizens, members of minorities have constitutional negative and positive rights. However, as minority groups, they lack these rights. The nondiscrimination and equality that negative rights guarantee individual citizens are helpful to members of minorities conceived as individuals but not as collectives. Therefore, the problem is not that African states do not guarantee nondiscrimination and equality; the problem is that no provisions are made to ensure that apart from guaranteeing negative rights, the positive rights of minorities are also guaranteed (Gilbert 2013, 417).

Empirically, nondiscrimination and equality are not sufficient to guarantee the well-being of minorities. While these negative rights are important, it has become commonplace to also argue for positive rights and minority-specific rights—both negative and positive rights of minorities. The notion of minority rights crucially goes beyond mere negative rights to also advocate positive rights (Gilbert, 2013 416), which place onus on governments to make certain provisions for minorities. While the negative right of nondiscrimination ensures the equality of minorities with other groups in the state, positive rights ensure that minorities are not only treated as equals with other groups but also enabled to remain different and flourish as a different group with their own particular identities (Ibid.).

Therefore, for African states to be seen as protecting the rights of minorities, and for African states to actually guarantee the rights of minorities, it is not enough for African states to claim that they do not discriminate against minorities and minorities are treated equally with other groups. African states must also make positive provisions to ensure that minorities are enabled to flourish as minorities with their own different identities. Alarmingly, even the constitutional guarantee of nondiscrimination and equality is largely merely theoretical. In practice, many minorities across the continent are marginalized, discriminated against, dominated, and do not have equality status.

In spite of sub-Saharan Africa being littered with cases of minority discrimination, only Cameroun, the DRC, and Uganda made explicit provisions for the protection of minority rights in their constitutions (Heyns and Kaguongo 2006, 674). Even in these countries, minority rights are only guaranteed in theory but not in practice. Given that in sub-Saharan Africa the remaining forty-five countries have no constitutional provisions to safeguard the rights of minorities, the glaring reminder we get from this scenario is that sub-Saharan African states are not sanguine about minority rights. As Kwasi Prempeh (2013) aptly argues, "[E]thno-regional elites and constituencies in Africa have not been keen about 'minority rights'; they have been a great deal more interested in obtaining a fair and equitable share of national power, wealth and opportunities than in legal protection of group-based 'rights' per se" (441).

Scholars provide two different kinds of arguments why African states generally do not accept minority rights. One kind of argument says that African states reject minority rights because they think minority rights cause or engender balkanization, privileged groups, and an ethnic jigsaw puzzle, which in turn lead to the disintegration of the state. This kind of argument can be termed *internal explanation* in the sense that it explains the rejection of minority rights based on certain internal dynamics in African states. The other kind of argument says that African states reject minority rights because they think that minority rights are neocolonial and neo-imperial weapons of Western domination. This kind of argument can be termed *external explanation* in the sense that it explains the rejection of minority rights based on certain external dynamics outside African states. Some scholars rely on the internal explanation, while other scholars rely on the external explanation.

The internal explanation includes the balkanization argument, the privileged argument, and the ethnic jigsaw puzzle argument (Gilbert 2013, 434). The balkanization argument says that the recognition of minority rights can be counterproductive to nation building or national interest (430–31). Balkanization, as the name suggests, refers particularly to the disintegration of the Balkans in the general disintegration of the Ottoman Empire. In recent times, the term *balkanization* brings to mind the disintegration of Yugoslavia after Tito's demise. Today, balkanization generally refers to the disintegration of a formerly united multiethnic political and geographical entity into various smaller ethnic political and geographical units. "The fear of 'balkanisation' is particularly acute in the context of Africa where ethnic identity is still considered significant" (Ibid.). It is widely believed that since the end of the cold war, African states—in the quest to guarantee national unity—see minority rights as a means of disaggregating African states into ethnic units (ibid.).

The privileged argument says that the state will be creating a group of privileged right holders if it recognizes minority rights (Gilbert 2013, 430–31). Post-independence, the colonial tribal legacy played two roles in Africa. On the one hand, it enabled some political leaders to use ethnicism or tribalism as a means to gain power and perpetuate themselves in power. On the other hand, it generated a wave of reactions in which there was a conscious and strategic effort to fight and conquer tribalism. Consequently, seeing tribalism as a colonial legacy and a "nonmodern" negative phenomenon, most states on the subcontinent "actively engaged in an exercise of nation-building to ensure the unity of their emerging countries. In such nation-building exercises, ethnic identity was viewed as treacherous" (430). Although these exercises were well intentioned, they had the negative effect of being an important part of the reason why there was a conscious prevention of the formulation of robust constitutional provisions to protect minority rights on the subcontinent (Ibid.).

The ethnic jigsaw puzzle argument says that "since everyone in Africa belongs to a specific tribe or clan and since every country is composed of a myriad of different ethnic groups, to some extent, 'everyone is a minority'" (Gilbert 2013, 430–31). This argument does not deny that there are minorities; however, it says that "everyone, to some extent, belongs to a minority group" (Ibid.). The ethnic jigsaw puzzle argument is implausible on two grounds. First, although everyone belongs to an ethnic group, some ethnic groups are larger or more influential or more powerful than others. Therefore, it is apt to say that it is not every ethnic group that is a minority group; some are minorities, while others are majorities. Second, some people are minorities and others are majorities not on the ethnic dimension but on other dimensions such as religion, LGBTQ, disabled people, and so on. Based on the ethnic jigsaw puzzle argument, African states fear "a domino effect under which, if you provide some form of special protection based on ethnicity, then everybody will soon start to claim specific rights" (Ibid.). The fear of a domino effect might be "genuine" in the sense that the protection of certain rights based on ethnicity might lead to demands for the protection of other rights based on religion, gender, and so on. Nevertheless, except when and where the state is genuinely severely incapacitated, the onus is on the state to protect such rights.

What we can deduce from the balkanization, the privileged, and the ethnic jigsaw puzzle arguments is that in some cases the rejection of minority rights was due to the genuine belief that minority rights may lead to national disunity. However, in other cases the rejection of minority rights was not due to any genuine belief that minority rights may lead to national disunity. Such rejection was a by-product of certain political games in which there was no genuine belief in the idea of national unity itself. The idea of national unity was used as a means to acquire and retain power. Prempeh's (2013) observation highlights how this political game is played. So, although lengthy, the observation is worth noting. First, Prempeh argues:

> Group-based claims and political formations were anathema to postcolonial Africa's founding elites. Early official hostility to political mobilisation on the basis of ethnicity stemmed from a fear that recognition or encouragement of such activity might challenge and undermine the inchoate national identity that fragilely held the new states' ethnically heterogeneous populations together. Thus, among the first constitutional and legislative changes enacted by Africa's postcolonial governments were the proscription of political parties allegedly organised along ethnic lines and the removal of structural safeguards that had been inserted in independence constitutions to preserve a realm of territorial autonomy for ethnic-regional sub-national communities. (438)

Second, Prempeh (2013) argues that "[a]lthough justified in the name of 'national unity,' these measures were also aimed at the time at suppressing political opposition, the most formidable of which tended to represent ethno-regional interests and constituencies, and often supported demands for provincial devolution or federalism. The ideology of national unity was similarly deployed by Africa's state elites to underwrite both the one-party state and presidential autocracy" (438).

The case of minorities in Africa is a case of double jeopardy. On the one hand, when they want to "divide and rule," African governments play some groups against others. In this case, while some minorities might be the beneficiaries of the divide and rule strategy, others may be at the receiving end. On the other hand, when they want to "unite and rule," African governments press for the elimination of identities and differences that they think work against nation building and national unity. In this case, minorities also suffer because while they may enjoy nondiscrimination and equality, they dare not press for minority-specific positive rights because these will be seen as counteracting nation building and national unity. As Alemante Selassie (1992) succinctly puts it, "African governments, believing that multiple cultures and languages foster divided loyalties and a sense of separateness, have too frequently assumed that nation-building requires supplanting the individual's ethnic and other particularist ties" (18).

The external explanation includes "external sovereignty" and "Western antecedents." It is very unhelpful to neglect the question of sovereignty when discussing reasons why African states are not receptive to minority rights. Sovereignty has two sides; the one side is internal sovereignty, and the other side is external sovereignty. When analyzing the rejection of minority rights in Africa, a focus on the internal dynamics is tantamount to a focus on internal sovereignty, and a focus on the external dynamics is tantamount to a focus on external sovereignty. Due to the link between internal and external sovereignty, apparently focusing on one and neglecting the other will not be of much help in understanding why minority rights are generally rejected by African states. A failure to acknowledge or respect the link between internal and external sovereignty was after all the dominant approach in the academic fields of law and political science, and largely, at least until recently, philosophy. We see this dominant approach in the subfields of international law (specifically international public law), international relations, and largely (at least until recently) in political theory and political philosophy. In spite of the link between internal and external sovereignty, scholars, jurists, diplomats, politicians, and others saw the two as separate entities. Unquestioningly taking this separation as fait accompli in their normative assessments of sovereignty, the aforementioned scholars and practitioners made a sharp distinction between two separate domains of normative theorizing—namely, intranational justice and international justice (Pogge 2003).

Now, let me briefly expatiate on the distinction between internal and external sovereignty by appealing to the distinction between intranational and international relations. This distinction will buttress, or at least shed light on, the way the notions of internal and external sovereignty are discussed in this chapter. Intranational and international relations

> were traditionally seen as constituting distinct worlds, the former inhabited by persons, households, corporations and associations within one territorially bounded society, the latter inhabited by a small number of actors: sovereign states. National governments provided the link between these two worlds. On the inside such a government was a uniquely important actor within the

state, interacting with persons, households, corporations and associations and dominating these other actors by virtue of its special power and authority—its so-called internal sovereignty. On the outside, the government was the state, recognised as entitled to act in its name, to make binding agreements in its behalf, and so on—its so-called external sovereignty. (Pogge 2003, s.p.)

These two sides of sovereignty—the internal and the external—account for the two different dynamics of rejection of minority rights by African states. All the internal dynamics for rejecting minority rights in Africa are issues of internal sovereignty. However, external sovereignty also affects how African states deal with minority rights. When African states perceive minority rights to be Western ideology or Western imposition, many of them fight back or at least many of them will be on the defensive by rejecting minority rights on the grounds that as sovereign states they are no less than Western states, and Western states are no more than them. For African states, this principle of equality demands that they do not bow to Western pressure. Moreover, the international relations principle of noninterference, which is predicated on the institution of sovereignty, is a consequence of this principle of equality.

To say that certain Western antecedents in Africa significantly contribute to African states "jealously guarding" their sovereignty is not far-fetched. There is no known conception or theory of minority rights in Africa. The focus was on communitarian rights rather than minorities. The focus was on "explicitly" duties and "implicitly" rights of individuals rather than minority rights (the duty of one individual is conversely the right of another individual and the community). However, today, that African states generally reject minority rights is not merely due to the concept not being African historically or due to the concept being Western historically; it is rather due to certain spatiotemporal circumstances, chief among which is the historical relationship between Africa and the West and the process that characterized this relationship. In other words, for African states, there is no objective definition of the notion of minority rights; it is defined in relational and contextual terms. Relationally and contextually it is defined in terms of the historical relationship and the process that characterized the historical relationship between Africa and the West. In this sense, the concept of minority rights is not seen as an objective concept that deals with the marginalization, discrimination, and domination of certain groups of people by other groups of people. Rather, the concept is seen as just another invented weapon in the arsenal of the West to continue the domination of Africa by "other means" and in "other ways."

It is a widely held view that the colonialists extensively exploited ethnic identities to sustain and strengthen their political domination of the subcontinent (Gilbert 2013, 428). Africans were not seen as people inhabiting proper political societies or states; rather, they were simultaneously seen as stateless persons and as persons inhabiting apolitical societies populated by tribes (Ibid.). In spite of the presence of robust kingdoms and related political entities, the colonialists falsely claim that such political entities were characterized by tribal domination in which strong "tribes" dominate weak "tribes" (Ibid.). The above strategy simultaneously enabled the colonialists to discount the political institutions of the so-called tribes and to divide, conquer, and rule the so-called tribes (Ibid.). However, the colonial practice of divide and rule, which gave preferential treatment to some ethnic groups to the detriment of other ethnic groups, and then set the preferred ethnic groups against the rest, left lasting consequences and has continued to influence the current ethnic rivalries on the subcontinent (428–29). The strategy, in its current form, has metamorphosed into "a tradition of mixing ethnicity and constitutionalism to ensure the dominance of some groups over others" (429–30).

Historically, African states have been dominated by Western states. While in the past the domination of African states by the West was largely in the form of hard power, in recent times it has taken the form of hard power, soft power, or smart power. A brief explication of the concept of power and the derivative concepts of hard power, soft power, and smart power will help us understand the skepticism of African states. Power is "the ability to affect others to get the things you want (through . . .) coercion, sticks; . . . payments, carrots; or . . . attraction and persuasion" (Nye 2011a, 46). Joseph Nye (2011b) introduced the distinction between hard power, soft power, and smart power into the lexicon of global politics. For Nye, hard power has to do with "coercion and payment," while soft power has to do with "persuasion and attraction" (xiii). In hard power, coercion is largely seen as military force, while payment is seen as economic resources. Soft power entails (1) others valuing and cherishing you, (2) you successfully convincing others to accept your arguments, or (3) both (1) and (2); hence, others become amenable to you affecting them to get the things you want. While smart power "refers to the ability to combine hard and soft power into . . . strategies in varying contexts" (xiv).

In view of the historical domination of Africa by the West through the use of hard power, no wonder African states see minority rights as reengineered power politics that takes the form of soft power or which is part of a smart-power strategy. For African states, whether this power politics takes the form of hard power, soft power, or smart power, the aim is always the same; the domination of Africa by the West. In global politics and at the global arena, although it is not only states that promote minority rights, African states seem to think that whatever means that are used to promote minority rights and whoever promotes minority rights can be traced to Western states. When NGOs in Africa promote minority rights, African states see these NGOs as puppets of Western states. When INGOs based in the West promote minority rights in Africa, African states see these INGOs as vicars of Western states. When multilateral institutions promote minority rights, African states see these institutions as mere aggregates of Western states. And when Western states promote minority rights in Africa, then African states see them as neo-colonialists or neo-imperialists.

One may ask, to what extent are these so-called external dynamics really external? Are the so-called external dynamics not African leaders' "representation" of Western ideologies? Are the so-called external dynamics not how African leaders relate to their own representations of Western ideologies? If so, then the so-called external dynamics are not external and as such cannot offer any causal explanation or interpretation of the reasons for the rejection of minority rights in Africa in terms of explanation of external dynamics, but only in terms of explanation of internal dynamics. To the above questions and claim, I will respond that while African leaders' representation of Western ideologies is an internal dynamic, and while how African leaders relate to such representation is an internal dynamic, the ideologies themselves are external dynamics. Therefore, in cases like this, while we may not have purely external dynamics, we may not have purely internal dynamics too; what we have here is a combination of both internal and external dynamics. However, since such representations and how such representations are related to by African leaders are motivated by what I have described as "Western antecedents"; it is not far-fetched to say that the so-called external dynamics are really external dynamics.

I agree that in principle, the internal explanation can provide a complete explanation at least in some sense. I also agree that in principle the external explanation can provide a complete explanation at least in some sense. However, I contend that neither the internal explanation alone nor the external explanation alone can provide a complete explanation in the sense of having an explanation that can simultaneously account for both the internal and the external dynamics. In this sense, an explanation that can account for both internal and external dynamics is more robust than an explanation provided by the internal explanation alone and an explanation provided by the external explanation alone. The reasons for believing that the internal explanation alone and the external explanation alone do not provide a complete explanation are as follows.

1. Some African states may reject minority rights based on internal dynamics. Some may reject minority rights based on external dynamics. However, others may reject minority rights based on both internal and external dynamics.

2. In view of (1), it is not only internal dynamics that are responsible for the rejection of minority rights in Africa; external dynamics are also responsible.
3. In view of (1), it is not only external dynamics that are responsible for the rejection of minority rights in Africa; internal dynamics are also responsible.
4. In view of (2) and (3), relying on internal dynamics alone or external dynamics alone to explain the rejection of minority rights in Africa is reductionistic.

Rephrasing the above contention in other words will offer clarifications. I agree that some African states can reject the idea of minority rights based on internal dynamics alone. In this sense, although internal dynamics alone are not necessary for the rejection of minority rights, they are sufficient for such rejection. In addition, I agree that some African states can reject minority rights based on external dynamics alone. In this sense, although external dynamics are not necessary for the rejection of minority rights, they are sufficient for such rejection. Nevertheless, other African states can reject minority rights based on both internal and external dynamics. Therefore, when analyzing the rejection of minority rights in Africa, mainly focusing on one kind of dynamics leaves a vacuum that can only by filled by analyzing the other kind of dynamics.

The internal dynamics seem to be more logical and empirical, and, consequently, more prominent. By this I mean the internal dynamics concern the concrete, immediate, and continuous struggle for nation building, while the external dynamics concern the distant and indirect machinations of a supposed malevolent actor. However, any methodological tendency or temptation to focus on the internal dynamics and be blind to the external dynamics must be resisted no matter its lures. Therefore, while I do not doubt the cogency of the internal dynamics, I am not sanguine about the potency of the dynamics to constitute a robust explanation for the rejection of minority rights in Africa. For this reason, I think we need the external dynamics explanation, if not as much as we need the internal dynamics explanation at least to complement the internal dynamics explanation. To pretend that only internal dynamics are responsible for the rejection of minority rights in Africa, and to pretend that external dynamics have no part to play in the rejection of minority rights in Africa, is tantamount to "explanatory nationalism"—the tendency to explain undesirable social, political, or economic situations "exclusively in terms of causal dynamics that are domestic to the societies in which they occur" (Pogge 2010, 24–25). However valid and useful, the internal dynamics explanation must be complemented by the external dynamics explanation if we are to have a robust explanation for the rejection of minority rights by African states.

The external dynamics represent the behavior of African states in international politics. What African states make of minority rights is influenced by their historical relationship with Western states. Therefore, it is partly in the context of the historical relationship between African states and Western states that we find what minority rights mean for African states. This argument appeals to contextualism. Contextualism is a derivative of the acknowledgment that (1) "behaviour, attitudes and strategic choices take place inside particular social, political, economic and even cultural contexts" (Steinmo 2008, 127) and (2) context "has a direct consequence for the decisions or events" (Ibid.). In the "contextual analysis," context is understood to be "(1) the era, period, or time; (2) the place or space, and; (3) the conditions or circumstances; which make up the milieu in which a relevant global actor (for instance, a state) acts or behaves or in which relevant global actors (for instance, states) act or behave" (Abumere 2015, 60). In other words, context represents the spacio-temporal circumstances that shape the content and scope of the behavior of actors in global politics (61). Contextual analysis acknowledges that other dynamics also shape the behavior of states in global politics; but it deems context to be the principal dynamic.

However, in view of the features and functions of minority rights, the questions African states may ask about minority rights are not questions with ego/alter or self/other connotations and denotations in relation to the West such as the following: Are minority rights not Western? Do minority rights not originate from the West? Did Westerners not invent minority rights? Are minority rights not another Western weapon of domination? These are wrong questions! The questions African states may be asking—that is, the significant questions—are the following. In their descriptive function, do minority rights help us understand the situation of a certain set of people, and is it true that these people are being marginalized, discriminated against, or dominated by other people? If the question is answered in the affirmative, then the following question would be as follows: In their prescriptive function, is the resolution proposed by minority rights helpful in dealing with the situation? If this question too is answered in the affirmative, then African states' approach to minority rights may not be based on the context of the subcontinent's historical relationship with the West. In other words, African states may not see minority rights as a particular and harmful Western phenomenon but rather as a universal and helpful human phenomenon.

Similarly, when the above questions are answered in the affirmative, African states' approach to minority rights may not be based on the fear of national disunity through balkanization, privileged, and ethnic jigsaw puzzle arguments. In other words, African states may not see minority rights as a harmful phenomenon that is likely to disunite the state. Rather, they may see minority rights as a vehicle through which injustice against powerless or less powerful groups can be prevented or remedied and through which powerful or more powerful groups can be prevented from discriminating against or dominating powerless or less powerful groups based on group identity.

In the preceding and penultimate arguments, I move from how African states *actually* see minority rights in view of the aforementioned internal and external dynamics to how they *may* see minority rights in view of the functionality of minority rights. Therefore, the arguments are simultaneously consistent with the truth that minority rights trigger the fear of national disunity and with the truth that African states see minority rights as a source of national disunity. Furthermore, it is simultaneously consistent with the truth that minority rights are a piece of Western ideology and with the truth that African states see minority rights as a piece of Western ideology. However, my contention is that minority rights may be judged based on neither their place of origin nor their fears of statesmen; rather, they may be judged based on their features and functionality.

Judging minority rights based on their functionality is not alien to African states. Nevertheless, when African states judge minority rights based on functionality, they see the function of minority rights as disintegration of states or subjugation of the continent. The conclusion that the function of minority rights is the disintegration of the state is reached because the judgement is not purely based on functional grounds. It is rather eclipsed by the assumption that the promotion of subnational identities and diversity rather than one national identity and unity is tantamount to the promotion of national disunity. While the conclusion that the function of minority rights is subjugation of the subcontinent is reached because the judgement is based on the assumption that African states must be suspicious of minority rights because of the place of origin of minority rights, my argument is that the functionality judgement is devoid of or detached from the national disunity and place of origin assumptions. While the functionality judgement is objective, the national disunity and place of origin assumptions are subjective.

DIPLOMATIC STRATEGIES

To get African states to accept the idea of minority rights, certain foreign policies and diplomatic strategies can be employed as it is done in the case of human rights. Chief among these instruments are aid incentives and the threat of sanctions—both comprehensive and targeted sanctions (I reject comprehensive sanctions because of their documented disastrous consequences). However, I contend that these strategies, when used by Western states, can lead to negative consequences for minority rights. This is because apart from rejecting the idea of minority rights on the grounds of balkanization, privileged, ethnic jigsaw puzzle, external sovereignty, and Western antecedents, another form of reaction from African states is to turn the protection of minorities or the guarantee and safeguard of minority rights into a chess game that brings the reward of aid in international relations.

When Western states are concerned about minority rights on the continent, African states will base their guarantee of minority rights on the aid they receive from Western states, and Western states will base the aid they give to African states on the condition that minority rights are guaranteed. For Western states, the more African states guarantee minority rights, the more aid the latter receive, and the less the latter guarantee minority rights, the less aid they receive. And for African states, the more aid they receive, the more they guarantee minority rights, and the less aid they receive, the less they guarantee minority rights. While this diplomatic, foreign policy, or international political strategy might incentivize African states to guarantee minority rights, it is a flawed approach in the following senses.

First, based on this approach, the protection of minority rights becomes merely a hypothetical imperative; and as such, it become merely conditional. If, and when, a Western state changes its foreign policy of giving aid to a certain African state, then the latter stops guaranteeing minority rights. And when a certain African state decides not to care anymore about whether it receives aid or not from a Western state, then the former stops guaranteeing minority rights. Second, contrary to the aforementioned, the protection of minority rights can be treated as a categorical imperative rather than as a mere hypothetical imperative. According to Immanuel Kant (1996[1785]),

> all imperatives command either hypothetically or categorically. The former represent the practical necessity of a possible action as a means to achieving something else that one wills (or that it is at least possible for one to will). The categorical imperative would be that which represented an action as objectively necessary of itself, without reference to another end. (4: 414)

For Kant (1996[1785]), if an "action would be good merely as a means to something else the imperative is hypothetical; if the action is represented as in itself good, hence as necessary in a will in itself conforming to reason, as its principle, then it is categorical" (4: 414).

My reasons for arguing that the protection of minority rights ought to be treated as a categorical imperative are based on my prior contention that minority rights can be judged based on their features and functionality. I think the features and functionality of minority rights reveal that guaranteeing minority rights is, in Kantian terms, "objectively necessary of itself" and "in itself good." As explained in the introductory section, minority rights "have two key features: first, they are intended to recognise or accommodate the distinctive needs of non-dominant . . . groups; and second, they do so by adopting minority-specific measures, above and beyond the non-discriminatory enforcement of universal individual rights that apply regardless of group membership" (Kymlicka, n.d.). In addition, minority rights perform two theoretical functions. First, they describe a normatively wrong, unjust, or immoral situation—that is, they describe the situation of a set of people who are normatively wrongly, unjustly, or immorally marginalized, discriminated against, or dominated by another set of people. Second, they prescribe a normatively right, just, or moral resolution to the situation.

When the protection of minority rights is treated as a categorical imperative, minority rights will be seen at once as (1) rights that are universal and (2) rights that ought to be guaranteed. In this sense, minority rights will not be seen as Western ideology (or Chinese ideology, Indian ideology, African ideology, etc.) but as an idea of humanity. Therefore, guaranteeing minority rights will not be seen as something that only Western states do, or as something that African states can afford not to do, or as something that African states will only do if they are sufficiently incentivized by Western states. Guaranteeing minority rights will be seen as something that we as humanity do because it is just what we ought to do. There is, as Kant (1996[1785]) says, "only one categorical imperative and it is this: act only in accordance with that maxim through which you can at the same time will that it become a universal law . . . act as if the maxim of your action were to become by your will a universal law of nature" (4: 421).

The reverse side of the aid incentive is the threat of sanctions. Simply put, both aid incentives and the threat of sanctions constitute carrot and stick diplomacy. The threat of sanctions from Western states can make African states safeguard minority rights. However, the threat of sanctions will fail to work if (1) Western states are not actually prepared to impose sanctions on African states that fail to guarantee minority rights or (2) if African states do not actually care about whether Western states impose sanctions on them. Fundamentally, even when Western sanctions work, African states guaranteeing minority rights because of the threat of sanctions still makes the protection of minority rights a hypothetical imperative rather than a categorical imperative. Minority rights has become something that African states will only guarantee if they are threatened with sanctions rather than something they will guarantee because they ought to. Absent the threat of sanctions, absent the guarantee of minority rights!

In a pragmatic or realistic sense, aid incentives and the threat of sanctions will help promote minority rights. It may seem idealistic, rather than realistic, to eschew aid incentives and the threat of sanctions from the normative endeavor to see that minority rights are guaranteed in Africa. Nevertheless, minorities will be better served if African states come to accept the protection of minority rights as a categorical imperative rather than as a hypothetical imperative. If it is correct that sometimes the road to justice passes through injustice, perhaps likewise we might also be hopeful that although aid incentives and the threat of sanctions may render the protection of minority rights a hypothetical imperative in the short run, the result might be different in the long run. Perhaps, eventually, the strategies may result in a situation whereby due to certain spacio-temporal circumstances or a combination of dynamics such as the passage of time, change of contexts, socialization, cognitive adaptation, and so on, the protection of minority rights might be accepted as a categorical imperative. When this sociopsychological stage is reached, then aid incentives and the threat of sanctions will be redundant.

Although I think that incentivizing the protection of minority rights may lead minority rights to be regarded in the wrong way, at least in the short run—that is, the protection of minority rights will not be seen as something African states do because minorities ought to be protected—I admit that perhaps such hypocrisy of African states may result in some gradual changes in the long run. Again, I admit that if the alternative is that minority rights are not protected, hypocritically protecting minority rights is better than not protecting minority rights. While I think that incentivizing the protection of minority rights makes minority rights conditional, I admit that if the alternative is that minority rights are not protected (e.g., the Chinese model), conditional respect for minority rights is better than no respect at all for minority rights.

I concede that while aid and targeted sanctions (comprehensive sanctions have been documented to have disastrous consequences for the people they are supposed to help) might not always work, this in itself is not a sufficient reason against trying to use such instruments; not using them might not always work either. In other words, although I think that minorities will be better served if African states come to accept the protection of minority rights as a categorical imperative rather than as a hypothetical imperative, I admit that perhaps this might not be a feasible option in the short run. Nevertheless, while I do not discount the question of feasibility in the short run, I am not only interested in the pragmatic and the short run; I am also interested in the ideal and the long run. Therefore, despite the limitations of incentivizing the protection of minority rights, my argument is not that it is always better not to incentivize the protection of minority rights than to incentivize the protection of minority rights. My argument is that since the incentivizing of the protection of minority rights is likely to make African states see minority rights as a negative Western ideology, Western states ought to be very cautious in trying to incentivize the protection of minority rights in Africa.

The question of whether Western states should incentivize the protection of minority rights in Africa is independent of the plausibility or implausibility of the external dynamics explanation. This is because the question will always arise, and it will always require an answer, irrespective of the plausibility or implausibility of the external dynamics explanation. Nevertheless, if the external dynamics explanation is plausible, then Western states' foreign policies of incentivizing the protection of minority rights in Africa will strengthen the claim that African states partly see minority rights as a neocolonial or neo-imperialist weapon. In other words, it will strengthen the claim that African states see minority rights as a weapon-in-disguise that the West uses against Africa in a Machiavellian fashion.

In summary, first, I argued that at the theoretical and methodological level, when explaining why African states reject minority rights, we should neither disregard the balkanization, privileged, and ethnic jigsaw puzzle arguments nor the external sovereignty and Western antecedent arguments. I explained why neither the balkanization, privileged, and ethnic jigsaw puzzle arguments (the internal dynamics explanation) nor the external sovereignty and Western antecedent arguments (the external dynamics explanation) constitute a robust explanation for the rejection of minority rights in Africa. Based on this premise, I argued that we need to focus on the two kinds of explanations in order to have a robust explanation for the rejection of minority rights in Africa.

Second, I argued that at the practical and policy level, when dealing with minority rights, African states can disregard the balkanization, privileged, and ethnic jigsaw puzzle arguments and the external sovereignty and Western antecedent arguments. I averred that in spite of the balkanization, privileged, and ethnic jigsaw puzzle arguments and the external sovereignty and Western antecedent arguments, African states ought to judge minority rights based on the features and functionality of minority rights. Then, in light of the features and functionality of minority rights, I concluded that African states may see the protection of minority rights as a categorical imperative rather than as a hypothetical imperative, and see minority rights as a universal human and helpful phenomenon rather than as a particular and harmful Western phenomenon or a harmful source of disunity.

Finally, I think if African states simultaneously reflect on the conditions of many minorities on the subcontinent and the features and functionality of minority rights, they will realize the necessity of protecting minority rights and the urgency the protection requires. Furthermore, I think in view of the necessity and urgency, African states will realize that although the balkanization, privileged, and ethnic jigsaw puzzle arguments and the external sovereignty and Western antecedent arguments are justifiable grounds for the rejection of minority rights, they can be superseded by the functionality of minority rights.

REFERENCES

Abumere, Frank Aragbonfoh. 2015. "Context as the Principal Determinant of the Behaviour of States in Global Politics." *International Journal of Peace and Conflict Studies* 2, no. 3: 57–68.

Gilbert, Jeremie. 2013. "Constitutionalism, Ethnicity and Minority Rights in Africa: A Legal Appraisal from the Great Lakes Region." *International Journal of Constitutional Law* 11, no. 2: 414–37.

Heyns, Christof, and Waruguru Kaguongo. 2006. "Current Developments: Constitutional Human Rights Law in Africa." *South African Journal on Human Rights* 22, no. 4: 673–717.

Kant, Immanuel. 1996[1785]. "Groundwork of The Metaphysics of Morals." In *Immanuel Kant*: *Practical Philosophy*, translated and edited by Mary J. Gregor. Cambridge: Cambridge University Press.

Kymlicka, Will. n.d. "Minority Rights." *Encyclopedia Princetoniensis*: *The Princeton Encyclopedia of Self-Determination*. http://pesd.princeton.edu/?q=node/256. Accessed: June 19, 2017.

Nye, Joseph S. 2011a. "The Future of Power." *Bulletin of the American Academy*, Spring. https://amacad.org/publications/bulletin/spring2011/power.pdf

Nye, Joseph S. 2011b. *The Future of Power*. New York: Public Affairs.

Pogge, Thomas W. 2003. "What is Global Justice?" Oslo, Norway. http://pages .uoregon.edu/koopman/courses_readings/pogge_what_is_global_justice.pdf

Pogge, Thomas W. 2010. *Politics as Usual: What lies behind the Pro-Poor Rhetoric.* Cambridge: Polity Press.

Prempeh, Kwasi H. 2013. "Constitutionalism, Ethnicity and Minority Rights in Africa: A Reply to Jeremie Gilbert." *International Journal of Constitutional Law* 11, no. 2: 438–43.

Selassie, G. Alemante. 1992. "Ethnic Identity and Constitutional Design for Africa." *Stanford Journal of International Law* 29, no. 1: 1–56.

Steinmo, Sven. 2008. "Historical Institutionalism." In *Approaches and Methodologies in the Social Sciences*: *A Pluralist Perspective*, edited by Donatella della Porta and Michael Keating, 118–38. Cambridge: Cambridge University Press.

Chapter Seven

The African Union and Normative International Relations

In chapters 4 and 5, I explained how and why the minority rights framework has not worked very well in Africa. While in chapter 6, I started by explaining that a major reason why proponents of the minority rights framework tend to simultaneously overestimate the framework and underestimate its lack of practicability is their failure to recognize that African states have widely rejected the framework, and this rejection of the framework in turn compounds and exacerbates an already bad situation. I proceeded to explain that this does not mean that the framework is wholly rejected. Nevertheless, what it means is that the framework is neither dominant nor pervasive. Then, I concluded that any attempt to comprehend the problem of domination and discrimination on the continent must take into consideration the compound nature of the problem.

Having taken into consideration the compound nature of the problem (see chapter 6), in this chapter and in chapter 8—in view of the failure of the minority rights approach as discussed in the fourth and fifth chapters and the compound nature of the problem as discussed in chapter 6—I argue for normative international relations among African states as a realistic resolution to the domination of, and discrimination against, migrant minorities. The normative international relations may include the adoption of minority rights, but it will not be limited to the adoption of minority rights. Essentially, it represents a constructivist reliance on norms in international politics in spite of the anarchical nature of international politics.

Nevertheless, I am conscious, and I admit, that normative international relations is not a new theory—it is not even a theory at all in the sense in which realism and neorealism; liberalism and neoliberalism; social constructivism or constructivism; the English School and critical theories such as Marxist theory, postcolonial theory, feminist theory; and so on are theory. In view of the consciousness and admission, to untangle normative international relations in ways that will make it adaptable to Africa, I shall untangle the relationship between normative international relations and realism and statism, internationalism, and cosmopolitanism and idealism within the context of human rights (individual human rights) and group rights (minority rights) protection in international politics and global politics in a globalized world.

In addition to the above task, the same consciousness and admission that give rise to my first task also give rise to my second task. Specifically, the second task stems from a consciousness and admission that normative regional relations are often not actionable. As one of the reviewers of this book aptly observes, in spite of "the existence of international structures and institutions," normative international relations may not necessarily

> constitute a significant resolution of minority and identity discrimination. The existence of these normative structures has not prevented the terrible acts of minority and identity repression we hear about on the news almost on a daily basis. The Rwandan genocide is a recent and most tragic example of how norms can be disregarded when regional and international realpolitik takes the stage.[1]

So my second task is to show how to navigate through the turbulent waves or troubled waters of international and global politics, and through the undulating terrain of regional integration diplomacy within the vicissitudes of globalization in order to arrive at an African Union that guarantees protection of minorities and migrants. The aforementioned two asks are the subject matter of this chapter and chapter 8.

So far, in my argument for normative international relations among African states as a realistic resolution to the domination of, and discrimination against, migrant minorities, I have argued that the normative international relations may include the adoption of minority rights, but it will not be limited to that. In other words, as already mentioned, normative international relations represent a constructivist reliance on norms in international politics in spite of the anarchical nature of international politics. Essentially, in this chapter and chapter 8, I shall delineate the scope and explain the content of normative international relations among African states.

Building on the discussion in the preceding chapters, in this chapter I shall analyze the process and show the mechanism through which the AU can arrive at normative international relations. To do this, first, I shall discuss the process such normative international relations can go through. Second, I shall show a mechanism that can midwife normative international relations in the AU. Third, I shall acknowledge the endeavors the AU has already made and is still making to protect migrants through normative international relations and political and legal frameworks.

THE ROAD TO NORMATIVE REGIONAL RELATIONS

The Westphalian system remains the most consequential political phenomenon in our world, and it divides the world into sovereign geographical territories whose borders serve as barriers between citizens and noncitizens. I think that the Westphalian system has the capacity to engender othering, and the consequences are dire for the *other* in view of the exclusionary function of boundaries, borders, and margins, and in terms of current political phenomena, resurgent nationalism, populism, xenophobia, and Afrophobia. As Seyla Benhabib (2004) succinctly puts it:

> In a territorially bounded nation-state system, that is, in a "state-centric" international order, one's legal status is dependent upon protection by the highest authority that controls the territory upon which one resides and issues the papers to which one is entitled. One becomes a refugee if one is persecuted, expelled, and driven away from one's homeland; one becomes a minority if the political majority in the polity declares that certain groups do not belong to the supposedly "homogeneous" people; one is a stateless person if the state whose protection one has hitherto enjoyed withdraws such protection, as well as nullifying the papers it has granted; one is a *displaced person* if, having been once rendered a refugee, a minority, or a *stateless person*, one cannot find another polity to recognize one as its member, and remains in a state of limbo, caught between territories, none of which desire one to be its resident. (55; emphasis in original)

As long as the Westphalian system remains the most consequential political phenomenon in our world, and as long as it divides the world into sovereign geographical territories whose borders serve as barriers between citizens and noncitizens, the possibility of othering and the problem of domination and discrimination, and even the danger of dehumanization, will always be present in our world. "The nation-state system . . . always carried within itself the seeds of exclusionary injustice at home and aggression abroad" (Benhabib 2004, 61). Tragically, we experience the darkest of times when our agency and spatio-temporal circumstances allow the possibility of othering to become the banality of evil.

In our world today, certain feature of globalization—namely extensity, intensity, and velocity, are considered to be shifting the world from a Westphalian statist world, through a semi-Westphalian internationalist world, to a non-Westphalian global world. This means that "the trajectory of world history and world politics are believed to be revealing a progressing shift beginning from the Westphalian system, going through international system and international society, and eventually leading to a cosmopolitan system" (Abumere 2019a, 19). This presupposes that Westphalian statism and internationalism are fading away due to the "circumstances of cosmopolitanism"

(Waldron 2000, 239)—that is, "the background conditions and presuppositions that inform and motivate the case for a cosmopolitan framework of law and sovereignty . . . [i.e.] the processes and forces of globalisation that increasingly enmesh us in overlapping communities of fate" (Held 2002, 23).

In other words, there is a belief that the nation-state is fading "as the necessary organizing principle of all global relationships and their histories" (Rosenberg 2004, 191). Consequently, it can be asserted that globalization requires a different and novel form of explanation that is not centered on the state as the focus of explanation (Finney 2005). On the one hand, the current situation of world politics (resurgent nationalism, populism, and xenophobia, and Afrophobia in Africa) negates the assertion that the trajectories of world history and world politics are moving from Westphalianism, through internationalism, to cosmopolitanism. From the United States to Brazil, or Europe and beyond, populism contradicts the claim that Westphalianism is on the decline while internationalism and cosmopolitanism are in ascendance. On the other hand, the trajectory of the post–Second World War world history and world politics until the past decade and this decade seems to indicate that internationalism and cosmopolitanism are not in terminal decline. This suggests that it may be plausible to contend that resurgent nationalism, populism, xenophobia, and Afrophobia are an aberration while globalization remains the norm (Abumere 2019a, 19). Nevertheless, in spite of globalization, our world has not evolved to a stage at which one can remotely, talk less of confidently, call it a cosmopolitan world. At best, it might be called an internationalist world containing either an international system or an international society.

According to Hedley Bull (2002), an international system is a mere system of states where "two or more states have sufficient contact between them, and have sufficient impact on one another's decisions, to cause them to behave—at least, in some measure—as parts of a whole" (9). Bull explains that states transit from an international system to an international society "when a group of states, conscious of certain common interests and common values, form a society in the sense that they conceive themselves to be bound by a common set of rules in their relations with one another, and share in the working of common institutions" (13). In Africa, whether the internationalist world is an international system or an international society or an oscillation between the two depends on how comprehensive and effective regional and subregional multilateral organizations are. After all, as Alexander Wendt (1992) famously argues, "[A]narchy is what states make of it" (391).

Wendt (1992; 1999) accepts the realist claim that international politics is anarchical but rejects the realist claim that the anarchical nature of international politics equals the absence of norms in international politics. Instead, he posits three cultures of anarchy: the first one based on the political theory of Thomas Hobbes (the Hobbesian culture), the second one based on the political theory of John Locke (the Lockean culture), and the third one based on the political theory of Immanuel Kant (the Kantian culture). "In a Hobbesian culture, states perceive or understand one another as enemies and consequently relate with one another as enemies. In a Lockean culture, states perceive or understand one another to be rivals and consequently relate with one another as rivals. While in a Kantian culture, states perceive or understand one another to be friends and consequently relate with one another as friends" (Abumere 2019b, s.p.). Therefore, as opposed to the aforementioned realist claim, "the anarchical nature of international politics does not necessarily negate norms, but the norms accepted or rejected by states determine how states act in international politics" (Ibid.).

In view of the constructivist argument by Wendt (1992)—that is, accepting that "anarchy is what states make of it" (391)—I aver that migration is what African states makes of it. What member states of the AU make of migration depends on whether they see the AU and other subregional organizations as a Hobbesian arena filled with enemies that only settle for a modus vivendi, a Lockean organization of rivals that compete against one another, or a Kantian union of friends who cooperate with one another. This argument appeals to contextualism. As already mentioned in chapter 6, contextualism is a derivative of the acknowledgment that (1) "behaviour, attitudes and strategic choices take place inside particular social, political, economic and even cultural contexts" (Steinmo 2008, 127) and (2) context "has a direct consequence for the decisions or events" (Ibid.). In this "contextual analysis," context is understood to be "(1) the era, period, or time; (2) the place or space; and; (3) the conditions or circumstances; which make up the milieu in which a relevant international actor (for instance, a state) acts or behaves or in which relevant international actors (for instance, states) act or behave" (Abumere 2015a, 60). Put differently, context is representation of the spatio-temporal circumstances that shape both the scope and the content of the behavior of states in international politics (61). In my contextual analysis, I acknowledge that apart from context, other dynamics also shape the scope and content of the behavior of states in international politics. Nevertheless, I think that context is primus inter pares among the other dynamics. In view of contextualism and globalization, and the optimistic view (described in the third chapter), it can be argued that in spite of the current discrimination against migrants, in the future there might be a divergence from discrimination to accommodation of migrants due to cooperation among the member states of the AU. This expected divergence is based on the grounds that in the past, African states and Western states were, to a large extent, members of an international system; in the present, they are, to a large extent, members of an international society, and in the future, they are likely to be members of a cosmopolitan world. Such optimism may not be far-fetched because cooperation already exists in multilateral organisations such as . . . the African Union (AU) at the regional level. Furthermore, at the sub-regional levels, cooperation already exists in multilateral organisations such as the Economic Community of West-African States (ECOWAS), Economic Community of Central African States (ECCAS), East African Community (EAC), Southern African Development Commission (SADC), Common Market for Eastern and Southern Africa (COMESA), Arab Maghreb Union (AMU), Community of Sahel-Saharan States (CEN-SAD) and Intergovernmental Authority on Development (IGAD). (Abumere 2020, 343)

As I mentioned in the third chapter, domination and discrimination are rife on the continent, but at the same time pan-Africanism is the order of the day on the continent. "Pan-Africanism is a description of African political elites' internalisation of the norm that Africans are one, and as such, Africans ought to support, and cooperate, with one another. In other words, unity ought to be the right kind of relationship among Africans, and African leaders must always act harmoniously, seeking compromise rather than confrontation" (Abumere 2020, 347; see Tieku 2013, 17). On regional matters such as discrimination against migrants, pan-Africanism simultaneously discourages disagreements among African leaders, encourages consensus among them, and pressurizes them to align with the consensus (Clapham 1996).

In conformity with the norm of pan-Africanism, African governments go as far as often sacrificing the interests and preferences of their states. Setting the normative standard of behavior for African states, governments, and their representatives, pan-Africanism does

not only encourage African political elites to show loyalty in public to continental unity; it also makes it hard for those elites to oppose openly an issue that commands broad support. Decision-making is often made easy by the self-regulation of the norm. It is the powerful effect of the norm that allows African states to develop common positions on crucial international issues. It often encourages African governments to engage in block voting in international forums. Indeed, it dictates actions of African governments in international politics especially in the absence of obvious material concerns. (Tieku 2013, 17–18)

In face of the discrimination against migrants, and in spite of the pessimistic view on the fate of migrants, what pan-Africanism shows is that, even though the optimistic view might be far-fetched, the discrimination against migrants can still be resolved, and this is what gives rise to the realistic view. After all,

the central referent of international politics in Africa are group preferences formation, consensual decision-making procedures and the solidarity principle . . . except these three collective traits are taken into consideration, we will not be able to explain international politics in Africa. In other words, any African international relations theory that fails to consider the three collective traits in its explanation of international politics in Africa is bound to fail. Consequently, to employ norms at the African regional level, one must rely on the three collective traits. In sum, to employ norms at the African regional level, one must rely on pan-Africanism. (Abumere 2020, 347; see Tieku 2013, 11)

I shall conclude this section by opining that normative international relations among African states that are expressed in pan-Africanism will go beyond being a realistic resolution to the problem of domination of, and discrimination against, migrants. It has the potential to lead to a more comprehensive and effective AU. If or when this happens, then it might not be difficult to imagine how normative international relations among African states can make many of the intractable problems in Africa tractable. In other words, when the risks, losses, and benefits of resolving international, transnational, sub-regional, and regional problems are regionalized, intractable problems such as migration, the Corona Virus (COVID-19) pandemic, threats of violence, potential conflicts, and actual crises and conflicts will become less intractable and more tractable.

This pan-Africanism is the kind of pan-Africanism that Achie Mafeje (2008[2000]) calls for—that is, "a new Pan-Africanism that brooks neither external dependence nor internal authoritarianism and social deprivation" (113). In this new pan-Africanism, member states of the AU are encouraged not to see member states as enemies or the "other," and not even as rivals or competitors, but as friends and collaborators. In this case, they are not to see their boundaries, borders, and margins as limiting cases but as representing a microcosm of the AU. This transcending of limiting cases is made possible by the fusion of horizons, which is the subject matter of the next section.

FUSION OF HORIZONS

In everyday language, the term *fusion of horizons* suggests certain possibilities—namely, there are two or more horizons and they can be joined together or synthesized to become one. In this sense, horizons denote or connote standpoints past which we cannot see. While fusion denotes or connotes the combination or the joining together of the standpoints, in philosophy, horizon has certain denotation and connotations that are especially found in the phenomenology of Edmund Husserl, the phenomenology of Martin Heidegger, and the hermeneutics of Husserl's and Heidegger's protégé, Hans-Georg Gadamer.

In his phenomenology, Husserl (1973) explains that "perception has horizons made up of other possibilities of perception, as perceptions we could have, if we actively directed the course of perception otherwise: if, for example, we turned our eyes that way instead of this, or if we were to step forward or to one side, and so forth" (44). He categorizes horizons into three: internal horizon, external horizon, and temporal horizon. On the one hand, he refers to the characteristics that an object necessarily has because they are in the nature of the object as internal horizon. On the other hand, he refers to the horizons that establish the relationship between an object and its environment as external horizon. Then, he explains that the temporal nature or circumstances of the object are the temporal horizons (Vessey n.d., s.p.). Put differently, for Husserl, on the one hand, the nature of an object—that is, the existence of the object—is its internal horizon. On the other hand, the special relation of the object to its environment is the external horizon. Then, the spatio-temporal nature of the object and its relations to time, space, other objects, and its environment are simultaneously the temporal horizon in one breadth and the internal and external horizons in the same breadth (Abumere 2015b, 35).

Husserl argues that temporal horizon is more important than internal and external horizons. For him, temporal horizon is more important than internal and external horizons because as perceivers we perceive all objects in terms of their temporality—that is, as temporal objects. Although objects are spatial objects—that is, they are extended in space—they are also perceived to be temporal objects—that is, they are also extended in time. Since we know the internal horizon of an object through our common expectations of future disclosures about the object, and since we know the external horizon of an object through the manifestation of the object's relation to its environment, temporality is the crucial link between objects and other horizons (Vessey n.d., s.p.). In essence, for Husserl, without temporal horizon, it will be impossible to have internal and external horizons. For this reason, he explains that "future disclosures and relations, including the history of the object that made the object the sort of object that it is and put it in the place where it is, are in essence temporal" (Abumere 2015b, 36).

Building on Husserl's temporal horizon, Heidegger (1996) explains that temporality is "the possible horizon for any understanding of being" (xix). For him, horizon is "that towards which each *ecstasis* is intrinsically open in a specific way . . . the open expanse towards which remotion itself is outside itself" (Heidegger 1982, 267; emphasis in original). *Ecstasis*, also spelled as *ekstasis*, stands for transcendence or transcendental. Hence, for Heidegger, horizon is that toward which each transcendence or transcendental is intrinsically open in a specific way—that is, horizon is the open expanse of the transcendent or the transcendental in which remotion itself is outside itself.

The aforementioned historical background is helpful because it gives us insight into the meaning of fusion of horizons. In philosophy, the term *fusion of horizons* is associated with Gadamer. It is common knowledge that Gadamer's hermeneutics is a derivative of Heidegger's phenomenology and ultimately Husserl's phenomenology. Although, unlike Husserl who focuses on perception and unlike Heidegger who focuses on time, Gadamer focuses on linguistics. Moreover, certainly Gadamer did not invent the words *fusion* and *horizons*. Since he borrowed the words from their everyday language usage, his usage of the words bears similarities with the everyday usage. However, his usage of the term has a certain philosophical conceptualization, and it is with such conceptualization that I am concerned in this book. I devote the remainder of this section to an explication of that conception.

Gadamer was sanguine about the importance of the temporality of horizons. However, that was the early Gadamer. The later Gadamer (1997) explains that the temporality of horizon is not helpful in explaining the importance of "the otherness of the other" and the essential role that language plays as conversation (45). For him, interpretive distance does not always have to be a historical distance. As he explains, temporal distance does not always help us defeat erroneous memories and images and their resonance and warped uses (Abumere 2015b, 36–37). Other horizons, internal and external horizons, are very helpful, and sometimes even more helpful than temporal horizon, in defeating erroneous memories and images and their resonance and warped uses. Nevertheless, temporal distance remains very important because certain changes become apparent to us and certain differences become observable to us only through temporal distance (Gadamer 1997, 45).

Fusing one's horizons with the horizons of others means that one is able to change standpoints and step out of one's own horizon, and "the merely changing of standpoints entails the possibility of having different horizons and the mere stepping out of our horizons entails the possibility of having broader horizons" (Gadamer 1997, 45) In a nutshell, the defining characteristic of horizon is flexibility, not rigidity. For this reason, Gadamer (1989) does not see horizon as a nonshifting borderline; rather, he thinks horizon actually shifts with us and encourages us to go forward (245).

In the final analysis, Gadamer (1989) explains that "the historical movement of human life consists in the fact that it is never absolutely bound to any one standpoint, and hence can never have a truly closed horizon. The horizon is, rather, something into which we move and that moves with us. Horizons change for someone who is moving" (304). Concisely, fusion of horizons is simultaneously a rejection of objectivism, on the one hand, and universalism, on the other hand. On the one hand, it is a rejection of objectivism because it discourages us from discounting our horizon and objectifying the horizon of the other. At least it does not encourage us to discount our horizon and objectify the horizon of the other. On the other hand, it is a rejection of universalism because it discourages us from seeing a singular horizon as the sole holder of the truth, the whole truth, and nothing but the whole truth. At least the fusion of horizons does not encourage us to see a singular horizon as the sole holder of the truth, the whole truth, and nothing but the whole truth. Consequently, fusion of horizons entails that we are not closed up in a closed horizon (Abumere 2015b, 36). It promotes an understanding truth that is open to modification and further clarity.

Prima facie, fusion of horizons seems to be Hegelian dialectics of, say, being + nothingness = becoming or thesis + antithesis = synthesis, which itself becomes a new thesis. However, such characterization of fusion of horizons is wrong (Abumere 2015b, 36–37). We arrive at a fusion of horizons only when we realize that the context of our discourse can be seen from a perspective that is different from ours and the complementarity of these different perspectives are helpful in reaching a novel conclusion (Vessey n.d., s.p.). When this is done, we develop a new perception of the existing information or even acquire new information, thereby revaluating our previous conclusions, becoming aware of the weaknesses of our previous conclusions, gaining new understanding of our discourse, and ultimately fusing our horizon with the horizon of others as coparticipants in the discourse (Ibid.). Therefore, at the end of the discourse, we minimize the weaknesses of our previous conclusions, improve our previous understanding, and form new perspectives. Consequently, the previously limited horizon becomes a broadened horizon (Ibid.).

Gadamer (1989) says, "[I]t requires a special effort to acquire a historical horizon" (305). Therefore, fusion of horizons is a difficult task. It is human nature to highly value our position, and in view of this high valuation of our position, it is also human nature to want to hold on to our stance even when we are confronted with more valuable values that logically refute our stance. Unless we are aware that we are fallible, and our position is logically refutable, we may not be conscious that our position is not, cannot be, and ought not to be absolute. What is true of our position is also true of the position of the other. Nonabsoluteness applies not only to our position but also to the position of the other. Therefore, fusion of horizons encourages us neither to jettison our position in favor of the position of the other nor to jettison the position of the other in favor of ours. Working with the assumption that both positions are reasonable—that is the positions contain certain plausible and positive elements that are worth fusing—fusion of horizons demands that we fuse both positions. In this sense, the fusion of horizons operating principle is that neither of the positions is so worthless to the extent that it does not contain any plausible or positive elements that is worth fusing with the other position (Abumere 2015b, 36–37).

There are many criticisms of the Gadamerian conception of fusion of horizons. Eric Donald Hirsch's (1967) criticism seems to be the most potent among the criticisms. Hirsch contends that the Gadamerian concept of horizon negates the possibility of any fusion of horizons. He asserts that a reader cannot fuse his or her own horizon and that of the text together. For this fusion to be possible, the reader must have comprehended the original perspective of the text and integrated the perspective into his or her own perspective. Since fusion of horizons is impossible unless the reader has already comprehended the original perspective of the text, and since once the reader has already comprehended the original perspective of the text that perspective automatically becomes part and parcel of the reader's own perspective, then fusion of horizons is impossible (Abumere 2015b, 36–38).

Hirsch argues that "if the original perspective of the text is beyond our horizon, then we cannot understand the text. If this is the case, then fusion of horizons is impossible. As long as we are limited by our own horizon, then we cannot break the barrier of this limitedness in order to fuse our horizon with that of the text" (Abumere 2015b, 38). For Hirsch, to argue that the reader can break the barrier of the aforementioned limitedness in order to fuse his or her horizon with the horizon of the text is equivalent to arguing that the reader was not in the first place limited at all. If so, then there was no horizon in the first place (Hirsch 1967, 254).

In spite of the apparent potency of Hirsch's criticism of Gadamer, the former would have been right and the latter would have been wrong if the latter used horizon in the ordinary language sense of the word. However, as Husserl (1990) did in his phenomenology as already explained earlier, Gadamer reconceptualizes horizon—as already explained—to play a technical role in his hermeneutics. Just as Husserl does not place emphasis on the ordinary-language meaning of horizon as a limit, so also Gadamer does not place emphasis on the ordinary-language meaning of horizon as a limit. Rather, Gadamer places emphasis on the technical or philosophical meaning of horizon "as that which we can enlarge, as that which gives us pointers to something else and somewhere else and as that which we can go outside of in order to reach some new place" (Abumere 2015b, 38). Moreover,

the "horizon" is the larger context of meaning in which any particular meaningful presentation is situated. Inasmuch as understanding is taken to involve a "fusion of horizons", then so it always involves the formation of a new context of meaning that enables integration of what is otherwise unfamiliar, strange or anomalous. In this respect, all understanding involves a process of mediation and dialogue between what is familiar and what is alien in which neither remains unaffected. (Malpas 2009, 32)

Therefore, although horizon denotes or connotes the reader's particular limit at a particular time and place—that is, within a given spatio-temporal circumstance—it neither confines the reader to that limit nor eliminates any possibility of the reader transcending that limit to a boundless milieu. It recognizes that the reader has the opportunity within space and time—that is, the spatio-temporal potential—to walk ahead and see further (Vessey n.d., s.p.).

Fusion of horizons passes the test of Hirsch's criticism in the sense that there is no infusibility problem with the Gadamerian conception of fusion of horizons. Even if there is an infusibility problem in the sense in which Hirsch understands it, this will not negate the essence of the Gadamerian conception of fusion of horizons; it will only show the limitation of the Gadamerian conception of fusion of horizons. Moreover, on the one hand, unlike Hirsch, I do not conceive of fusion of horizons in the ordinary-language sense of the concept. On the other hand, like Gadamer, I conceive of fusion of horizons in the technical or philosophical sense of the concept. Nevertheless, I do not take Gadamer's conception to be dogmatic.

Within the AU, the ultimate result of fusion of horizons is the acceptance of norms that will govern the relationships and interactions among member states. When, simultaneously, AU member states are bounded together by norms and their relations and interactions are bound by norms, then they will do away with the realist-rationalist fundamentalism that is characterized by the epistemic conception of states as ontologically self-interested and self-regarding actors (Abumere 2019b, s.p.). Instead of the aforementioned realist-rationalist fundamentalism or the epistemic conception of states as ontologically self-interested and self-regarding actors, a constructivist conception of AU member states as other-regarding members of the AU may emerge. As an other-regarding member of the AU, a member state will be amenable to behaving in standards that the AU and other members deem to be appropriate (Ibid.).

In African regional relations, norms will serve as "collective expectations for the proper behavior of actors with a given identity" (Katzenstein 1996, 5). In other words, in African regional relations, norms will serve as "generalized standards of conduct that delineate the scope of" an actor's "entitlements, the extent of its obligations, and the range of its jurisdiction" (Raymond 1997, 126). I concede that "[t]here is no general agreement on whether norms extensively and ubiquitously shape the behaviour of actors in international politics, and likewise we do not know to what extent norms shape the behaviour of actors in international politics" (Abumere 2019b, s.p.). However, I am sanguine that even though not always to a large extent, at least to some extent norms constrain the behavior of actors "in international politics just as law, morality or norm constrains the behavior of individual members of society" (Ibid.).

In the AU, when member states choose to abide by norms, this does not mean that they will cease to pursue goals that they are interested in. While they will still pursue their goals, the means they will use to achieve the goals will no longer inevitably be mere self-regarding and other-disregarding (Abumere 2019b, s.p.)—that is, considering only their own interests even when pursuing such interests is detrimental to other member states. For example, when member states abide by norms, they will not inevitably rely "on materialist means or hard power" (Ibid.). Furthermore, they will "not see materialist means or hard power as the only means to achieve goals everywhere and at all times" (Ibid.). In regional relations, while member states of the AU "may rely on material means or hard power somewhere and sometimes," in view of normative international politics they will be "willing to achieve their goals by other means, namely norms" (Ibid). Ultimately, the "willingness to achieve goals through norms is what makes the realistic resolution (Ibid.) of the problem of discrimination against migrants possible.

AFRICAN UNION'S NORMATIVE ENDEAVORS

Having discussed fusion of horizons as a mechanism that can midwife normative international relations in the AU, I shall acknowledge the endeavors the AU has already made and is still making to protect migrants through normative international relations, and political and legal frameworks. As I mentioned in the third chapter, the AU has been moving toward the free movement of goods, services, capital, and persons in a bid to achieve a comprehensive regional integration. In January 2018, the AU introduced both the AfCFTA and the FMP. Recently, in April 2019, the establishment of the AfCFTA came into effect. In addition to AfCFTA, building on similar arrangements at the subregions, such as the ECOWAS, the SADC, the EAC, and so on, in early 2018, the AU's "Assembly of Heads of State and Government adopted the Protocol to the Treaty Establishing the African Economic Community Relating to the Free Movement of Persons, Right of Residence and Right of Establishment (the Free Movement Protocol)" (Sharpe 2020, s.p.).

This shows that, as I mentioned in the third chapter, that the AU is committed to a comprehensive regional integration and has taken important steps to realize it. Moreover, in 2016, the AU

decided to move towards a "borderless" Africa with seamless intracontinental migration. The bloc created a single continental passport and gave it first to national leaders, with a plan to distribute it more widely and enable Africans to move around the continent without a visa. Two years later, the effort was codified in the AU Protocol on Free Movement of Persons. (Okunade 2021, s.p.; emphasis in original)

In late 2019, the AU assessed the implementation progress of the FMP and reported that thirty-three states have signed the FMP Protocol—"[m]issing among the signatories to the FMP were all the North African countries; nearly half of the SADC countries, including Namibia, Botswana, South Africa, and Zambia; Ethiopia in the horn of Africa; Nigeria in West Africa; and Cameroon in Central Africa" (Hirsh 2020, 3).

However, since the FMP is required to be ratified by fifteen states for it to come into force, the AU still has a long way to go to get the required ratifications because only four states, namely Mali, Niger, Sao Tone and Principe in West Africa and Rwanda in East Africa have ratified it.

The hesitance to commit to the FMP Protocol points to a range of concerns about giving up sovereign protections regarding the movement of people and about the implementation plan for the Protocol. There are concerns about the impact of higher levels of immigration on the domestic economic and security environments. In general terms, because of the design of the Protocol and its accompanying "Roadmap," ratification of the treaty could be interpreted to entail the virtually immediate implementation of Phase One, "the right of entry and abolition of visa requirements" in regard to all countries which have concluded the ratification process. (Hirsh 2020, 3)

In spite of the aforementioned hesitation to commit to the FMP Protocol, the African Charter on Human and Peoples' Rights (the Banjul Charter) and the FMP Protocol still serve as political and legal frameworks (the Banjul Charter more so than the FMP protocol) for the protection of migrants. The Banjul Charter established an African Commission on Human and Peoples' Rights, which came into force on 2nd November 1987 "to promote human and peoples' rights and ensure their protection in Africa." Article 2, Chapter 1, of the Banjul Charter stipulates that "[e]very individual shall be entitled to the enjoyment of the rights and freedoms recognized and guaranteed in the present Charter without distinction of any kind such as race, ethnic group, color, sex, language, religion, political or any other opinion, national and social origin, fortune, birth or other status." While Article 19 of the same chapter says, "All peoples shall be equal; they shall enjoy the same respect and shall have the same rights. Nothing shall justify the domination of a people by another."

Furthermore, Paragraph 4, Article 12, Chapter 1, of the Banjul Charter stipulates that "[a] non-national legally admitted in a territory of a State Party to the present Charter, may only be expelled from it by virtue of a decision taken in accordance with the law." While Paragraph 5, Article 12, of the same chapter says, "The mass expulsion of non-nationals shall be prohibited. Mass expulsion shall be that which is aimed at national, racial, ethnic or religious groups." Then, Article 28, Chapter 2, says, "Every individual shall have the duty to respect and consider his fellow beings without discrimination, and to maintain relations aimed at promoting, safeguarding and reinforcing mutual respect and tolerance."

Paragraph 1, Article 4, of the FMP Protocol says that "[s]tate Parties shall not discriminate against nationals of another Member State entering, residing or established in their territory, on the basis of their nationality." While Paragraph 1, Article 6, of the FMP Protocol says, "In accordance with this Protocol, nationals of a Member State shall have the right to enter, stay, move freely and exit the territory of another Member State in accordance with the laws, regulations and procedures of the host Member State." Then, Paragraph 1, Article 16, says, "Nationals of a member State shall have the right of residence in the territory of any Member State in accordance with the laws of the host Member State." Paragraph 3 of the same Article says, "States Parties shall gradually implement *favourable* policies and laws on residence for nationals of other Member States" (emphasis mine).

In addition, Paragraph 1, Article 17, of the FMP Protocol stipulates that "[n]ationals of a Member State shall have the right of establishment within the territory of another Member State in accordance with the laws and policies of the host Member State." Paragraph 2 of the same Article says, "The right of establishment shall include the right to set up in the territory of the host Member State: (a) a business, trade, profession, vocation; or (b) an economic activity as a self-employed person." While Paragraph 1, Article 20, says, "The mass expulsion of non-nationals shall be prohibited."

A BRIEF RECAPITULATION

I have been arguing for normative international relations among African states as a realistic resolution to the problem of domination of, and discrimination against, migrants. Normative international relations has the potential to lead to a more comprehensive and effective AU. So it is not far-fetched to think that normative international relations among African states may make many of the seemingly intractable problems on the continent more tractable. One of such problems is discrimination against minorities, especially migrants.

In the fifth chapter, I presented one way of resolving the problem of domination and discrimination, while in chapter 8 I shall present another way. In the fifth chapter, the resolution I prescribed is strategic alliances and balance of power. I conceded that ultimately, normatively, a human rights framework and a minority rights framework should be the long run possible resolution because they are more sustainable and more acceptable than strategic alliances and balance of power. However, I prescribed strategic alliances and balance of power as the short run realistic resolution because pragmatically they are easier to adhere to than a human rights and minority rights framework. Therefore, adopting strategic alliances and balance of power in the short run creates space and time for us to work toward a rights framework in the long run.

Beginning with this chapter and ending with chapter 8, I untangle the relationship between normative international relations and realism and statism, internationalism, and cosmopolitanism and idealism within the context of human rights (individual human rights) and group rights (minority rights) protection in international politics and global politics in a globalized world. Then, I show how to navigate through the turbulent waves or troubled waters of international and global politics, and through the undulating terrain of regional integration diplomacy within the vicissitudes of globalization in order to arrive at an AU that guarantees protection of minorities and migrants.

In chapter 8, I make three proposals. First, I propose that, in Africa, based on the principle of pluralism, national, subregional, and regional (and even global governance) systems should work in concert (Woods et al. 2013, 2) to protect the minority rights of migrants. Second, I propose that, based on the principle of subsidiarity, when the national, subregional, and regional (and even global governance) systems are working in concert, matters of the minority rights of migrants should be dealt with by the lowest authority or closest authority to the migrants that is most efficient and capable of dealing with the matters. In other words, "[I]ssues ought to be addressed at the lowest level capable of addressing them . . . some problems can be handled well and efficiently at the local, national, sub-regional and regional levels reducing the number of issues that need to be tackled at the international and supranational level" (United Nations 2014, s.p.). Third, I propose that the national, subregional and regional (and even global governance) systems should respect what I refer to as the principle of violation and responsibility. This principle presupposes a negative duty of no harm, a positive duty of remedy, and the notion of commensurability.

REFERENCES

Abumere, Frank Aragbonfoh. 2015a. "Context as the Principal Determinant of the Behaviour of States in Global Politics." *International Journal of Peace and Conflict Studies* 2, no. 3: 57–68.

Abumere, Frank Aragbonfoh. 2015b. *Different Perspectives on Global Justice: A Fusion of Horizons*. Bielefeld: PUB—Publication at Bielefeld University.

Abumere, Frank Aragbonfoh. 2019a. "World Government, Social Contract and Legitimacy." *Philosophical Papers* 48, no. 1: 9–30.

Abumere, Frank Aragbonfoh. 2019b. "Norms." In *The Palgrave Encyclopedia of Global Security Studies*, edited by Scott N. Romaniuk, Manish Thapa and Péter Marton. Cham: Palgrave Macmillan.

Abumere, Frank Aragbonfoh. 2020. "Introducing Normativity in African International Politics." *Politikon: South African Journal of Political Studies* 47, no. 3: 342–60.

African (Banjul) Charter on Human and Peoples' Rights (Adopted 27 June 1981, OAU Doc.CAB/LEG/67/3 rev. 5, 21 I.L.M. 58 (1982), entered into force 21 October 1986).

Benhabib, Seyla. 2004. *The Rights of Others: Aliens, Residents, and Citizens.* Cambridge: Cambridge University Press.

Bull, Hedley. 2002. *The Anarchical Society: A Study of Order in World Politics*, third edition. London: Palgrave.

Clapham, Christopher S. 1996. *Africa and the International System: The Politics of State Survival.* Cambridge: Cambridge University Press.

Finney, Patrick. 2005. "Introduction: What is International History." In Palgrave Advances in International History. Ed. Patrick Finney. London: Palgrave: 1–35.

Gadamer, Hans-Georg. 1989. *Truth and Method.* New York: Crossroad.

Gadamer, Hans-Georg. 1997. "Reflections on My Philosophical Journey." In *The Philosophy of Hans-Georg Gadamer*, edited by Lewis Edwin Hahn, 3–63. Peru, IL: Open Court.

Heidegger, Martin. 1982. *The Basic Problems of Phenomenology.* Bloomington: Indiana University Press.

Heidegger, Martin. 1996. *Being and Time.* Stambaugh, J. (trans.). Albany, SUNY Press.

Held, David. 2002. "Law of States, Law of Peoples: Three Models of Sovereignty." *Legal Theory* 8, no. 1: 1–44.

Hirsch, Jr., Eric Donald. 1967. *Validity in Interpretation.* New Haven: Yale University Press.

Hirsh, Alan. 2020. "A Strategic Consideration of the African Union Free Movement of Persons Protocol and Other Initiatives Towards the Freer Movement of People in Africa." South African Institute of International affairs, University of the Witwatersrand, Johannesburg.

Husserl, Edmund. 1973[1931]. *Cartesian Meditations.* Den Hague: Martinus Nijhoff.

Husserl, Edmund. 1990[1913]. *Ideas.* Dordrecht: Kluwer Academic Publishers.

Katzenstein, Peter J. 1996. "Introduction: Alternative Perspectives on National Security." In *The Culture of National Security: Norms and Identity in World Politics*, edited by Peter J. Katzenstein, 1–27. New York: Columbia University Press.

Mafeje, Achie. 2008[2000]. "Africanity: A Combative Ontology." *CODESRIA Bulletin 3rd and 4th*: 106–10.

Malpas, Jeff. 2009. "Hans-Georg Gadamer." *Stanford Encyclopaedia of Philosophy*, Spring edition. https://plato. stanford.edu/entries/gadamer/

Okunade, Samuel. 2021. "Africa Moves towards Intracontinental Free Movement for Its Booming Population." Migration Information Source, Migration Policy Institute, January 21, 2021. https://www.migrationpolicy.org/article/africa-intracontinental -free-movement

Protocol to the Treaty establishing the African Economic Community relating to the Free Movement of Persons, Right of Residence, and Right of Establishment (FMP Protocol), African Union (AU) Commission, Addis Ababa, Ethiopia, January 2018.

Raymond, Gregory A. 1997. "Neutrality Norms and the Balance of Power." *Cooperation and Conflict* 32, no. 2: 123–46.

Rosenberg, Emily S. 2004. "Considering Borders." In *Explaining the History of American Foreign Relations*, second edition, edited by Michael J. Hogan and Thomas G. Peterson, 176–93. Cambridge: Cambridge University Press.

Sharpe, Marina. 2020. "The Free Movement of Persons with the African Union and Refugee Protection." *RefLaw*, May 25, 2020. https://reflaw.org/the-free-movement -of-persons-within-the-african-union-and-refugee-protection/

Steinmo, Sven. 2008. "Historical Institutionalism." In *Approaches and Methodologies in the Social Sciences: A Pluralist Perspective*, edited by Donatella Della Porta and Michael Keating, 118–38. Cambridge University Press, Cambridge, 2008.

Tieku, Thomas Kwasi. 2013. "Theoretical Approaches to Africa's International Relations." In *Handbook of Africa's International Relations*, edited by Tim Muruthi, 11–20. New York: Routledge.

United Nations (UN). 2014. "Global Governance and Global Rules for Development in the Post-2015 Era." Committee for Development Policy, Department of Economic and Social Affairs, New York.

Vessey, David. n.d. "Gadamer and the Fusion of Horizons." Accessed: June 8, 2013. https://www. davevessey.com/gadamer_Horizons.htm.

Waldron, Jeremy. 2000. "What is Cosmopolitan?." *The Journal of Political Philosophy* 8, no. 2: 227–43.

Wendt, Alexander. 1992. "Anarchy is What States Make of It: The Social Construction of Power Politics." *International Organization* 46, no. 2: 391–425.

Wendt, Alexander. 1993. *Social Theory of International Politics*. Cambridge: Cambridge University Press.

Woods, Ngaire, Alexander Betts, Jochen Prantl, and Devi Sridhar. 2013. "Transforming Global Governance for the 21st Century." Occasional Paper 2013/09, UNDP Human Development Report Office, September 2013. http://hdr.undp.org/sites/ default/files/hdro_1309_woods.pdf, Accessed: June 19, 2017.

NOTE

1. I am indebted and grateful to the reviewer for this comment and the entire observation in this paragraph and in the next paragraph. It is due to the observation that I embark on the twofold task in this chapter and in chapter 8. In other words, the consciousness and admission which spur me to embark on the tasks stems from the reviewer's observation. So, I owe such consciousness and admission to the reviewer.

Chapter Eight

Future of Normative International Relations in Africa

I shall begin by reiterating that there is a plethora of discrimination against minorities and migrants on the continent (and of course, outside the continent). From Algeria to Zimbabwe, the African continent is littered with horrible cases of minority discrimination. The violation of the group rights of minorities is one of the tragedies of the continent. When the violation of the rights of minorities is coupled with the violation of the human rights and group rights of migrants, then we have an even greater tragedy.

The aforementioned violations should prompt us to revisit the question of how to protect adequately or guarantee effectively the rights (both the international human rights and the minority rights) of minorities and migrants (especially children) in a world that is simultaneously Westphalian, international, and global. Corresponding to the Westphalian, international, and global nature of the world, there are three models of rights regimes—namely, the statist model, the internationalist model, and the cosmopolitan model. The statist and internationalist models are largely the reality of the world, while the cosmopolitan model largely represents an aspiration. That is because the Westphalian system that divides the world into sovereign geographical territories and the international system that coordinates the competition and cooperation among the sovereign geographical territories are not only the order of the day but also the most consequential political phenomena in our world. Consequently, rights regimes either work within these systems or justify why they have to work outside the systems. In this chapter, I concede that any *realistic* approach to the problem of minority rights must accommodate the statist and internationalist models. Simultaneously, I concede that the cosmopolitan model is the *ideal* model for the protection of the minority rights of children. Therefore, I reconcile the three models and then propose a realistic approach to minority rights.

THE STATIST AND INTERNATIONALIST MODELS

The statist model "gives the state free reign in the constitution of political and economic relations" (Held 2002, 1). The internationalist model "seeks to delimit political power and extend the liberal concern with limited government to the international sphere" (Ibid.). While the cosmopolitan model "conceives international law as a system of public law which properly circumscribes not just political power but all forms of social power" (Ibid.). Corresponding to these three models of sovereignty, there are three models of rights—namely, statist, internationalist, and cosmopolitan (Donnelly 2007, 30). Some people hold the view that legitimacy resides inside the state, and outside the state, there is no legitimacy. If this view is correct, then it seems the only legitimate model of rights will be the statist.

I concede that the major sources of state legitimacy—consent, beneficial consequences, democratic approval, and public reason—may be "thicker" in the sovereign state and "thinner" in the international society and the global institutional order. There is no agreed-on particular threshold that must be reached before legitimacy can be considered to be present outside the sovereign state. On the grounds of the thickness and thinness of legitimacy, it is wrong to conclude that legitimacy is present in the sovereign state and absent outside the sovereign state. The correct question to ask is to what extent is legitimacy outside the state. Whether legitimacy is present to a larger extent or to a lesser extent outside the state, the implication is that at least legitimacy is extendable to the international society and the global institutional order. Consequently, the statist model of rights is not the only legitimate model.

However, the traditional, de facto, de jure, and most prominent model is the statist model. From the Universal Declaration on Human Rights (UDHR), to the International Covenant on Civil and Political Rights (ICCPR), to the International Covenant on Economic, Social and Cultural Rights (ICESCR), to the UNCRC, to other major, minor, and regional declarations and covenants, the state is taken to be the guarantor of rights. This statist conception of rights is at least partly due to the realist understanding of international politics as an anarchical realm devoid of hierarchy—that is, a nonhierarchical international world where states are the only principal and significant actors.

Contra realists, (neo)liberals have argued that states are not the only important actors in global politics. They argue that other actors such as MNCs/2, supranational organizations, and so on, and certain other institutions, are also relevant or important actors in global politics. Moreover, there are factual claims that MNCs such as Alphabet Inc., Apple, Microsoft, and so on have more influence than states such as Chad, Niger, Togo, and so on. Therefore, states—if ever they were the only guarantors, obligors, and enforcers of human rights and minority rights—are no longer the exclusive guarantors, obligors, and enforcers of human rights (Donnelly 2007, 30) and minority rights.

While it is true that states are not the only actors and are not the only significant or important actors in global politics, it is also true that largely they are still the most important actors in the twenty-first century. But the important point is that statists, except extreme statists or those we may call hardcore statists, have come to accept that although, by and large, states remain the most important actors at the international realm in the twenty-first century, states are not the only important actors. Some statists acquiesce that there are other significant actors at the international arena, and some statists accept that individual human rights and minority rights do not have to do with states alone. Nevertheless, generally, statists conclude that "there is no significant, independent international community, and certainly no international body with the right to act on behalf of [individual] human rights" (Donnelly 2007, 30) and minority rights. In other words, while they agree that there is an international system at the international arena, they disagree that that international system constitutes "much of an international society" (Ibid.).

Based primarily on the principle of sovereignty, and secondarily on the consequent principle of noninterference, the statist model conceives of individual human rights and minority rights in the following two senses. First, as claims that citizens, residents, others, and groups who are within the geographical and jurisdictional territory of a particular state have against such a state. Second, as duties or obligations that such a state owes its citizens, residents, others, and groups who are within its geographical and jurisdictional territory. Statists insist that individual human rights and minority rights "remain primarily a matter of sovereign national and (ought to continue to be) a largely peripheral concern of international (interstate) relations" (Donnelly 2007, 30).

Although the statist model has been, and still is, the predominant model, not just in the protection of (individual) human rights but also in the protection of (group) minority rights, the limitation of this model is beginning to dawn on the international community. In this vein, the OSCE (1991) affirmed that the discrimination against minorities and minority rights matters are too important to be left to domestic politics alone, for they are "matters of legitimate international concern and consequently do not constitute exclusively an internal affair of the respective State" (chap. II, para. 3)

The internationalist model is middle-of-the-road between the statist model and the cosmopolitan model (Donnelly 2007, 30). As a middle-of-the-road model, internationalism tends to be moderate when put on the same spectrum with statism and cosmopolitanism. In addition, as a middle-of-the-road model on the same spectrum with statism and cosmopolitanism, internationalism can tend either toward statism or toward cosmopolitanism. When it tends toward cosmopolitanism, we have a weak internationalism; when it tends toward statism, we have a strong internationalism (Ibid.); and when it tends toward neither cosmopolitanism nor statism but rather sits perfectly in between the two, then we have a moderate internationalism.

For the internationalists, the international arena is not just a mere international system where states—at least to some extent—behave as part of a whole due to their engagements, contacts, or interactions with one another being systemic to, at least, a reasonable extent. In other words, it is not a mere system of states where "two or more states have sufficient contact between them, and have sufficient impact on one another's decisions, to cause them to behave—at least in some measure—as parts of a whole" (Bull 2002, 9). Rather, the international arena is an international society or a society of states (Donnelly 2007, 30). The international society "exists when a group of states, conscious of certain common interests and common values, form a society in the sense that they conceive themselves to be bound by a common set of rules in their relations with one another, and share in the working of common institutions" (Bull 2002, 13).

For the internationalist, the international society, which "is essentially the society of states" (Donnelly 2007, 30), is crucially supplemented by international actors such as NGOs and individuals, to the extent that they have been formally or informally incorporated into international political processes (Ibid.). In this international model, although "norms . . . may vary considerably" (Ibid.) given whether we have a moderate, weak, or strong internationalism, more importantly, international individual human rights and minority rights activities are "permissible only to the extent authorised by the norms of the society of states" (Ibid.).

Some commentators say that the human rights regime is at the heart of the internationalist model (Held 2002, 9). Nevertheless, the model is inadequate due to the "circumstances of cosmopolitanism" (Waldron 2000, 236–39)— "the background conditions and presuppositions that inform and motivate the case for a cosmopolitan framework of law and sovereignty . . . [i.e.] the processes and forces of globalisation that increasingly enmesh us in overlapping communities of fate" (Held 2002, 23).

THE COSMOPOLITAN MODEL

The statist and internationalist models are state centric, while the cosmopolitan model is person centric. Unlike the statist and internationalist models, the starting point of the cosmopolitan model is not states but individuals. This is the case because the primary focus of cosmopolitanism is the individual rather than states or organizations. The centrality of cosmopolitanism in general and moral cosmopolitanism in particular is the well-being of the individual, and the tenets of cosmopolitanism are individualism, universality, and generality (Pogge 2008, 175). The postulation of individualism is that "the ultimate units of concern are human beings or persons" (Ibid.). The postulation of universalism is that "the status of ultimate unit of concern attaches to every living human being equally" (Ibid.). While the postulation of generality is that "this special status has global force. Persons are ultimate units of concern for everyone" (Ibid.).

In view of the primary focus, centrality, and tenets of cosmopolitanism, it can be argued that minority rights, conceived of as universal moral claims rather than as mere legal claims, seem better suited to a cosmopolitan conception of world politics (Donnelly 2007, 30). In this conception of world politics, individuals, persons, or human beings are seen less as members of a particular polis—citizens of a particular state—and more as members of the universal cosmopolis—citizens of a global political community (Ibid.).

However, the cosmopolitan model is not without its attendant limitations. For instance, if I were to adopt legal cosmopolitanism rather than moral cosmopolitanism, I would be charged with clamoring for a world government or a world state, because legal cosmopolitanism "is committed to a concrete political ideal of a global order under which all persons have equivalent legal rights and duties—are fellow citizens of a universal republic" (Pogge 2008, 175). Legal cosmopolitanism is quite unfeasible and problematic because it tends toward a world government with serious negative consequences (Kant 1991; Rawls 1999, 36). In addition, it tends toward seeing individual human rights and minority rights as mere legal phenomena.

If our main concern is with how the conception and enforcement of minority rights ought to be, then we have to go beyond mere legality and focus more on morality. This journey, taking us from legal cosmopolitanism, leads us to moral cosmopolitanism. The latter does not necessarily negate the former. The latter may oppose or support the former depending on "certain empirical circumstances" (Pogge 2008, 175). The latter is more abstract, while the former is more concrete; and the latter—due to its abstractness—is weaker than the former, and in turn, the former—due to its concreteness—is stronger than the latter (Ibid.).

If moral cosmopolitanism—as explained in its central idea—is mainly concerned with individuals, of what use is it to minority rights when the greater threat to minority rights is not from individuals as such but from institutions that are far more powerful than individuals? While individuals are the central focus of moral cosmopolitanism, it nevertheless focuses on institutions too. However, the focus on institutions is not for the sake of the institutions; institutions are focused on to ensure that they do not harm human beings and to ensure that they promote the well-being of human beings. In this sense, moral cosmopolitanism can be interactional or institutional depending on "the nature of the moral constraints to be imposed" (Pogge 2008, 176).

On the one hand, in interactional moral cosmopolitanism, individuals and collective agents have "direct responsibility for the fulfilment of human rights" (Pogge 2008, 176). In this sense, individuals and collective agents are the obligors, protectors, and enforcers of minority rights—that is, they are the ones who have the duty to respect the individual human right and minority right claims of other individuals. On the other hand, in institutional moral cosmopolitanism, the responsibility to respect individual human right claims and minority right claims is assigned to institutions (Ibid.). These two conceptions of moral cosmopolitanism are not mutually exclusive. In fact, the "institutional and interactional conceptions are compatible and thus may be combined in a mutually complementary way" (Ibid.). Therefore, the obligors, protectors, and enforcers of the minority rights of racial, ethnic, religious, and linguistic minority children will be neither individuals and collectives alone nor organizations and states alone, but both the latter and the former.

In terms of the violations of individual human rights and minority rights, my analysis neither deals with interactional factors alone nor deals with institutional factors alone, but both factors. Hence, rather than employ either interactional moral cosmopolitanism alone or institutional moral cosmopolitanism alone, I employ both conceptions in my analysis. This is of double advantage because in view of the interactional conception, individual human rights and minority rights "impose constraints on conduct," and in view of the institutional conception, individual human rights and minority rights "impose constraints, in the first instance, upon shared practices" (Pogge 2008, 176). Therefore, in our social world, cosmopolitanism imposes interactional and institutional constraints on conducts and practices that harm the well-being and well-becoming of racial, ethnic, religious, and linguistic minority children.

RECONCILING THE STATIST, INTERNATIONALIST, AND COSMOPOLITAN MODELS

Having already discussed the statist and the internationalist models in the penultimate section, in the preceding section I explained why the cosmopolitan model is preferable to the statists and the internationalist models. In this section, I will reconcile the three models. There are three ways to look at the three models. First, we can look at them as descriptive models describing the nature or situation of the conception and enforcement of individual human rights (Donnelly 2007, 30) and minority rights in our world. Second, we can look at them as prescriptive models prescribing what the conception and enforcement of individual human rights (Ibid.) and minority rights in our world ought to be—that is, how we should conceive and enforce rights. Third, we can simultaneously look at them as both descriptive and prescriptive. In this sense, they simultaneously tell us what the conception and enforcement of rights in our world is and what it ought to be.

Between the three models, the statist model has the most descriptive power. As earlier mentioned, the UDHR, ICCPR, ICESCR, UNCRC, and other major, minor, and regional declarations and covenants conceive of the state as the principal obligor, protector, and enforcer of rights. On the one hand, Jack Donnelly (2007) says that the "rights reality that we face today is one of considerable state sovereignty, with modest limits rooted principally in the international society of states" (31). This reality is true of minority rights. In this case, it seems that while statism has the most descriptive power, internationalism is the next in line, and cosmopolitanism is relegated to the bottom. On the other hand, Donnelly argues that "some sort of internationalist model—or a very heavily hedged statism—provides the most accurate description of the place of . . . rights in contemporary international relations" (Ibid.). In other words, for Donnelly, "[A] relatively weak internationalist model, with modest international societal constraints on state sovereignty, describes the nature of the contemporary international politics of . . . rights and is likely to continue to do so for at least the next several years" (Ibid.).

Moreover, there are existing positive and negative phenomena that favor the statist model and the internationalist model, respectively. On the positive side, for instance, the existence of regionalism, quintessentially the European Union, is a case that supports the internationalist model. On the negative side, certain phenomena negate the cosmopolitan model but support the statist model. For instance, the emergence of Donald Trump in the United States, and the resurgence or surge of nationalism in parts of Europe such as Austria, France, Germany, Hungary, Italy, Poland, the Netherlands, and the United Kingdom (BREXIT).

However, that statism and internationalism are currently faring better than cosmopolitanism in terms of descriptive power does not necessarily mean that they will always fare better, or they will fare better in the future (Donnelly 2007, 31). More importantly, it does not necessarily mean that the statist model or the internationalist model, rather than the cosmopolitan model, "is the best, or even a good, way to treat human rights [and minority rights] in international relations" (Ibid.) or in global politics. Moreover, "the universality of human rights fits uncomfortably with a political order structured around sovereign states" (30). For this reason, normatively and prescriptively, the cosmopolitan model—which reaches the heights of its powers when it comes to universality—is the *ideal* for the protection of the minority rights of migrants.

In principle or in theory, Africa's approach to the protection of the minority rights of migrants can mainly be described as normative and prescriptive rather than descriptive. However, realistically or in practice, Africa cannot afford to eschew descriptiveness. Nevertheless, opting for prescriptiveness does not necessarily mean entirely eschewing descriptiveness. What it means is that descriptiveness can be employed at the service of prescriptiveness. Given this approach, the statist and internationalist models are conceptually and normatively inadequate. Due to their universal nature, the minority rights of migrants in particular and individual human rights in general do not fit comfortably "with a political order structured around sovereign states" (Donnelly 2007, 30). By virtue of their universality, the minority rights of migrants transcend the territorial boundaries of sovereign states. These rights are universal rights whose holders transcend the boundaries of sovereign states; correspondingly, its obligors transcend sovereign states. Here, the term *universal* does not refer to human rights that all persons possess—that is, universal individual rights that all persons possess—by virtue of being human. Rather, it refers to group rights that all migrants possess by virtue of being minorities and migrants.

I have shown that since the cosmopolitan model reaches the heights of its powers when it comes to normativeness and prescriptiveness, therefore the cosmopolitan model is the *ideal* for the protection of the minority rights of migrants. However, let me reiterate that even at the height of its normative and prescriptive power, the cosmopolitan model has its limitations. The limitations are evidently of serious concern if we adopt legal cosmopolitanism. Since what I recommend is moral cosmopolitanism, the limitations may not appear to be of serious concern. Yet even moral cosmopolitanism lacks the practical force of statism and internationalism. In other words, as the morally ideal model, the cosmopolitan model possesses a theoretical force that the other models lack. Nevertheless, it lacks the practical force that the other models have because the other models are more in tune with the practical realities of international and global politics.

In summary, the cosmopolitan model is idealistic, while the statist and internationalist models are realistic. On the one hand, that the cosmopolitan model is idealistic does not mean that it is feasible. It only means that it is the morally preferred model. On the other hand, that the statist and the internationalist models are not the morally preferred models does not mean that they have no usability whatsoever. It only means that although they are useful, they are still less morally preferable to the cosmopolitan model. Although the cosmopolitan model is the ideal, the other models are the status quo. While it is desirable to move from the status quo to the ideal, it is also important to know that any approach that disregards the status quo is likely to be a project in futility. Therefore, to combine the three models, I propose the principle of subsidiarity as the organizing principle of the global governance of human rights in our Westphalian, internationalist, and global world.

The principle of subsidiarity, as Samanthan Besson (2016) aptly says, "is *en vogue* in international human rights law" (70). Its origin can be traced back to Aristotle, Thomas Aquinas, and Johannes Althusius (Feichtner 2007). Pope Leo XIII's Rerum Novarum, Pope Pius XI's Quadragesimo Anno (Carlen 1981), and post-Cold War (unified) Germany contributed to the development of the principle. It came to prominence in 1991 when it was included as one of the key principles of the European Union's Maastricht Treaty and subsequently in Article 5.1 and 5.3 of the Lisbon Treaty. Some argue that several decisions of the Supreme Court of the United States also contributed to this prominence (Follesdal 2013, 37).

There are different traditions of subsidiarity that include Althusian, confederalist, economic federalism, Catholic personalism, and liberal contractualist (Follesdal 2013, 41–49). Essentially, the principle of subsidiarity regulates the allocation and use of authority in a political and legal order where there is dispersal of authority between a center and different units (37). In its most comprehensive conception, subsidiarity is

> a principle of justice that requires larger communities to protect the legitimate autonomy of smaller communities, to provide them with the assistance (subsidium) needed to fulfil their ends, and to co-ordinate and regulate their activities within the common good of the larger community, of which they are a part and which is also necessary to the flourishing of their individual members. (Carozza 2016, 53)

Therefore, subsidiarity is neither mere localism nor mere devolution, nor mere "utilitarian principle of efficiency in the allocation of powers" (Carozza 2016, 53).

Paolo Carozza (2003) argues that the basis of subsidiarity is neither contractual nor utilitarian, but rather personalistic (42). He means that the foundation of subsidiarity is that every human person inherently has an inalienable dignity, by virtue of which his or her value takes ontological and moral precedence over the state or other social groupings. Therefore, ultimately, the telos of every form of society, from the family to the state to the global institutional order, should be the enablement of the flourishing of the human person (Ibid.). In the same vein, the principle sees a world in which smaller communities are able to realize their telos by virtue of the support they receive from "larger" or "higher" groups, which they are part of, while a key duty of the "larger" or "higher" groups is to enable the smaller groups to realize their telos (43).

The aforementioned conception of subsidiarity has two implications for larger or higher groups; it simultaneously imposes on them a negative duty of restriction and a positive duty of provision. On the one hand, it restricts them from intervening or interfering in smaller groups when the latter are capable of fulfilling their telos without any aid from the former. On the other hand, it requires them to assist the smaller groups when the latter are incapable of fulfilling their telos without any aid. Therefore, subsidiarity is a paradox in the sense that simultaneously it limits the powers of larger or higher groups, yet empowers larger or higher groups; it limits their intervention, yet requires it; and it stipulates both negative and positive duties for larger or higher groups (Carozza 2003, 44). Deducing from the foregoing, subsidiarity requires a certain degree of normative coherence in the larger group for the larger group to be able to fulfil its functions (55). However, such normative coherence is absent due to the fragmentation of contemporary international law, which makes it lack the nested and pyramidal structure in subsidiarity's envisioned embedded society (57).

In the application of the principle of subsidiarity to international human rights law, we face a problem that has to do with the apparent tension between the affirmation of universal human dignity and the respect for the diversity and freedom of different cultures and societies (Carozza 2003, 38) whose views and practices may clash with the universal human dignity. In this vein, Leonard Besselink (1998) criticizes subsidiarity based on three desiderata (639, 668, 678). The first desideratum—the legal objection—says that, by creating room for pluralism, subsidiarity will weaken the "uniform and full effect" (678) of international human rights law. The second desideratum—the political objection—says that "the doctrine of legal and political pluralism would mean a definitive end to the doctrine of supra-nationalism, based as the latter is on a subaltern relationship" (Ibid.). While the third desideratum—the philosophical objection—says that, by creating room for pluralism, subsidiarity "is tantamount to positing that fundamental rights are not really fundamental rights; taken to its logical conclusion, the assertion means that rights are not rights at all" (Ibid.).

The philosophical objection is where the universality of human rights and the particularity of cultures are really at stake. The objection can be, and has been, rebutted in different ways. A prominent rebuttal is that the "fundamentalness" of human rights is based on the grounds that without human rights, both the dignity of the human person and the common good are unrealizable. Consequently, the "universality" of human rights is based on the grounds that without human rights, the realization of human dignity and the common good in every society will not be possible (Carozza 2003, 71–72; Perry 1998,

65). Therefore, the objection is an expression of Besselink's (1998) failure to understand the true meaning of the term *universal* in its role as an adjectival qualifier of "human rights." When the term *universal* is properly understood, the fact that different societies have different "particulars" and that these particulars ought to be accommodated in the application of human rights do not negate the universality of human rights (Stackhouse 1999).

Furthermore, it may be far-fetched to argue as Erhard Denninger (1999) does that as bearers of rights, human beings can only be properly understood in their "situatedness" as members of specific political orders, hence the necessary congruence between universal human rights and respect for pluralism. Put differently, "although the point of reference of human rights is every human being in general, as concrete subjects of rights those human beings can be understood only within particular legal orders and value systems" (Carozza 2003, 71). Nevertheless, John Finnis (1980) is apt to argue that although human rights are universal, in the application of human rights in different spatio-temporal societies, the particulars of those societies will definitely shape how the bearers of the rights are conceived and in turn what the rights mean to them (218–21).

Another problem we face in the application of the principle of subsidiarity to international human rights law is the incongruence between the state centricness of international law and the cosmopolitan normative individualism of human rights. According to Andreas Follesdal (2013), from the perspective of cosmopolitan normative individualism, some conceptions of subsidiarity are justifiable; however, such conceptions are not congruent with state-centric international law (55). He argues that subsidiarity is state centric—that is, states dominate other forms of societies, and the interests of the former dominate the interests of the latter and other concerns (41).

To paraphrase Finnis (1980), subsidiarity, in its state centricness, depends on states as the quintessential communities whose end is to promote the common good of human beings (members of a *polis*) and where the needs of such human beings or members are met (147–50). Included in this centrality is "the primacy of state consent in creating legal obligations and an understanding of the main social function of public international law as securing the interests of states" (Follesdal 2013, 55). Testament to this state-centric nature of international law is that "[s]tates remain dominant masters of treaties: They enjoy veto rights, and immunity except in areas explicitly agreed. Treaties only bind states that have agreed to do so" (55).

Two doctrines engender the centrality of states in international law and in the application of the principle of subsidiarity. These doctrines are restrictive interpretation and margin of appreciation. In international law, the "doctrine of restrictive interpretation in favour of state sovereignty entailed that treaties should be interpreted so as to minimize the restrictions on state sovereignty"

(57). The problem is not that treaties never benefit individual persons; one can even argue that treaties are likely to benefit individuals who are members of liberal democracies where respect for international human rights is sacrosanct. However, the problem is that "problems of a mismatch between the interests of states and those of their citizens do arise—even in democracies—partly since interpretations are largely left to the judiciary, and treaty negotiations that could check such interpretations are typically handled by the executive of each state" (58). Therefore, in states where respect for human rights is already a problem, the doctrine of restrictive interpretation is likely to compound the problem.

Furthermore, in the application of the principle of subsidiarity, the margin of appreciation favors states when it comes to the determination of whether states have complied, to what extent they have complied, or whether they have sufficiently complied with international law. The merit of this doctrine is that it caters for the following need:

> [T]he rampant value pluralism and variations in natural and social conditions across states globally does counsel a certain leeway concerning how states should best respect and promote various objectives—including human rights. The room for discretion is especially important with several partly conflicting objectives, ranging from conflicts among human rights to conflicts between human rights and other important objectives. (58–59)

However, we do not know "how and where to draw the limits of such a margin, partly due to different assessments of risks" (58–59). This indeterminacy is likely to play into the hands of authoritarian governments that are ever looking for ways to circumvent international human rights law.

Finally, subsidiarity is not always state centric; it can also be person centric (see Follesdal 2016). For instance, comparatively, the European Court of Human Rights is more state centric and less person centric, while the Inter-American Court of Human Rights is more person centric and less state centric in their interpretations of international human rights law. In state-centric subsidiarity, dictatorships can take advantage of subsidiarity. But in person-centric subsidiarity, dictatorships cannot take advantage of subsidiarity. Whether in state-centric or in person-centric subsidiarity, when dictatorships are taking advantage of subsidiarity, the courts—especially the human rights courts—will have to intervene.

THE GOVERNANCE OF MINORITY RIGHTS IN NONCOMPLIANT AND PARTIAL COMPLIANT STATES

In the preceding section, to use the strengths of each model to compensate for the weaknesses of the other models, I proposed subsidiarity as the organizing principle of the global governance of (individual) human rights and (group) minority rights (hereafter, both the individual and the group rights shall be referred to simply as rights) in our Westphalian, international, and global world. However, although subsidiarity can be person centric, it is prone to state centrism. The problem with state centricness in noncompliant and partial compliant states is that it creates room for them to violate human rights. This unintended consequence of the state centricness of subsidiarity happens because of the following reasons.

State centrism gives preference to the interests of the sovereign state rather than the actual persons who live in the state. Consequently, the stability of the state takes precedence over the rights of persons. In addition, state centrism places the onus of protecting human rights almost solely on states. Placing the onus of protecting human rights almost solely on states leads to a twofold problem. First, in noncompliant and partial compliant states, state centricness is advantageous to authoritarian governments that are ever looking for ways to circumvent international human rights law. Consequently, state centricness may end up compounding already-existing human rights problems in non-compliant and partial compliant states. Second, in some cases, some states may fail to protect human rights not because the states are unwilling but because they are too weak.

Nevertheless, in its application to international human rights law, a key strength of the principle of subsidiarity is that it creates room for pluralism. Therefore, I propose that, in Africa, based on the principle of pluralism, national, subregional, and regional (and even global governance) systems should work in concert (Woods et al. 2013, 2) to protect the minority rights of migrants. This will resolve the major problems with the state centricness of the statist and internationalist models. By virtue of their state centricness, the statist and internationalist models give preference to the interests of the sovereign state rather than the actual persons who live in the state. Consequently, the stability of the state takes precedence over the rights of persons, in our case, the minority rights of migrants.

Another consequence of state centricness is that, by virtue of their state centricness, the statist and internationalist models place the onus of protecting the minority rights of migrants solely on states. However, this leads to a two-fold problem. First, in some states (e.g., notably African and Middle East states), state centricness is advantageous to authoritarian governments that are ever looking for ways to circumvent international human rights law. Consequently, state centricness may end up compounding already-existing rights problems in such states, in our case, the minority rights of migrants. Second, in some cases, some states may fail to protect the minority rights of migrants not due to unwillingness but because the states are too weak.

Therefore, I propose that, based on the principle of subsidiarity, when the national, subregional, and regional (and even global governance) systems are working in concert, matters of the minority rights of migrants should be dealt with by the lowest authority or closest authority to the migrants that is most efficient and capable of dealing with the matters. In other words, "[I]ssues ought to be addressed at the lowest level capable of addressing them . . . some problems can be handled well and efficiently at the local, national, sub-regional and regional levels reducing the number of issues that need to be tackled at the international and supranational level" (United Nations 2014, s.p.). This will simultaneously accommodate the state centricness of the statist and internationalist models and transcend state centricness when necessary.

Then, I propose that the national, subregional, and regional (and even global governance) systems should respect what I refer to as the principle of violation and responsibility. This principle presupposes a negative duty of no harm, a positive duty of remedy, and the notion of commensurability. Then, it goes on to say that, first, any actors that violate the rights of migrants should be held responsible for the violations. Second, ab initio the actors are prima facie "commensurately responsible" to the extent or degree of the violations. Third, the "commensurate responsibility" should only be a *pro tanto* obligation, therefore leaving room for more demanding obligations that the actors may have depending on different contexts.

PRELIMINARY CONCLUSION

I think the fundamental determinants of the appropriate approach to the problem of the minority rights of migrants are theoretical plausibility, practical possibility, and moral reasonableness. First, an approach to the problem of the minority rights of migrants might be practically possible and morally reasonable; but if it is not theoretically plausible, that approach cannot be convincingly and successfully argued for. And if it cannot be argued for, then it is likely not going to be accepted. Therefore, an approach to the problem of the minority rights of migrants must be theoretically plausible.

Second, an approach to the problem of the minority rights of racial, ethnic, religious, and linguistic minority children might be theoretically plausible and morally reasonable, but if it is not practically possible, it will make no difference to the lives of migrants, and in their societies. Consequently, such an approach will be a project in futility. Hence, crucially, any approach to the problem of the minority rights of migrants must be practically possible.

Third, an approach to the problem of the minority rights of migrants might be theoretically plausible and practically possible, but if such an approach is not morally reasonable it might even aggravate the injustice it is meant to remedy, alleviate, or eradicate. Therefore, above all else, any approach to the problem of the minority rights of migrants must be morally reasonable.

On the one hand, to the extent that an approach helps us deal with the problem of the minority rights of migrants on the theoretical, practical, and moral levels, to that extent it is theoretically plausible, practically possible, and morally reasonable. On the other hand, to the extent that an approach fails to help us deal with the problem of the minority rights of migrants on the theoretical, practical, and moral levels, to that extent it is theoretically implausible, practically impossible, and morally unreasonable.

With the aim of proposing a realistic approach to the protection of the minority rights of migrants, I discussed the statist, internationalist, and cosmopolitan models of rights regimes. I argued that although the cosmopolitan model is the ideal, the statist model is the realistic one, while the internationalist model is middle-of-the-road between the two—each model has its own comparative advantage. Consequently, with the aim of reconciling the three models, I neither negated nor affirmed any of the models at the expense of the other models; I treated all the three models as complementary. Based on the reconciliation, I proposed a realistic approach that reflects pluralism, subsidiarity, and the principle of violation and responsibility. Therefore, my approach meets the three desiderata of theoretical plausibility, practical possibility, and moral reasonableness.

REFERENCES

Besselink, Leonard F. M. 1998. "Entrapped by the Maximum Standard: On Fundamental Rights, Pluralism and Subsidiarity in the European Union." *Common Market Law Review* 35, no. 3: 629–80.

Besson, Samantha. 2016. "Subsidiarity in International Human Rights Law: What is Subsidiarity about Human Rights." *The American Journal of Jurisprudence* 61, no. 1: 69–107.

Bull, Hedley. 2002. *The Anarchical Society: A Study of Order in World Politics*, third edition. New York: Palgrave.

Carlen, Claudia, ed. 1981. *The Papal Encyclicals 1903–1939*. Raleigh: McGrath.

Carozza, Paolo G. 2003. "Subsidiarity as a Structural Principle of International Human Rights Law." *Scholarly Works* 564: 38–79.

Carozza Paolo G. 2016. "The Problematic Applicability of Subsidiarity to International Law and Institutions." *The American Journal of Jurisprudence* 61, no. 1: 51–67.

Denninger, Erhard. 1988. *Dirriti dell'Uomo e Legge Fundamentale*. Torino: Giapichelli.

Donnelly, Jack. 2007. *International Human Rights*, third edition. Boulder: Westview Press.

Feichtner, Isabel. 2007. "Subsidiarity." *Oxford Public International Law*. http://opil.ouplaw.com/view/10.1093/law:epil/9780199231690/law-9780199231690-e1477 Accessed: June 1, 2018.

Finnis, John. 1980. *Natural Law and Natural Rights*. Oxford: Clarendon Press.

Follesdal, Andreas. 2013. "The Principle of Subsidiarity as a Constitutional Principle in International Law." *Global Constitutionalism* 2, no. 1: 37–62.

Follesdal, Andreas. 2016. "Subsidiarity to the Rescue for the European Courts? Resolving Tensions between the Margin of Appreciation and Human Rights Protection." In *Join, or Die: Philosophical Foundations of Federalism*, edited by Heidemann Dietmar and Katja Stoppenbrink. Berlin: Walter de Gruyter.

Held, David. 2002. "Law of States, Law of Peoples: Three Models of Sovereignty." *Legal Theory* 8, no. 1: 1–44.

Kant, Immanuel. 1991. "Perpetual Peace: A Philosophical Sketch." In *Kant: Political Writings*, edited by Hans Reiss, 93–130. Cambridge: Cambridge University Press.

Organization for Security and Cooperation in Europe. 1991. *Report of the CSCE Meeting of Experts on National Minorities*. CSCE (Commission on Security and Cooperation in Europe), Geneva, Switzerland. http://www.osce.org/hcnm/14588?download=true. Accessed 30 June 2017.

Perry, Michael J. 1998. *The Idea of Human Rights: Four Inquiries*. Oxford: Oxford University Press.

Pogge, Thomas. 2008. *World Poverty and Human Rights: Cosmopolitan Responsibilities and Reforms*, second edition. Cambridge: Polity Press

Rawls, John. 1999. *The Law of Peoples with The Idea of Public Reason Revisited*. Cambridge: Harvard University Press.

Stackhouse, Max L. 1999. "Reflections on 'Universal Absolutes.'" *Journal of Law and Religion* 14, no. 1: 97–112.

United Nations (UN). 2014. "Global Governance and Global Rules for Development in the Post-2015 Era." Committee for Development Policy, Department of Economic and Social Affairs, New York.

Waldron, Jeremy. 2000. "What is Cosmopolitan?" *The Journal of Political Philosophy* 8, no. 2: 227–43.

Woods, Ngaire, Alexander Betts, Jochen Prantl, and Devi Sridhar. 2013. "Transforming Global Governance for the 21st Century." Occasional Paper Series, 2013/09, Human Development Report Office. United Nations Development Programme, September 2013.

Conclusion

I shall conclude the discussion in this book by simultaneously recapitulating and reiterating what I said at the beginning of the book. At the beginning of the book, I said that minority domination and discrimination can be a complex and multifaceted subject. Nevertheless, since the fundamental problems with minority discrimination are those of identity and difference, inclusion and exclusion, the scope of and the grounds for discrimination, and, above all, rights and justice, I set out to deal with minority discrimination in light of the situation of migrants on the African continent. There is a complexity to the discrimination against migrants in Africa that does not only make the problem different from many cases of discrimination but also makes it an important case to discuss. In the discrimination against migrants in Africa, there are multiple majority groups (host or receiving countries and their institutions and citizens) dominating a multitude of minority groups (migrants); and some nationalities are simultaneously victims and perpetrators or prey and predators. This makes the problem different from many other cases of discrimination in which it is usually one majority against one or few minorities.

As I said at the beginning of the book, the complex nature of the problem of discrimination against migrants reflects certain conditions that make the very specific kinds of discrimination against migrants in Africa possible. In view of the conditions, in the short run one may be forced to adopt stopgap solutions to the problem while at the same time accepting that ultimately a human rights framework and a minority rights framework should be the long run possible resolution. However, walking step by step, from the short-run solution to the long-run solution is an arduous journey because the discrimination problem is intractable. The intractability of the discrimination problem does not mean that resolving the problem is impossible. Conscious that the host or receiving countries and their institutions and citizens have the capacity to interfere arbitrarily in certain choices migrants are in a position to make, I proposed a realistic resolution to the problem.

I started the discussion in this book by stating my aim of combining moral philosophy, political philosophy, political theory, and international relations to explore the possibility of using normative international relations as a realistic resolution to the problem of domination of, and discrimination against, minorities, specifically or, especially, migrants on the African continent. To this effect, I explained the grounds of domination of, and discrimination against, minorities and migrants; the nature of the domination of, and discrimination against, minorities and migrants; and why the domination of, and discrimination against, minorities ad migrants seem to be an intractable problem. Then, I explained that in cases of domination of, and discrimination against, minorities, minority rights are the go-to solution. However, I showed why minority rights is not a realistic resolution to the domination of, and discrimination against, minorities and migrants in Africa.

Consequently, without negating minority rights but not relying on minority rights, I argued for normative international relations (which includes the adoption of minority rights but does not depend on minority rights) among African states as a realistic resolution to the domination of, and discrimination against, minorities and migrants on the African continent. Having argued that the starting point of any realistic resolution to the problem must entail the adoption of normative international relations, I explained that to have normative international relations that transcends realist-rationalist fundamentalism, African states must be amenable to a fusion of horizons. This is not a policy book with a set of policies or recommendations that are actionable. Nevertheless, the book tells us where to start from if we are to have a set of policies that are actionable.

Index

About the Author

Frank Aragbonfoh Abumere is a philosopher and political scientist who specializes in ethics, political philosophy/political theory, international politics, and African/Africana Studies. His latest work is *Global Justice and Resource Curse*: *Combining Statism and Cosmopolitanism* (London: Routledge, 2021). He is the Cmelikova Visiting International Scholar at the Jepson School of Leadership Studies, University of Richmond (United States), and an adjunct professor at Arrupe Jesuit University (Harare). Until recently, he was a visiting professor at the Centre for Studies in Ethics and Politics, Vita-Salute San Raffaele University (Milan). Prior to visiting San Raffaele University, he was a senior member of St Anthony's College (University of Oxford); an academic visitor at African Studies Centre, Oxford School of Global and Area Studies (University of Oxford); and a visiting research fellow at the Department of International History, London School of Economics and Political Science. He was also the leader of the Developing World/Global South research unit of the Globalizing Minority Rights Research Group at the Department of Philosophy, The Arctic University of Norway, and a lecturer (assistant professor) at the Department of Philosophy, Ebonyi State University, Nigeria.

Lightning Source UK Ltd.
Milton Keynes UK
UKHW011851230822
407714UK00004B/45